I'm Radcliffe! Fly Me!

I'm Radcliffe! Fly Me!

The Seven Sisters and the Failure of Women's Education

by LIVA BAKER

Macmillan Publishing Co., Inc.

NEW YORK

Collier Macmillan Publishers

LONDON

A Woman's college! maddest folly going!

What can girls learn within its walls worth knowing?

—Florian in Gilbert and Sullivan's *Princess Ida*

Macmillan Publishing Co., Inc.
866 Third Avenue, New York, N. Y. 10022
Collier Macmillan Canada, Ltd.

Library of Congress Cataloging in Publication Data

Baker, Liva.
   I'm Radcliffe, fly me!

   Bibliography: p.
   Includes index.
   1. Higher education of women—United States.
I. Title.
LC1756.B34   376'.65'0973   76–16172
ISBN 0–02–506310–3

FIRST PRINTING 1976

Printed in the United States of America

For Sara

Contents

I'm Radcliffe! Fly Me!

1

The Moons of Venus They're Not.

AT THE CLOSE of the eighteenth century it was authoritatively declared that the ability to calculate an eclipse was less than useful to a woman who needed to know how to keep cream from feathering on a hot day.

"Knowledge is a fine thing, and Mother Eve thought so," Abigail Adams reminded her sister in 1791, "but she smarted so severely for hers, that most of her daughters have been afraid of it since. . . ."[1]

Although she would not live to savor fully its fruits, Mrs. Adams (whose self-acquired education was extraordinary for colonial America, when wives of distinguished men still signed their names with a cross) stood at the brink of a second American revolution, this one a revolution of the mind in which Eve's daughters would finally share, so that at the close of the nineteenth century the historical anomaly that one sex should live in intellectual poverty while the other prospered was recognized as just that: a historical anomaly.

One of the most significant factors in this change in attitude was the establishment in the latter half of the nineteenth century of the seven prestigious women's colleges known formally as the

Seven College Conference,* informally as the woman's Ivy League, and colloquially as the Seven Sisters: Barnard, Bryn Mawr, Mount Holyoke, Radcliffe, Smith, Vassar, and Wellesley.

Born in intellectual radicalism, the Seven overcame all manner of resistance in order to take women's education out of the female seminaries, where it had been essentially decorative, and to endow it with academic respectability. Beginning life with all the fervor and dedication of youthful revolutionaries and denying by their very existence that anatomy is intellectual destiny, they led the way in women's intellectual emancipation.

The adventure was not, however, an unqualified success. Intellectual emancipation alone would not suffice, and before they could follow through with the social, political, and economic emancipation that was necessary if the sexual equation ever was to be balanced, the adrenalin ran out, and they became, over their first hundred years, the victims of their own ethos. Today, each institution has either recently celebrated or is approaching the celebration of its centennial,** and the question for the second hundred years is whether these seven can still serve a meaningful purpose or whether, like the reddlemen of Thomas Hardy's

---

*The Seven College Conference, a confederation in the loosest sense, was established in 1915 by Mount Holyoke, Smith, Vassar, and Wellesley as the Four College Conference which Barnard, Bryn Mawr, and Radcliffe subsequently joined. Over the years it has had varying degrees of cohesiveness which peaked about 1927 when the administrative heads of all seven—presidents or deans—stumped the country together in search of endowment funds. In recent times it included, in addition to informal periodic meetings of administrative officers to discuss common experiences and problems, cooperative admissions programs. Vassar's decision to go fully coeducational in 1969 and the Harvard–Radcliffe decision in 1975 to combine their admissions offices under a new policy of "equal access" for men and women to the 1,600 places in the freshman class, has reduced the participants in Seven-College admissions programs to five; however, the seven presidents and the deans, physicians, alumnae officers, faculty members, and so forth, intended to continue their association in areas other than admissions.

** In chronological order: Mount Holyoke Female Seminary opened in 1837, was chartered as a full-fledged college in 1888; Vassar opened in 1865, followed by Smith and Wellesley in 1875; Radcliffe opened in 1879 as the "Society for the Private Collegiate Instruction for Women," was chartered as Radcliffe College in 1894; Bryn Mawr opened in 1885 and Barnard in 1889.

Wessex, they are doomed to obscurity, their past proud achievements recalled and recorded only by sentimental alumnae.

Each of the Sisters has some distinctive features. Writing in the *Woman's Home Companion* in November 1920, Helen M. Bennett attempted to distinguish between five of the seven psyches: ". . . Smith College turns out the doer; Wellesley, the student; Vassar, the adventurer; Bryn Mawr, the social philosopher; Mount Holyoke, the conservative. . . . There is a standard joke to the effect that 'If you give a piece of work to graduates of the women's colleges, the Vassar girl will sit down and talk about it, the Bryn Mawr girl will philosophize over it, Mount Holyoke will pray over it, Wellesley will go down to the library and read all about it, and Smith will go out and do it. . . .' "[2]

There is, however, a family resemblance, sharing as they do common origins, a common dedication to women's education, liberal arts, and the residential institution, and making "Seven Sisters" something more than colloquial shorthand.

The women's colleges had common roots in the feminism following the Civil War which, like most wars, had challenged some old prejudices and broken down some traditions to open new opportunities to women. At the same time participation in the abolition movement had given women not only a heightened consciousness of their own capabilities but had sharpened theirs and society's awareness of some analogies in the positions of women and Negroes. (Interestingly enough, the movement had a parallel a century later when, equality for neither women nor Blacks having yet been achieved, the new feminism followed close behind the Civil Rights movement of the 1960s.) And the Sisters were conceived out of a common cause: middle-class women's demand for higher education which, much later, was to contribute to the success of the campaign for suffrage and to coincide with an urgent national demand for primary and secondary school teachers —to teach males, of course.

They had, however, no common precedent in this country, where most of the schools that existed for girls in the nineteenth century emphasized the "accomplishments": painting, dancing, singing—a fine arts curriculum that had not yet been raised to academic respectability. The prototype was the medieval monastery, that early scene of feminist stirring, where, for the first time on an institutional level and in a socially acceptable fashion, women could and did receive serious academic instruction, and where they could and did lead lives of scholarship.

Not everyone in nineteenth-century America agreed that a woman ought to have a real college education. "Has she strength of brain enough to receive it?" asked Vassar president John Howard Raymond in a letter to *Godey's Lady's Book* in July 1870, articulating the doubts of many young women and their parents. "Has she sufficient moral earnestness and energy of purpose to carry her through? Will thorough training do for her what it does for a man? Will it not destroy feminine grace and delicacy? Will it not break down her physical health? Will it give clearness, breadth, force and fertility to her mind; dignity, weight, refinement and symmetry to her character?"[3]

Thoroughly persuaded of the merits of higher education for women, Raymond had ready answers to these questions. There were a few other visionaries like him who were willing to invest their fortunes and reputations in the unlikely possibility that his questions could be answered satisfactorily. One was the dedicated school teacher Mary Lyon who, almost single-handedly, founded Mount Holyoke Female Seminary in 1837 and was already contemplating the time when the experiment would become a full-fledged college for women—which it did a half century later, although Miss Lyon did not live to see it. Another enthusiast was Henry Fowle Durant, a successful Boston lawyer who abandoned his practice when he could not square the law with the Gospels, and whose largesse was responsible for the creation of Wellesley College. Indeed, as he confided to a Wellesley English professor, Durant envisioned among the hills around Lake Waban, "On that hill an Art School, down there a Musical Conservatory, on the elevation yonder a Scientific School, and just beyond that an Observatory, at the farthest right a Medical College. . . ."[4] (His women's university never materialized, however; Wellesley remains today an undergraduate institution.) Then there was Joseph Wright Taylor of Pennsylvania, a Quaker physician who had long understood the need for the education of women and who left his substantial fortune to the founding of Bryn Mawr.

Most Americans, however, were convinced neither of the desirability nor of the utility of higher education for women. Matthew

Vassar, the Poughkeepsie, New York, brewer and benefactor of
the college that bears his name, intended to endow a local hospital
until he was persuaded to finance a college "for young women
which shall be to them what Yale and Harvard are to young
men."[5] The spinster Sophia Smith, whose brother had declared
that not a cent of *his* money would ever go toward women's
education, had originally intended to leave her wealth to Amherst
College. She actually did endow a professorship at Andover Theological Seminary[6] before her pastor, John M. Greene, persuaded
her to change her will in favor of a new women's institution, to
be named Smith College and to be built in Northampton, Massachusetts. Barnard College was established only after a long and
bitter struggle among Columbia's trustees and administration. And
Radcliffe College was founded more as a compromise than an
earnest educational adventure, a compromise between the Harvard sisters and daughters who were eager for education and the
Harvard establishment that would have no part of them.

The first four years for each college—a proving time—were
no less difficult. Physically, the institutions were not always completed by opening day. Tradition has it that the first Wellesley
girls to arrive in their basques and bustles in September 1875 had
to pull up their skirts and walk a plank to the door of the college
building because the front steps had not yet been set in place.

Lacking precedent, even nomenclature became a problem.
Incoming students were called all manner of names. To avoid calling them "freshman," Elmira College, which had preceded Vassar,
used "protomathian" and Rutgers Female College (later Douglass
College) used "novian." Vassar decided on "first-year student."
By the third edition of the Vassar catalogue, however, the first-
year student had become a freshman, President Raymond having
argued successfully with the trustees that the "man" in "freshman"
was a generic term, as in "human" and even in "woman." A century later, in the wake of the new feminism, Smith dealt with the
problem of department heads by labeling them, not chairmen or
chairwomen or chairpersons, but, simply, "chairs."

In nineteenth-century America a college education for women
was a little less shocking than a life of prostitution, and the girls
who enrolled in the earliest classes in these newfangled institutions
had to fight skepticism, prejudice, and constant reminders that a

college education would destroy their chances of marriage—which, in 1870 and following, was the only respectable thing for a woman to do. Among the adventuresome little group of strangers who gathered on a night in early September 1875 in Dewey House at newly opened Smith College to get acquainted by the light of candles stuck in potatoes, there was one whose father had been warned he would have to buy her coffin before her diploma. Still, there was no dearth of applications, and two hundred more applicants than the college could hold applied for admission to Wellesley in September 1875, beginning a trend that has allowed Wellesley—and her Sisters—to maintain high (the highest until Yale and Princeton began to admit women in the late 1960s) standards of selection.

Some students could work the quadratic equations on the entrance examinations, but could not conjugate French irregular verbs; others, vice versa. Most of Wellesley's first admissions had not achieved what was considered college-level preparation. Some of the earliest of the Seven Sisters—Vassar and Wellesley—found it necessary to establish preparatory departments to maintain the standards of the New England men's colleges. (By the time Bryn Mawr opened in 1885, the increasing popularity of higher education for women had in turn increased the availability of preparatory education, and such remedial measures could be abandoned. Bryn Mawr, in fact, was able to establish a graduate school.*

First-rate faculty was difficult to hire and keep—then as now. Woodrow Wilson, a young associate professor of history struck a not uncommon chord when he noted, on joining Bryn Mawr's first faculty in 1885: "I should, of course, prefer to teach young men, and if I find that teaching at Bryn Mawr stands in the way of my teaching afterward in some men's college, I shall, of course, withdraw."[7]

Smith was able to recruit some moonlighters from nearby

---

* Although a very few masters degrees are granted by the other five, Radcliffe and Bryn Mawr—alone among the Sisters—have sponsored systems of graduate education: Radcliffe through Harvard, Bryn Mawr through its own small graduate school. In both cases, however, the institutional center of gravity is the undergraduate college, and the focus is on undergraduate education.

Amherst, and Mount Holyoke drew heavily on visiting lecturers from Wesleyan, Dartmouth, Williams, and Massachusetts Inititute of Technology (MIT) to supplement the teaching corps of its own graduates. Harvard professors repeated their lectures to Radcliffe students across the Yard (a major condition of the Great Compromise and a major cause of Radcliffe's later troubles), and Barnard's original ageement with Columbia stipulated that the women's institution, whose graduates were to receive Columbia degrees, use only Columbia instructors.

But not all of the Seven were so fortunate. Vassar opened with a total of six advanced degrees among its faculty of thirty, including President Raymond, LL.D., who, as was customary at the time, combined the roles of administrator, active scholar, and teacher. Wellesley's founder, whose commitment to the education of women included the corollary that they ought to be taught by women, had imposed a particularly tiresome requirement on the college officers at a time when qualified women were extremely rare: that they hire an all-woman faculty, including the president. Nevertheless, Wellesley opened with a faculty of about thirty women, some college-trained, some self-taught. (Today the Wellesley faculty remains more than half women,* all highly trained, with the Ph.D. a requirement for appointment.)

Curriculum was a riddle. What, these struggling institutions asked themselves, was a "thorough, well-proportioned, and liberal education, adapted to woman's wants in life?" Matthew Vassar articulated his dilemma to his friend Sarah Josepha Hale, editor of *Godey's Lady's Book*, prior to Vassar's opening, continuing:

"Shall a certain number of years of study, or a certain amount of attainments, be required for a Diploma?

"*How far* prosecute the Ancient Classics?

"Best means of aesthetic culture?

---

* According to the 1974–75 catalogues, Barnard led the Sisters with 59.1 percent women on the faculty. Wellesley followed with 55.1 percent women and was followed in turn by Smith (40.4 percent), Mount Holyoke (40.3 percent), Bryn Mawr (40 percent), and Vassar (39.5 percent). Radcliffe continues to be wholly dependent on the Harvard faculty, which remains heavily male. (All figures include part-time and full-time faculty members, and exclude physical education faculty members and visiting professors.)

"How much the Art of Conversation?

"Should *Dancing* be encouraged?"[8]

The earliest of the Seven Sisters compromised. Departments were modeled on those of the older private men's institutions, those custodians of the liberal arts whose elitist philosophy assured their absence from the educational democratization which had begun to sweep the country by the 1870s. Adopting the same elitism, the women's colleges offered rhetoric, ancient and modern languages, mathematics, the sciences, natural history, history and political economy, philosophy, and theology. To these were added courses in the traditionally feminine accomplishments: music, drawing, and painting. Gradually these last were either dropped, at least as courses taken for credit, or were enriched academically and made full-fledged music and art courses, a respectable part of the liberal arts curriculum.

The students proved their academic mettle early. Amherst professors who taught at Smith "affirmed that the average scholarship of the young women was higher in the same studies than in Amherst classes," reported President L. Clark Seelye of Smith of the first graduating class (1879). "More restraints were needed for the diligent than coercive stimulants for the indolent."[9] Accreditation came quickly, with the New England Association of Colleges and Preparatory Schools, on its organization in 1885, admitting women's institutions on equal terms with men's. National recognition followed in 1899 when President William McKinley accepted honorary LL.D's at Smith and Mount Holyoke. College, acknowledged one educator, has not made woman "a bluestocking, or a stick or a brute."[10]

By the turn of the century, the intellectual experiments were no longer experimental. The pioneering was, in effect, done. Rigid adherence to high academic standards was facilitated by the large number of applicants and anticipated some future meritocratic system. This, combined with the women's mastery of curriculums as demanding as those of leading men's institutions, had proven that whatever other deficiencies they possessed, women as a sex were the intellectual equals of men, a fact heavily underscored in recent times by the achievement of women at newly coeducational Yale and Princeton: At Yale, from 1970 to 1974, women consistently earned higher grades than men;* and at Princeton, in June 1975, women were chosen valedictorian and salutatorian of the university's 228th commencement.

What, however, were women to do with their newfound intellectual wealth? Marriage prospects seemed to have declined in direct proportion to the quality of a girl's education. One midwestern farmer described the disillusioning experience of his Vassar-educated daughters this way: "All the young men among the storekeepers or the rich farmers around, who might have been agreeable acquaintances, and that would have made good matches for ordinary girls—why, they have nothing in common with a girl that's spent four years studying Latin and Greek and history. . . . The girls don't take any pleasure in their company, and the boys are afraid of them. . . . I guess I'll have a lot of college-educated old maids on my hands. . . ."[12]

Except in the schoolhouse, where demand was running ahead of the supply and where most early Seven Sisters graduates were able to find jobs, professional opportunities had not kept pace with educational opportunities, and although the young Smith woman had been given the same academic equipment as that given the young Amherst man, the same doors at the banks, factories, law offices, and medical schools were not opened to her.

The next step appears obvious. If women were ever to achieve *human* dignity, there had to be a demand for a restructuring of the economic, social, and political orders which continued to discriminate against participation by women, although women had been prepared, at least intellectually, to participate.

Here the women's colleges demurred. The adventure ended. Confusion in the institutional psyche as to what they were educating women for—the institutions being subject to some of the same ambivalences as their students—was solved by coming down hard on the side of tradition, a solution which became self-perpetuating. So if a college education gave a woman stature among other women, it did little for her status in the larger society, a conse-

* A comparison of men's and women's grades, 1970–71 through 1973–74, indicates that an average of 3.8 percent *more* women than men achieved honors or A's in all courses, while an average of .44 percent *fewer* women than men failed.[11]

quence which served not only to reinforce her own self-image of inferiority, but which began to work on the institutions themselves, endowing them ultimately with an appearance of academic as well as social timidity. A Vassar education could never be to young women, as the old New York brewer had hoped, what a Yale or Harvard education was to young men except in the sense that each variety was institutionally self-perpetuating, committed to the status quo, a position the men's colleges which had everything to conserve could afford but which Vassar could not, if it was truly to serve women who had nothing to conserve. Still clinging to the women's colleges was the faint odor of chivalry, the code which was one of the finest products of medieval Europe but also one of its most socially debilitating. It legitimized worship of women's bodies but not their intellects or judgments, and women grasped at it for what they thought was a strengthening of their position but was in fact a weakening. The code, which was the inspiration of the upper classes, became the aspiration of the middle classes, and so it persisted into the nineteenth century in many forms, including the atmosphere of the schoolhouse.

It was a triumph of consumerism. While availability of European monastic education eventually filtered down from the offspring of nobility and country gentry to the fishmonger's daughter and servant girl, education of these latter in America was left largely to the public institutions which were emerging in the last half of the nineteenth century. Education at the Seven Sisters, with its predilection for the classical humanism of the Renaissance which assumed a certain academic elitism, followed the historical imperative that restricted education generally to the leisured upper and middle classes, with the emphasis on middle classes, the Roosevelts and their ilk still preferring to send their daughters to finishing schools abroad. And as the desirability of education for middle-class women increased, a symbiotic relationship developed between the institutions and the members of that vast and influential class whose social conservatism sometimes seemed at variance with its laissez-faire politics and economics, a relationship which militated strongly against any alteration in the status quo, a prominent feature of that class being its rigid opposition to social change.

It was almost as if there existed a kind of unspoken and perhaps even subconscious nonaggression pact: The women's colleges would provide educated wives but not professional competition for the men of Amherst, Yale, Harvard, Dartmouth, Princeton, and the rest; in return the men's institutions assumed a distant but real paternal interest in the Sisters, serving as sources for administrators, trustees, faculty, and, not least, financial support as alumnae husbands. The inevitable uncertainties of the women's-college graduates, heightened and sharpened by a superior education that ultimately proved irrelevant to the larger society, were assuaged by the promise of leadership in good works for social causes, offering the women self-validation and society a free ride.

Another prominent characteristic of the middle class is its preoccupation with a kind of fundamentalist morality, and there was some fear on the part of the women's colleges—which have a low threshold for social pain—that radicalism might somehow be equated with sexual deviance, an explanation which is still sometimes offered for an absence of institutional involvement in women's concerns that has on occasion bordered on antifeminism.

And so, deferring, as is institutionally customary, to the historical imperatives, the intellectual heretics became establishment: academic, social, political, economic—and psychological. The Sisters became leading purveyors of the social ecology, failing to deny the societal stereotypes or to complete the revolution they had begun. They abdicated leadership of the larger society and became its mirror, a mirror that reflected all that feminism was against: passivity, timidity, docility, conformity, and self-denigration.

Early curriculums required an Ivy League identity to demonstrate academic quality. Trapped by their self-images of feminine inferiority, the Sisters became educational wallflowers, continuing to offer the academic fare of the men's institutions, following whatever repackaging trends were in fashion, and leaving the white papers to their betters—the Harvards, the Amhersts, the Flexners, the Hutchinses, and the Kerrs. One by-product of this academic timidity is the irony in the equal disregard in their curriculums by men's, women's and coeducational institutions of the same half of the human race.

The women's colleges offered an elaborate selection of extracurricular activities and exploited the fact that in the absence of

men—who traditionally dominated the coeducational campuses—
all those activities were accessible to women as tools with which
to learn organizational skills and to test leadership capacities.
Lacking, however, the input of the traditionally dominant faction
of society, it seemed more like playing house. Further, in the name
of psychological support, there was a vital element missing—
competition, on which middle-class boys traditionally have been
nurtured as preparation for competitive careers. As a substitute for
competition the women were offered the cooperative enterprises
on which little middle-class girls traditionally have been nurtured
from the time they begin to play nurse in preparation for a lifetime
of adaptability to the lives and careers of others, a perpetuation of
a double standard which is easily and often carried to psychological absurdity. As one woman put it: "How can I let off steam?
A man just slams his fist into the wall. It's acceptable for him to
get mad, but I'm afraid if I do, I'll just be considered emotionally
unfit for the job."[13]

The Sisters claimed that they trained leaders; and they did to a
limited extent. Each of the Seven has its Katherine Hepburn
(Bryn Mawr '28), or its Helen Keller (Radcliffe '04), Josephine
Hull (Radcliffe '99), Margaret Mead (Barnard '23), and Frances
Perkins (Mount Holyoke '02), who has been replaced in official
college public relations by Connecticut's and the country's first
woman governor to be elected in her own right, Ella T. Grasso
(Mount Holyoke '40; A.M., '42). The elitism was more than
token, but something less than the institutions pulling their own
weight, and the other 140,000 living alumnae have generally been,
and are, the *wives* of society's leaders or the leaders of *women*. Essentially, the Sisters produced an officer corps of American women
but failed to produce much dissatisfaction with the roles defined
and dictated by tradition, a failure that has had consequences for
the entire society.

Within the institutions there were and are, of course, individuals
of more daring. Bryn Mawr's second president, Martha Carey
Thomas (1894–1922),* carried her feminism—which has come

---

* Carey Thomas, as she was known, having dropped the "Martha" early,
came from a middle-class Baltimore family. She had clawed her way, over her
father's opposition to her higher education, to an A.B. from the newly coeducational Cornell in 1877, later to a Ph.D. *summa cum laude* from the

down to us in larger-than-life proportions—into suffrage and all sorts of unchic organizations, as well as into the Bryn Mawr chapel where she is said to have urged students, if they must marry, to plan their babies for August bornings, in order to leave the rest of the year free for furthering their own budding academic careers. She is said to have described Bryn Mawr this way: "Our failures only marry."

Vida Scudder, Smith '84 and a member of the Wellesley faculty for forty years, championed labor's cause long before it was either fashionable or ladylike, and consequently suffered academic slights (more of that later). But the Carey Thomases and the Vida Scudders are rare; as institutions, the Sisters distrusted radicalism, and the radicals had no place on the boards of trustees (often in the early days dominated by clergymen) or among the administrators and faculties which signified RESPECTABILITY to skeptical parents and gave the institutions a conservative tone that never has been abandoned.

One of the paradoxes pointed up by this conservatism is that although these Seven were born out of the two most significant human rights movements of the last century—abolition and women's suffrage—when these same movements (the Civil Rights and women's movements) resurfaced in the 1960s, the Sisters joined only half-heartedly and belatedly, their lack of interest serving to emphasize that over the first century of their existence they had assumed much the same position and some of the same retiring characteristics in the academic order that their clientele

---

University of Zurich, and finally to the presidency of Bryn Mawr College in 1894. As president, her authority was often tyrannical, her prejudices unreasonable, her decisions arbitrary, and the formation of the student government at Bryn Mawr was less an undergraduate exercise in politics than a rebellion against her despotism. Virginia Gildersleeve, longtime dean of Barnard, describes in her memoirs, *Many a Good Crusade*, an Atlantic crossing with Miss Thomas in 1919, when the two educators were on their way to England to aid in organizing an international association of university women: "The *Aquitania* was still fitted up as a troop ship. One afternoon a small fire developed in a pile of the straw mattresses on which the soldiers had slept. The smoke penetrated through the decks and reached me in my cabin where I was taking a nap. I remember smelling it, thinking vaguely, 'Oh, well, if it's a fire, Miss Thomas will see to it.' Whereupon, turning over, I continued my slumber."[14]

assumed in the social, political, and economic orders. They were followers, not leaders.

Education, declared Mount Holyoke's founder Mary Lyon in 1846, ought to be the pacesetter: "Like the moons of Venus . . . it should rise earlier and set later. . . ."[15]

What follows is intended to describe where women's education was, where it is, where it's going.

2

Coeducation Is Beside the Point.

F ROM THE BEGINNING, implicitly, and in some cases explicitly, the ultimate goal of the women's colleges has been to put themselves out of business. They have looked forward to the time when universal sexual equality would pronounce them obsolete. As Columbia president Frederick A. P. Barnard put it in one of his annual pleas for coeducation, his 1881 report to the Columbia board of trustees: "The Colleges for women recently established in the State of Massachusetts [Mount Holyoke, Smith, Wellesley] are, probably, all things considered, the best examples of their kind in the United States; but no thoughtful man can doubt that, had the money expended in their erection been given to Harvard University, with the condition that that institution should do the work which they are doing, the result would have been far more advantageous to the people of the State . . ."[1]

Duplication of educational facilities, said Bryn Mawr's president Carey Thomas, herself a product of early coeducation,* is "crimi-

---

* As a student at Cornell, Miss Thomas had already articulated some of her own doubts: "There is much," she wrote, "that is very hard for a *lady* in a mixed university and I should not subject any girl to it unless she were determined to have it. The educational problem is a terrible one—girls' colleges are inferior, and it seems impossible to get the most brilliant men to fill their chairs and on the other hand it is a fiery ordeal to educate a lady by coeducation. . . . It is the only way and learning *is worth it.*"[3]

nally wasteful";[2] not only was there "not enough money in the world to duplicate schools and universities for women," but by spreading the available scholarship thinner, "they would become less good."[4] The college of the future, Miss Thomas predicted with confidence, "will be coeducational."[5]

Miss Thomas did not have in mind the spineless though common-garden variety of coeducation which nearly a century later Betty Friedan described as administered by the "sex-directed educators":[6] a serious education for men and a marriage market for women. However, the fact that in 1968 the sociologist David Riesman, whose mother had been one of Carey Thomas' students at Bryn Mawr, could write with complete assurance that "most women find it easier to come to terms with male dominance at an integrated college than at a segregated one,"[7] may be some indication of why the future was a long time coming. Suffrage did not guarantee political equality, and Carey Thomas' stiffening of the entrance requirements to Bryn Mawr and her modeling of the Bryn Mawr curriculum on Harvard's did not open the same doors for Bryn Mawr women that were opened to Harvard men. It was not the way to make a balanced equation out of intellectual and professional equality.

In 1969, a hundred and four years after Vassar opened, it became the first of the Seven Sisters to try full coeducation, a status achieved through a series of events that ought not to go unnoticed in the literature of seduction.

Vassar went coeducational not because the social conditions were finally right (although for the first time in history they may very well have been, the youth culture that was leading sit-ins, waging political campaigns, starting campus revolutions, and staging peace marches being on the whole, egalitarian), but because finances dictated it. Economic determinism, which too often sacrifices inellectual to housekeeping concerns, has become a persistent theme in academic administration throughout the nation. The editor of *Change* tells how he and his colleagues editorially "called on the higher education establishment to begin thinking of how the nation's universities might yoke their strengths to deal with a long-term energy crunch. There was not a single letter in response. But when our editorials deal with bread-and-butter issues, the letters pour in. . . ."[8] In the mid-1960s, bread and butter had become a serious concern at most private colleges, including Vassar, her Sisters, and such prestigious men's institutions as Princeton, Yale, Dartmouth, Williams, Amherst, and Haverford.

At the beginning of the 1960s, the problem was less acute; there were 298 traditional women's colleges in the United States: 96 percent were private; more than 69 percent were church-affiliated; 25 percent were independent, nonprofit colleges. The remainder was made up of 12 public institutions, 10 of them in the South. Demand for the colleges' services, following the World War II baby boom, was running ahead of supply, and the economic outlook appeared favorable. The future of the private colleges looked bright.

By the mid-1960s, the future looked less bright. The economy had begun to slip. Public education was cheaper for the consumer. In 1964 the mean student expense at five selected public institutions was $2,190; at five of the Seven Sisters, it was $3,125.[9] Tuition cost remains today one of the major problems for private education. In spite of government aid and subsidies by the colleges themselves—Wellesley, for example, claims tuition fees cover only about 43 percent of the cost, with the college picking up the bill for the remaining 57 percent[10]—maintenance of high standards has continued to dictate fee increases. (Tuition, room, board, and student activities fees ran a total of $4,650 at Wellesley in 1974–75.) Consequently, private education stands on the brink of pricing itself out of the middle-class-income-family market on which it has traditionally relied for clientele.

In the mid-1960s, the cost factor, combined with easier accessibility and general improvement of educational quality, began to make public education an increasingly solid and attractive bargain and to provide intensifying competition for the best students. The balance had begun to shift. Before World War II, about 60 percent of all students attended private universities; by 1965, 65.6 percent were enrolled in *public* institutions. By 1971, the percentage in public institutions would rise to more than 70 percent; Ivy League applications would be down 6.7 percent and Seven Sisters down 2.5 percent.[11] Further, a Harvard admissions official, Humphrey Doermann, would have shaken up his colleagues with his comprehensive study of admissions trends and statistics. It revealed that in the counterpart of the Seven Sisters' applicant pool—the Ivy

League's—the number of male high school graduates who could score at least 550 on the verbal section of the College Entrance Examination Board's Scholastic Aptitude Test* *and* who came from families with incomes of at least $15,700 a year, was not between 80,000 and 200,000, as most admissions officials had thought, but was actually *less than half* that—much closer to 18,000 and in no case larger than 33,000. This finding had similar implications for Seven Sisters admissions officials.[12]

Faculty salaries have never been the strong point of the Sisters, although in fact the low rate of compensation has been, on occasion, used to separate the moneygrubbers from the teachers, implying less professional dedication on the part of the former. In 1921, Vassar received an unsolicited check for $25 from the United Association of Plumbers and Steamfitters, Local 180, with the explanation: "We believe in a fair rate of wages for all, and because Vassar professors are receiving less than professors and teachers in other colleges, we consider that this is a worthy object...."[14]

In 1965–66, the public universities were paying professors, on the average, nearly $2,000[15] a year more than were the independent liberal arts colleges (by 1974–75, the difference was still nearly $2,000), and good faculty, especially the younger ones, were being lured away from the private institutions by the higher salaries of the state universities, where the qualifications might be the same or even lower, but the rewards substantially greater.

Facilities—the libraries and the laboratories, which are more abundant in the university, public or private—count for more today than they did for Mr. Chips. Sociological and economic changes, plus the enormous increase in the body of knowledge, have turned college teaching from a calling to a profession, a "field for experts rather than artists,"[16] as Barnard's president, Rosemary Park, put it in 1966. Old loyalties to the local college community are being displaced by new loyalties to scholarly disciplines, professional mobility has become easier, and now—even more than when Woodrow Wilson went to work for what he considered a minor-league team—the Sisters run an increasing risk of becoming farm clubs.

---

* Nationally, from 1963 to 1971, scores on the same test averaged from 478 to 455.[18]

If the shift from private to public education was a strain on the state budgets and, ultimately, on the taxpayers, it was none the less real, and the high-priced private institutions, especially the undergraduate colleges, had to produce a rabbit if their act was to survive.

The problems of the women's colleges, which they shared with other institutions, were complicated by the obvious differences in their ability to raise money, a societal imperative that has changed little since Margaret Beaufort, mother of England's Henry VII, lavished her fortune on men's colleges at Oxford and Cambridge, the consequences of which seem to increase not mathematically but geometrically. Mary Lyon canvassed New England towns, door-to-door, for sheets, blankets, and donations as low as 6¢ so that Mount Holyoke Female Seminary could open in 1837; much later in the same century Carey Thomas cadged free passes on the Pennsylvania Railroad for her alumnae to ride out into the suburbs to solicit contributions for Bryn Mawr. But Harvard, for example, was able, by 1924, to collect $1,250,000 for a party to celebrate the great Charles William Eliot's ninetieth birthday. It remains a truism today that men assign contributions out of the total family income, and women lay aside what's left of the weekly grocery money.

Vassar's dollar problems were further complicated by her geographical isolation in a day when regional cooperation among educational institutions was increasing rapidly as one way to ease financial pressures. As the president of Yale was later to remark: "Of all the first-rate women's colleges, Vassar is one of the few that does not have a natural dancing partner in its own neighborhood."[17]

Marrying for money was one answer. Coeducation had obvious advantages for the admissions office; it seemed not only to double the applicant pool instantly, but also to lure back those women who were opting increasingly for public coeducation. There were also some nice social and educational overtones. Vassar, its president Alan Simpson was to declare in 1967, had "outlived its historical justification." Late-twentieth-century women, unlike their mothers and grandmothers, were accustomed to an open society. "They miss the male contribution to classroom discussion; they want to be able to talk freely and casually with men outside of

class and to share 'heir intellectual and social interests with them,"
Simpson added. "They believe that men are more likely to respect
the female intelligence and to understand as husbands the aspirations of educated women, if they have gone through their college
experience together."[18] (Even in 1967, is that *all?*)

Roger Ascham, tutor to Queen Elizabeth I of England, may
have been the last to describe in print the unmitigated joys of
teaching a diligent and sharp-witted woman.[19] In the twentieth
century, faculty generally preferred the more spirited responses,
psychological and social, of male students.

And by the mid-1960s coeducation was a respectable option for
middle-class women, although it lacked, perhaps, a certain
charisma inherent in eastern establishmentarianism. ("Vassar girls,
in general, were not liked by the world at large," commented
Mary McCarthy, Vassar '33, in her 1954 novel *The Group*.
"They had come to be a sort of symbol of superiority.")*[20]

Abroad, the University of Zurich had admitted women in 1868,
and Cambridge University in 1869 had opened Girton College
as an "annex" for women—the latter was to serve later as the
model for Radcliffe College. In the western United States, where
the prevailing winds were egalitarian—and, more important, the
need for an inexpensive pool of teachers was urgent—coeducation
in the lower schools had always been standard practice; hence
coeducation in colleges and universities was achieved without
much fanfare. Oberlin College pioneered, admitting women in
1837, less for the effects on women's intellectual status or professional opportunities than to bolster the institutional economy: Male
students worked the Oberlin farm in a nineteenth-century version
of financial aid that also reduced institutional operating costs;
women were cooks, seamstresses, laundresses, and waitresses; and
Oberlin became nearly self-supporting;[22] Antioch followed, as did
the state universities of Iowa, Utah, and Washington. By 1870, the
list also included the state universities of Wisconsin, Kansas, Indi-
ana, Minnesota, Missouri, California, and finally Michigan; a century later, in 1974, single-sex education was uncommon west of
Pittsburgh except in parochial schools.

* Vassar's revenge, as reported by Joseph Lelyveld of *The New York
Times* in 1964: "Vassar has shunned the word 'group' since publication of the
novel of that name. . . ."[21]

But the East, where admission of women to lower schools had been spotty at best and dependent on local prejudices, long retained its grim Puritan conservatism. Even Cornell, which owed its existence to both the Morrill Land Grant Act of 1862 and the largesse of wealthy Ezra Cornell, and whose semipublic status militated against exclusion of women, agonized for two years over whether or not to admit them. Physically, when the first application from a woman was received in 1870, the two-year-old university had no place to put her in the sea of male students for whom housing was still inadequate. Academically, Cornell was competing for students, faculty, and prestige with the older eastern educational pacesetters, Harvard and Yale, and it was feared that the admission of women would serve to lower Cornell's academic standards. And institutionally, the Cornell administration, having departed radically from the tradition of university sectarianism and having democratized the curriculum by giving such practical subjects as agriculture and engineering equal standing with the humanities, believed these innovations sufficient for the time being; Cornell could ill afford the added burden of coeducation. A long and enervating family quarrel ensued; but in the end, the views of the old Quaker founder and those of Cornell's first president, Andrew D. White—who had headed a committee of trustees to explore the question and concluded in favor of the adventure—prevailed, and the offer of Henry Sage, a trustee, of $250,000 to endow a college for women was accepted in 1872.

The strictly private institutions, far older than women's demand for higher education, remained largely single-sex. In October 1869, Charles William Eliot, at his inauguration as president of Harvard, set the tone for the East (and laid the foundations for many of Radcliffe's later troubles) by declaring himself irrevocably opposed to coeducation. "The difficulties involved," said this otherwise visionary educator in an otherwise majestic inaugural address, "in a common residence of hundreds of young men and women of immature character and marriageable age are very grave. The necessary police regulations are exceedingly burdensome."

In addition, Eliot warned, "the world knows next to nothing about the natural mental capacities of the female sex. Only after generations of civil freedom and social equality will it be possible to obtain the data necessary for an adequate discussion of woman's

natural tendencies, tastes, and capabilities." It was not, he said, the
responsibility of the Harvard Corporation to assume such a task.*[23]

Amherst, although no less a personage than the governor of
Massachusetts publicly offered to endow a scholarship for women,
followed fair Harvard's example,[24] as did Dartmouth and Brown.
The last, however, eventually established a separate "annex" for
women (Pembroke). And Harvard itself later gave its blessing—
but little cooperation—to a carefully chosen committee of Cambridge women who raised enough money to form an association
for the "Private Collegiate Instruction for Women," purchased a
house, hired a few Harvard professors, and in 1879 opened classes
to twenty-seven students. This was the "Harvard Annex" which
Harvard stubbornly refused to annex and which was chartered in
1894 as Radcliffe College.

It was clear that in the East coeducation at prestigious institutions was out. If women were to be educated beyond the normal
schools and "female seminaries" it would have to be elsewhere.
The answer was found in the establishment of separate colleges
for women, and following the establishment of these in the second
half of the nineteenth century, the heat was off the men's institutions. The issue of coeducation was tabled for nearly a century,
and with it, any question of balancing the sexual equation.

"Segregation," declared Mildred H. McAfee in 1937, shortly
after she had become president of Wellesley, "can be a very convenient social process. . . . So long as women were not threatening
the endowments, equipment, or established routine of men in their
colleges, the academicians could smile upon them and offer their
slightly quizzical but fundamentally amicable good wishes. . . . If
visitors came to scoff, they often remained to praise; and since

---

* Not generations later, but less than half a century later, Eliot ate his
words. "It is no longer necessary for Smith College to provide proof that
young women in good health can take a four years' college course without
impairing their physical vigor," he told the group assembled to see a former
professor of English, his friend William Allan Neilson, inaugurated as president of Smith in June 1918, "or that women can excel in the studies which
formerly made up the prescribed course in colleges for men, or that separate
colleges for women are to be preferred to colleges for men and women
together, or that a broad elective system is even more advantageous to young
women than to young men. These questions are settled now, and are no
longer discussed. . . ."[25]

there was no self-defense involved, they often admitted an ability it would have been hard to recognize publicly on a campus where male prestige might have been threatened. Segregation which allows the postponement of issues until both parties are prepared to face them has its energy-saving social function!"[26]

Over the first century of their lives, the Seven Sisters did little more than toy self-consciously with the idea of coeducation, postponing the moment of decision. "I believe that coeducation is the ultimate way," Marion Edwards Park, successor to Carey Thomas at Bryn Mawr, declared in 1933. "Just now, on the other hand, it is necessary for the development of women that they be made to feel responsible and important. No girl in a woman's college can fail to see that she is expected to take responsibility. Therefore I hold that in another half century woman will have more to contribute to joint education if for the interval she is educated separately."

To which Henry Noble MacCracken of Vassar added: "Women students at coeducational institutions are apt to defer to the current fashion in men's opinion, and their college life lacks the vigor and initiative of life at the separate college."[27]

Fifteen years after its own graduation, the class of 1934 also agreed. Only one in five of that year's graduates of all the Sisters who replied to a rare jointly sponsored questionnaire sent them in 1949 indicated they would have preferred coeducation.[28]

In 1963, Rosemary Park, Barnard's newly appointed fifth dean and second president, told the *Saturday Review*: "I am inclined to think that there is still a place for the women's college. Somehow, it is always more difficult for women than for men to achieve a sense of independent individuality. In the background of woman's mind, there is traditionally the thought that someone will take care of her, that some man will come along and give the answer. . . . We educate women at the wrong time, when the biological urge is strongest and the intellectual intent is not wholehearted. But we must educate at that time, because the mind is most supple, the memory strongest, the ability to take to new ideas unsurpassed. The women's college can do the best job of shaping the sound person who has achieved some intellectual, social, emotional, and financial independence before entering on a partnership. Coeds don't have as many opportunities to learn to stand on their own two feet. . . ."[29]

By 1963, however, the idea of coeducation had begun to elicit some interest, if not wild enthusiasm, in the women's colleges. The outlook for women had not changed, but the financial picture had. Two years before, Sarah Gibson Blanding, Vassar's only woman president, had predicted the demise of the women's institutions largely because of their wastefulness, which she classed as second only to that of hospitals. She warned the alumnae gathered at the Waldorf-Astoria in New York to celebrate the 100th anniversary of Vassar's charter by the New York State legislature that within a quarter of a century many of the independent women's colleges would have become parts of universities for men, have gone coeducational, become units of state universities, or been taken over by the government.[30] The second hundred years would undoubtedly be the hardest.

The same year, Miss Blanding was invited to lunch in New Haven, Connecticut, with A. Whitney Griswold, president of Yale, marking the first episode in Yale's ultimately abortive attempt to seduce one of the northeast corridor's most interesting academic spinsters.

A Yale trustee, Morris Hadley, who was married to a Vassar trustee, had suggested to Griswold and Miss Blanding that Yale and Vassar merge, with Vassar moving to New Haven and becoming coordinate to Yale. Griswold was apparently interested in the scheme, and he gave the Vassar president not only lunch, but a tour of the ten or twelve acres out near the Divinity School, where he had selected a possible site for the women's college campus. Miss Blanding said later (in 1973) she had had ambivalent feelings about moving to Yale. Nevertheless, a secret joint meeting of both boards of trustees was called to discuss the possibilities. The idea, however, was premature, and there was not much excitement generated. The project was abandoned, at least temporarily.

In 1964 Kingman Brewster, Jr., formerly of the Harvard Law School, became the seventeenth president of Yale, and Alan Simpson, formerly of the University of Chicago, became the seventh president of Vassar. Brewster began to talk a little more about Yale's interest in women's education. A Yale *Daily News* poll reported that 80 percent of the undergraduates and more than 80 percent of the faculty were in favor of coeducation, and Yale began to look around for someone to dance with. Vassar, something of a wallflower because of her isolation, but not exactly underendowed ($63 million and highly respectable academic credentials), appeared a likely and lively possibility. In his inaugural address, Simpson had pointed out the vices of the large university which tended too often to sacrifice undergraduate teaching to graduate students and research, and extolled the virtues of the small, independent liberal arts college whose priorities were precisely the opposite. Nevertheless, he proved suggestible to affiliation; marriage, in the mid-1960s, was still really the only respectable option for women.

A mutual acquaintance—never identified positively but thought to have been Julius Stratton, a former president of MIT, friend of the Yale president, and a member of the Vassar board of trustees —fixed up the president of the nation's third oldest college (after Harvard and William and Mary) with the president of the second oldest of the Seven Sisters (after Mount Holyoke) for a blind date in New York in December 1966. A few days later President Simpson retraced Miss Blanding's steps to New Haven, was given a similar tour of the Yale campus, and agreed to consult the Vassar trustees.

The coordinate college, which offered autonomy with its coeducation, was in vogue in 1966. Hamilton College in Clinton, New York, was in the final stages of establishing Kirkland as a coordinate women's institution; Kenyon College in Gambier, Ohio, was considering a similar plan. Williams College in Williamstown, Massachusetts, was looking around for feminine companionship, and Mills College in Oakland, California, was talking about establishing a coordinate men's institution.

Yale's interest in women's education had been given overtones of self-righteousness. "In the young women of the nation we have a huge supply of talent for which our educational institutions have insufficiently provided, and which our country has imperfectly utilized," declared the report of the President's Committee on the Freshman Year in 1962, the first official recognition of Yale's new commitment. "We think Yale has a national duty, as well as a duty to itself, to provide the rigorous training for women that we supply for men, and we recommend that the University keep in its view for ultimate adoption the entrance of women to the freshman class. . . ."

Yale's interest also had strong ties to the admissions office: "Virtually every candidate who turns Yale down," observed a Yale admissions official some time later, "goes to a coed school—we are hard put to defend our monastic atmosphere."

For Vassar, a major consideration was its faculty. Competition for the best was intensifying. The young and ambitious felt isolated in the small, independent liberal arts setting, particularly those in the natural and social sciences where contact with colleagues engaged in major research as well as access to libraries and laboratories was essential, and the usefulness of graduate students as research assistants and teaching apprentices was a not unpleasant fringe benefit.

By the end of December 1966, Yale and Vassar were almost engaged. Their boards of trustees had approved proposals to study the possibilities of the coordinate arrangement, and the Carnegie Corporation of New York—the same people who later brought you "Sesame Street"—contributed $160,000 to help finance the study.

As might have been expected, Yale's 4,000 undergraduate men and Vassar's 1,160 women were delirious. "Urban Renewal—at Last," said one Vassar banner. Yale men proclaimed the end of hitchhiking. Yale Chaplain William Sloane Coffin, Jr., set the proper moral tone: "There's a kind of phony maleness at an all-male school. Women can pull the rug out from under that." Sarah Gibson Blanding, retired now with a tractor Vassar had given her in appreciation of eighteen years of fund-raising, campus construction, and academic reupholstering, commented on this climax to events in which she had had an early hand: "I think Vassar and Yale could be absolutely stunning together. I'm all for it." And Mary McCarthy, reached in Paris, observed acidly: "They deserve each other."

Though 1967 was a memorable year for Vassar, it was less so for Yale, since it was assumed in New Haven that—like most marriages—Vassar would ultimately make the move but the impact would be considerably less on the larger and older men's institution. In Poughkeepsie, committees and study groups were formed to solicit student and alumnae opinion, to visit other coordinate women's colleges and other independent liberal arts institutions. Alan Simpson stumped the alumnae clubs—which, after all, control the purse strings in the end—coast-to-coast, and wrote letters in the *Vassar Quarterly*, the official alumnae magazine, to try to reach those women he had not seen, explaining the pressures of the 1960s and why "the Vassar-Yale study is the most promising immediate path to follow. . . ." Kingman Brewster trekked to Poughkeepsie to court the Vassar faculty, and department representatives from both institutions met to try to work out the delicate problems of academic protocol and the necessary structural changes.

The city of Poughkeepsie had been horrified at the possibility of Vassar's leaving, less because it was an old and honored cultural leader than because of the estimated $6 million which the college added annually to the local economy. Local legislators introduced bills in Albany to prohibit Vassar, which had been chartered under New York State law, from leaving the state, and the governor is said to have wooed the women's institution with some handsome offers to stay. But these were relatively insignificant considerations in the final decision.

In mid-summer 1967 a Vassar alumna on an around-the-world tour is reported to have gone into a Buddhist shrine and prayed that Alan Simpson be struck down. By that time the opposition to the merger had solidified largely within the ranks of the twenty thousand alumnae, and they had turned their Vassar-learned League of Women Voter tactics on the Vassar establishment. A newly organized group called the Alumnae for Vassar's Future took a full-page ad in the April 1967 *Vassar Quarterly* to ask "Is This Trip Necessary?" and proceeded to point out why it was not: Yale facilities were already overcrowded, the locale selected for Vassar was a congested area of New Haven separated from the Yale campus by a ten-lane highway, and undergraduate access to the star-studded Yale faculty was an illusion, the reality being reserved for seniors and graduate students.

"Is this a 'dazzling' option," asked the *Quarterly* ad. "Is it even a fair exchange for Vassar's own home which offers:

"Room to expand on its 200-acre campus.

"An additional 750 acres for possible development of a men's college or a graduate school.

"Close contact with full professors. . . .

"An opportunity to play a vital role in building a major aca-

demic complex in Vassar's area—now a serious goal of New
York State leaders."

The Alumnae for Vassar's Future begged other alumnae to
write. They did, and a dozen letters a day, most opposed to the
merger, were directed to the office of the chairman of the board of
trustees. At the annual alumnae association meeting in April 1967,
the women were deaf to President Simpson's warning that "you
can stay in Poughkeepsie and find yourself the victim of a silent
move, one not so dramatic, a move away from excellence." At
the June reunion, alumnae officers repeatedly attacked the scheme.
Before the alumnae were through that year, they had managed
with their outspoken and organized opposition to put the psychological, and potential material, cost of the merger far out of reach.

Equally important was the opposition of the Vassar faculty.
For all its newfound allegiances and ease of mobility, the faculty is
still the fundamentally permanent part of the institutional structure and its desires carry considerable weight in institutional
decision-making. The Vassar faculty, eyeing the fancy Yale facilities, had been a significant factor in the design for merger in the
first place. However, the likelihood that the Vassar men and
women would be second-class citizens in such a large, male-dominated institution was not so alluring, and meetings with the Yale
faculty had left the Vassar contingent unimpressed with the sin-
cerity of Yale's commitment to either undergraduate or women's
education and its willingness to accept the newcomers as anything approaching equals. It looked, they were certain, more like
a junior partnership which could easily be ignored in so large a
university complex. With their independence and status at stake,
merger meant death, and the Vassar faculty rejected it.

On September 1, the Vassar-Yale study group submitted its
report, and President Simpson gave his "considered recommendation to the Vassar board that the affiliation of Vassar with Yale,
though fraught with great problems, offered promises which
merited further study. . . ." Although deeply divided, the board
of trustees in the main disagreed with their president, and once
again, the project collapsed, this time for good.

There were some last-ditch rescue attempts by the two presidents
who had always believed details could be worked out, but these

ultimately failed. On November 20, 1967, a little less than a year after they met, Vassar announced the marriage was off. Vassar's decision was motivated, Mr. Simpson explained, by "loyalty to a place as beautiful as ours, confidence in the future of our region, desire to be mistress in our own house, our commitment to women's education, and faith in the Vassar spirit of discovery of new paths of excellence."

He revealed plans for graduate institutes and a coordinate men's college on the Vassar campus. "Full speed ahead in Poughkeepsie!" he cheered.[31]

By the late 1960, not coordinate, but *co*education was the wave of the future. By 1972 a survey by the Educational Testing Service's College Research Center revealed that of the 298 American colleges which had begun the decade so self-confidently as women's institutions, only about one-half—49 percent—were still operating as such; about 40 percent were officially coeducational, coordinate, or merged-coeducational; about 11 percent were out of business. In the northeast corridor, Sarah Lawrence and Bennington undertook full coeducational undergraduate programs in 1968, followed the next year by Connecticut College—which had been granting graduate degrees to men since 1959—and in 1971 by Skidmore.

The traditional men's colleges, suddenly self-conscious about sexual discrimination in academe, blushingly opened their doors to women: Colgate, Williams, Dartmouth, Trinity, Union, Wesleyan, and finally in late 1974, after seven years of agonizing, Amherst announced it would accept women sophomore and junior transfer students in the fall of 1975 and would begin accepting freshmen women in the fall of 1976. (Amherst received 309 applications from female upperclassmen the first year, of whom 85 enrolled; to accommodate the move to coeducation, which is to be gradual, the student body was to be increased from 1,300 to 1,500 by 1976).[32] Princeton, which had polled a selected group of high school seniors on their college preferences and found the preference for single-sex education wanting, said that the decision for coeducation, begun in 1969, "was taken at a time when there was beginning to be general recognition that the opportunities for the female half of the nation's population were less than equal and that this inequality meant both human denial and the loss of needed talents and skills. Continuing to limit undergraduate admission to men would have helped to sustain the inequities and indeed could have become a prime example of them. . . ."[33]

Confronted with similar problems, but not yet convinced of coeducation's merits, Bryn Mawr, Mount Holyoke, Smith, and Wellesley adopted a wait-and-see position. (Radcliffe and Barnard, coordinate colleges from the beginning, were at the time engaged in various stages of devising new relationships to the parent institutions.) The errant sister, Vassar—after considering, and then abandoning, the idea of establishing a coordinate men's college in Poughkeepsie—and Yale—after considering, and then abandoning, the idea of creating a new women's college in New Haven—decided, like so many others, to follow the route of full coeducation. There was little opposition at Vassar to this plan. What Alan Simpson frequently and fondly refers to as the "Vassar family" agreed on its sensibleness and desirability, and the Vassar faculty voted 101 to 3 in favor of coeducation. Compared to the alternatives, it was, Mr. Simpson later said, "sounder, simpler, quicker, and cheaper."[34]

At Yale, the going was slightly tougher—a coordinate college was one thing; women in the residential colleges and wearing Y's on their sweaters was something else. Kingman Brewster has been quoted as saying: "Much of the quality that exists at Yale depends on the support of people who don't believe strongly in coeducation."[35] However, in the fall of 1969, 580 women (230 freshmen, 350 transfer students) entered Yale.

Institutional character is never easy to change, and no doubt there will be complaints, not entirely groundless, of sex discrimination, overt and subtle, at Yale—and Dartmouth and Princeton and Williams and Amherst—for many years to come. It will be some time before women's academic interests are taken as seriously as men's, until the extreme male character of the institution is modified. However, the transition to coeducation was somewhat smoother at Yale than at Vassar. In brisk, no-nonsense fashion, Yale replaced one of the 12 male residential college deans with a woman; added a woman professor to the 2 already there, making a total of 3 women and 300 men of professorial rank;* assembled a

---

* In the entire faculty there were 52 women and 817 men. None of the women headed departments; the first woman to do so at Yale—Anne Coffin Hanson, art history—was not appointed until 1974.

committee on coeducation; added a gynecologist and a psychiatric social worker to the Department of Mental Health; opened the door of the admissions office; and called it coeducation.

Girls flocked to New Haven. The college received 2,847 completed applications for the class of 1973, offered admission to 288, or about 10 percent, of whom 230, or 80 percent, entered. Two out of five were semi-finalists in the National Merit Scholarship Competition. Sixty percent of them had scored about 700 on the verbal section of the Scholastic Aptitude Test (SAT), compared with 44 percent of the men; 50 percent of them had scored above 700 on the mathematical section of the SAT, compared with 53 percent of the men. Admissions officials at Seven Sisters institutions refused to release student SAT scores; however, the Yale women's scores are high (the national average on the verbal section that year was 463, on the mathematical, 493) and the gap between the men's and women's mathematical scores unusually narrow. While the University Committee on Coeducation clucked and fluttered, reporting that "for many women, the current environment does not provide an ideal setting in which to grow and develop as a person," only 15 girls out of the total 580, or 2.6 percent, had withdrawn by the end of the second semester of the first year of full coeducation.[36] (In the same year, for example, the attrition rate at Bryn Mawr, all female, was 8.1 percent.)[37]

The transition was more difficult at Vassar. While Yale, with hardly a ripple in its routine, had simply got on with the business of quality education, Vassar would play, this time, the seductress. True to the feminine stereotype that had made a historical reality out of chivalry, Vassar went out of its way to cater to what it supposed men wanted: athletics, pubs, game rooms, a sort of Marlboro country on the Hudson.

While administrative and faculty changes hardly even approached the national picture of traditional and unblushing discrimination against women in academia (it had never occurred to the administration of the men's and coeducational institutions that young people ought to be educated by both sexes), there was an attempt to alter the Vassar image. Key male administrators were imported: a vice presidency for student affairs was created and the position filled by a male (since replaced by a female); a new male admissions director, whose background was in advertising, replaced a woman director, and a news directorship, headed by a male, was grafted on to the public relations structure. The full-time faculty was not only expanded by 30 percent, but also heavily masculinized. The total percentage of full-time faculty women had fallen from 42.9 percent in 1967–68, the year before coeducation began, to 38.2 percent in 1973–74. In the same time span, women department chairmen had fallen from 38 percent to 19 percent; and at the first rung of the academic ladder—the assistant professorship where professors to the next generation are born—muscle in future faculties was aided by the reduction of female representation from 40 percent to 32 percent, while the lowly instructors, lecturers, and teachers in the campus nursery school—the non-ladder appointments—remained significantly and increasingly female: 50 percent in 1967–68, 70 percent in 1937–74.[38]

The college brooded about its identity, and in the name of image, lightened its commitment to its Sisters in the Seven College Conference of which it has been a member for half a century, taking itself completely out of the admissions sector and maintaining more casual ties with the other sectors. It spent $18,000 for a public relations firm to produce a frankly male-oriented recruitment movie featuring views of the campus, classroom discussion, a house party, a couple walking arm-in-arm, and narration by a young, urbane male assistant professor of philosophy, while it virtually ignored a legitimate Vassar claim to academic elitism: the excellence that had helped win for its alumnae *five* Pulitzer Prizes.*[39]

Being both an undergraduate institution and a women's college where societal pressures of various kinds have worked against serious involvement in the sciences, Vassar's institutional direction traditionally had been pointed toward the humanities and social sciences. The hard science majors, observed Mary McCarthy in

---

* Edna St. Vincent Millay in 1923 and Elizabeth Bishop in 1956 for poetry; Margaret Leech in 1942 and 1960 for history; and Lucinda Franks in 1971 for national reporting. More Pulitzer Prizes were awarded to Vassar women than to the women graduates of any other institution in the country. Radcliffe and the University of Wisconsin tied for second place, with four each; among the other five Sisters, Smith produced two, Bryn Mawr and Wellesley one each. Total Pulitzer Prizes awarded, 1917–1975, 683; total Pulitzer Prizes awarded to women, 1917–1975, 66.[40]

The Group, "were about the lowest stratum at Vassar. They were the ones . . . you would not remember when you came back for your tenth reunion: pathetic cases with skin trouble and superfluous hair and thick glasses and overweight or underweight problems and names like Miss Hassenpfeffer . . ."[41]

There were never as many courses offered in the hard sciences: 25.9 percent of the 235 courses offered in 1915–16, 28.6 percent of the 460 courses offered in 1930–31, and 14.2 percent of the courses offered in 1974–75 were in the physical and biological sciences and mathematics. There was, after all, less demand from women for science courses.[42] Of the 5,290 bachelors' degrees awarded from 1950 through 1966–67, 696, or 13.1 percent, were in the physical, biological, and mathematical sciences; 1,029, or 19.4 percent, were in English alone.[43] Of the 69 Vassar seniors who were awarded Woodrow Wilson Fellowships for graduate study between 1945 and 1967, only 2 were in the sciences (both biology); from 1952 through 1967–68, Vassar ranked seventh among the Seven Sisters in National Science Foundation graduate fellowships awarded. Of the 16 Vassar alumnae who were awarded fellowships by the John Simon Guggenheim Foundation from 1940 to 1973 (including Mary McCarthy who won a Guggenheim grant to write *The Group*), *none* of the fellowships was for research in the sciences.

Of the 17 Vassar faculty who were awarded Guggenheim grants between 1940 and 1975, one (male) was awarded a fellowship for research in the sciences. In the number of basic research grants awarded to faculty by the National Science Foundation from 1952 to 1974, Vassar ranked fifth among the Sisters with 16; Harvard–Radcliffe received 1,332; Smith 45; Bryn Mawr 44; Mount Holyoke 24; and Barnard and Wellesley 13 each.[44]

Vassar was clearly not the most exciting laboratory in academe, and it was one thing to want to redraw the societal picture of women by attempting to thrust leadership in the sciences upon Vassar graduates, at the same time remaking the curriculum into what was considered more attractive to men; it was quite another thing, in a time of economic hardship, to retool the entire enterprise.

Nevertheless, when the time came to implement the bright promises of new graduate programs at Vassar which Alan Simpson had made so confidently following the collapse of the Yale–

Vassar merger plan in 1967, the main ideas that were advanced involved the relatively unfamiliar but male-stereotyped scientific
disciplines. One such idea involved a graduate center for environmental studies and would have depended upon the cooperation of
the State University of New York (SUNY) at New Paltz; another proposed to offer professional education at the graduate
level in science, engineering, and industrial administration, and
was to have been developed in conjunction with Syracuse University, Union College, and IBM which had a facility in the neighborhood.

Another proposal, while not specifically science-oriented, would
have pursued other unfamiliar paths: Vassar, which had never
granted the Ph.D. and drew no more than a handful of M.A.
candidates to the campus at any one time, proposed a plan to establish an institute for the advancement of college and university
teaching which had as a stated goal the reform of the Ph.D. degree
system. At the same time the college turned down an offer from
a foundation to develop a teaching degree for instructors in two-
year and four-year colleges, a project with which an undergraduate liberal arts institution would have had some experiential and
theoretical familiarity.

Not surprisingly, the bright promises failed, after what President
Simpson described as a "history of false starts which have consumed time, money, and temper." They were, he declared, victims
of "bad luck and bad judgment," and an institutional impatience
"to fulfill the expectations so dramatically aroused in 1967."[45]

In October 1968, the projection had been the expansion of the
Vassar student body from 1,500 women to 2,400 men and women,
evenly divided, by the mid-1970s; in April 1974, with male applications for admission to the class of 1978 down 19 percent compared
with the previous year and female applications for the same class
down 7 percent, the director of admissions said the college seemed
"stuck" with an enrollment of 2,200, of whom only about one
third were men.*[46]

---

* Total completed applications to Vassar declined 24.1 percent between
the classes of 1975 and 1978; over the same time span, men's applications
declined by 16.9 percent, women's by 18.5 percent. At Yale, during this
period, total applications rose 5.3 percent; men's applications declined by
1.7 percent, women's rose by 23.4 percent.[47]

In February 1975, a Trustee Committee on Coeducation, having thoroughly investigated Vassar's condition and "reaffirmed its strong commitment to coeducation," made recommendations to the college community in three basic areas. In none of these recommendations was there any suggestion for improvement in academic quality, although during the recession of the mid-1970s, there had been deep concern at Vassar as well as elsewhere that quality was being sacrificed, perhaps overly so, to the financial emergency. In fact, the three areas singled out for improvement were admissions, athletics, and public relations and had nothing to do with the substance of academics. There was a good deal of overlap among the three, all of them boiling down to public relations.[48]

2

While their adventurous Sister was enduring the initial rigors and uncertainties of coeducation, Bryn Mawr, Mount Holyoke, Smith, and Wellesley, confronted with some of the same problems to which Vassar had decided coeducation was the answer, were reconsidering their own spinsterhood. These four came up with a very different solution—regional cooperation—to which they are committed in varying degrees but which offer, in addition to the presence of men (which may or may not be relevant) significant improvement in the quantity and quality of academics.

Although the details of each institution's experience vary, the general outlines are somewhat similar; that of Smith is not atypical. The antennae of Smith's early warning system had begun to pick up blips in 1964 when what much later became known as Five Colleges Incorporated* was exchanging students in a limited way, and a Smith faculty committee recommended an investigation of "the feasibility of extending coeducation at Smith."[49] In 1965, the Faculty Planning Committee was established, and the question of coeducation, among many others, was referred to it.

In February 1968, while this committee continued its explorations, Princeton University, with Smith cooperation, conducted

* The regional cooperative venture of Smith, Mount Holyoke, Amherst College, the Amherst campus of the University of Massachusetts, and by 1970, the new Hampshire College.

a survey of the interests, attitudes, and expectations of 4,680 seniors in 19 public and private secondary school from which both Princeton and Smith frequently drew students: 47 percent of the girls said that the presence of both men and women students would increase the attractiveness of a college "a lot"; another 27 percent said it would make a college "a little more" attractive; 20 percent said it would make no difference; only 5 percent said it would make a college less attractive. The previous fall, a questionnaire circulated to 777 randomly selected Smith students elicited 62 percent agreement with the statement: "Bringing men more completely and naturally into the academic and social life of the campus is fundamental to the improvement of the undergraduate life and program of Smith College"; by spring of 1969, the percentage had risen to 72. Translated, these statistics meant to Smith administrators that whatever women were left in the rapidly shrinking student pool preferred to be educated with men.[50] Both of these polls and a subsequent one, however, considered only social aspects of the college experience and ignored the possibilities of alternative spending of the money coeducation would require. For example, the first Smith poll in 1967 (repeated in 1968), included this question: "If Smith College were to be offered a bequest of twenty million dollars to introduce undergraduate education for men . . . which of the following would you favor? Refuse the bequest and retain a female undergraduate student body" or "accept the bequest and develop a plan for educating men at Smith College?" Students were not offered the option of allocating that hypothetical bequest to coeducation, improvement of academic quality, financial aid, or campus facilities.[51]

Among the Smith faculty surveyed in the spring of 1968, the advantages and disadvantages of coeducation were perceived as a coordinate of age, the figures breaking down along predictable lines: only 33 percent of those faculty members over fifty preferred coeducation; 48 percent of those between forty and forty-nine; 74 percent of those between thirty and thirty-nine; and 67 percent of those under thirty.[52] Unlike the students, however, the faculty were offered alternative ways of spending the money, and their answers became a significant factor in the final decision.

But that was later. For spring 1968, it was enough that there was interest and no serious opposition. The results of these surveys led the Faculty Planning Committee to recommend that the college give immediate attention to ways in which men could be admitted to Smith, and in the fall of 1968, the Ten-College Exchange—later the Twelve-College Exchange (Amherst, Bowdoin, Connecticut, Dartmouth, Mount Holyoke, Smith, Trinity, Vassar, Wellesley, Wesleyan, Wheaton, and Williams)—was announced. An informal arrangement that allowed students to enroll and live on each other's campuses for a semester or, at most, an academic year, with almost any excuse for wanting to, academic or social, acceptable, it was a frankly social as well as an academic experiment designed to explore the implications of coeducation for the institution as well as for the student.*

In the fall of 1968, a sample survey of Smith alumnae was conducted and that body—which had been so influential in the Vassar deliberations—was found to be split. About half of those replying to the questionnaire said that the advantages of coeducation would be outweighed by the disadvantages, and less than half said they would urge a son to apply to Smith, although the presence of men in classes, a substantial number agreed, would be academically and intellectually profitable.[53]

With students and faculty apparently favorably disposed toward coeducation and the alumnae not violently opposed, the time seemed right for a more comprehensive study of the desirability and the feasibility. The late Ely Chinoy, professor of sociology, was relieved of most of his academic duties and put in charge of the study; his report was made in the fall of 1969.

Although overall the Chinoy report was a balanced document with a high degree of objectivity, the general tenor of it inclined toward coeducation. Smith, the sociologist warned in his report—as Alan Simpson had warned the Vassar alumnae two years earlier—may experience some deterioration in the quality of its education, including "some difficulty in recruiting and holding a superior faculty if it does not admit men." In addition, "the quality of the student body . . . will not be as readily maintained if Smith

---

* By 1975, the momentum of the Twelve-College Exchange had slowed considerably, all but four of its members—Smith, Mount Holyoke, Wellesley, and Wheaton—having opted for coeducation. While it was much less utilized by students than previously, as one Wellesley dean put it, its abandonment would be felt in the admissions office.

continues as a college for women. . . . Most faculty members and students—and a substantial minority of alumnae—do in fact see much to be gained in coeducation,"[54] including heightened liveliness in the classroom, diversity of perspective, improvement of morale, increased seriousness of academic effort, and increased relevance of experience.

It was not, however, full speed ahead in Northampton. Smith's president, Thomas C. Mendenhall—whose mother was an early Smith alumna ('95), one of the first women to attend Johns Hopkins Medical School, and an early reformer of American childbirth practices—had reservations. "I believe," he commented in February 1970, after reading the Chinoy report, "that coeducation is a much more serious step for a woman's college than a men's because there are women for whom Smith is the opportunity to have a first-rate education slightly apart from competition. We must decide to what extent we have the obligation to maintain that option."[55] It was also, he might have added, a much more traumatic experience as well as a much more expensive one.

In the fall of 1970, an augmented College Planning Committee, which included representatives of the administration, faculty, students, alumnae, and trustees, was charged with reviewing the Chinoy report and making recommendations. At the same time a third poll of student opinion was taken.

The first poll, in the fall of 1967, indicated that most students (62 percent) wanted some form of coeducation at Smith; 18 months later, in the spring of 1969, the proportion has risen to 72 percent. Now, in the fall of 1970, the figures had reversed; less than half the students (45 percent) considered coeducation a desirable option for Smith, and 68 percent agreed that "the opportunity to live and work in a society of women is an important choice that should be kept available in American higher education." The College Planning Committee was inclined to credit the impact of the contemporary woman's movement, which was well underway by this time, with the dramatic change in student attitudes. This was useful but unlikely. Historically and currently, feminism has not found fertile soil on the campuses of women's colleges and is an improbable cause of such an abrupt about-face. Other, subsidiary explanations offered by the Committee are more likely: By fall 1970 the anti-institutionalism that was inherent in the disruptions of the 1960s had spent itself; even more important, the increasing presence of the local Five-College and the Twelve-College exchange programs made coeducation a less critical issue.[56] Whatever the cause, the implication was clear: Smith should remain single-sex.

This third poll appeared to loom large in the final Smith decision, its coincidence with the contemporary women's movement becoming part of official public relations. Perhaps more significant when push came to shove was, as it had been at Vassar, the factor of faculty desires. The Smith faculty, in the spring of 1968, had favored "in the abstract" Smith's becoming coeducational; however, admission of men students received first priority in the allocation of resources from only 7 percent of those polled. The capital expenditure necessary for the addition of a reasonable number of students, set at 700, was estimated at $9,600,000, which was a lot of money when other urgent demands—scholarships, faculty salaries, increased regional cooperation, physical improvements to the campus—were competing for it.[57]

Another large barrier to coeducation was the difficulty in recruiting qualified men, many of whom, Chinoy had said, "hesitate to come to what has been a college for women, perhaps for fear of being considered effeminate, perhaps because their motives might be suspect."[58] Unstated but undoubtedly a consideration was the less-than-instant success of the Vassar adventure.

In April 1971, the College Planning Committee recommended that Smith remain single-sex; in October 1971, the faculty approved the recommendation, and in February 1972, the board of trustees approved it. Smith College would remain a college for women only, with the one qualification that it should "keep the question of coeducation under review and should be prepared from time to time to modify its policies as may be indicated by changes in society and the educational system and by changes in its own circumstances."[59]

The Smith experience was not unique. At roughly the same time, three of her Sisters—Bryn Mawr, Mount Holyoke, and Wellesley—were also considering the desirability and feasibility of admitting men students, and all three, like Smith, decided in the end to remain colleges for women only. These four were able to obtain certain of coeducation's advantages without the expense and trauma of expansion and the problem of recruitment. Unlike Vassar they did have natural dancing partners in their own neighborhoods, partners furthermore with whom they could share a dance without immediately having to make lifetime commitments.

Wellesley's arrangement was perhaps the loosest. In the mid-1960s, Presidents Ruth M. Adams of Wellesley and Howard W. Johnson of MIT were lunching together periodically and recording their conversations in a secret "ice-cream file." In May 1967, in a joint statement, they announced a five-year experimental program for permitting students to take courses at either institution in the fall of 1968.[60] It was a straightforward symbiotic arrangement basically involving student cross-registrations (819 by 1974–75) and some faculty exchanges but little personal involvement by either institution. Nevertheless, it held some potential, and in 1975 officials at both institutions had begun to work on expanded curriculum coordination.

Bryn Mawr, a twenty-minute ride on the Paoli local from Philadelphia's 30th Street Station, had the educational facilities of a major metropolitan area at its disposal. In addition, Swarthmore, a small Quaker coeducational liberal arts college maintaining high academic standards, was only five miles away. Most important, only a mile away was Haverford, a small men's liberal arts institution with a more than respectable academic reputation, a Quaker background like Bryn Mawr's own, and matching financial problems.

World War II faculty shortages had forced limited cooperation among Swarthmore, Haverford, and Bryn Mawr. Swarthmore was still a member of the trio in the late 1960s, but the shorter distance between Haverford and Bryn Mawr had forged their bonds much closer, close enough in fact to deter Haverford, whose $2 million deficit over a five-year-period had encouraged the men's institution to flirt seriously with the idea of coeducation, from committing academic adultery. In January 1974, following fifteen months of deliberation, which included considerable opposition from Bryn Mawr, the Haverford Board of Managers announced that at least for the present, it would pursue coeducation through increased cooperation with Bryn Mawr.

The beginnings of their relationship had been inauspicious: at the peak of the women's suffrage movement, so Bryn Mawr legend has it, its feminist president, Carey Thomas, wrote to Isaac Sharpless, president of Haverford, asking him to keep his rowdies off Bryn Mawr property.[61] By the early 1970s, the two institutions were calling themselves the Two-College Community. A free shuttle bus carried Haverford men to Bryn Mawr classes and Bryn Mawr women to Haverford classes; in 1960 there were 57 Bryn Mawr registrations at Haverford and 31 Haverford registrations at Bryn Mawr; by 1974, these figures had increased to 918 and 1,286 respectively. Most extracurricular activities were integrated, and by January 1975, both Bryn Mawr and Haverford students could run for student government offices on the other campus. Following a national collegiate trend, in 1969–70 the two colleges began an experiment in coeducational living which by 1975–76 resulted in 189 Haverford men housed in Bryn Mawr dormitories and 189 women housed in Haverford dormitories.

The relationship is certainly not without problems, from seemingly simple mechanical matters of meal-plan coordination to philosophical squabbles between academic departments. A few cases of faculty reluctance to compete in the open market have resulted in protective tariffs to discourage cross-majoring. There have been inequities in the negotiability of academic credits, and the balance of trade varies from year to year and department to department. There are personality conflicts, and although by any measuring stick Haverford is at least the academic equal of Bryn Mawr, there is at Bryn Mawr a detectable if repressed air of condescension toward its partner. And Bryn Mawr's commitment to its graduate schools sometimes serves to reduce the totality of its commitment to Haverford.

As a result, some departments are loosely federated, cooperating minimally; others operate almost as one department. Consultation on faculty hiring varies; so does agreement on curriculum requirements. Even goals are sometimes in conflict.

Nevertheless, the growth of the Two-College Community has taken some of the social and economic pressures off both institutions; provided both student bodies with increasing numbers of options; expanded the facilities and enlarged the intellectual community for both with a minimum of expenditure, and there appears to be a strong willingness to further enlarge the areas of cooperation. The relationship is, however, thus far both economically and personally self-serving for both institutions, having more kinship with the common law than the till-death-do-us-part variety of marriage, and there appears to be a wariness of deepening the commitment.[62]

Perhaps the best-known and biggest of the regional plans to evolve during this period is what is now known formally as Five Colleges Incorporated. Mount Holyoke and Smith shared their central Massachusetts location with Amherst, a relatively small men's liberal arts college (1,252 students in 1973–74), and the Amherst campus of the University of Massachuetts, plus, by 1970, the newly established, coeducational Hampshire College, which was actually the creation of the other four institutions, its unstructured and innovative curriculum and life-style designed to add spice to the more traditional institutions in the Connecticut Valley.

Cooperation among the older members of the group started a long time ago. John M. Greene, the Amherst clergyman who persuaded Sophia Smith to endow Smith College as a women's institution, married Louisa Dickenson, a Mount Holyoke alumna in 1857, setting the stage for the contemporary relationships which have kept Amherst busy trying to dance with both, as evidenced by a local slogan: "Smith to bed, Holyoke to wed."*

On a more serious level, President Mary E. Woolley of Mount Holyoke observed just prior to her retirement in 1937 that the four Connecticut Valley institutions were physically closer than certain parts of New York University: "I believe it is time," she declared, "we were planning some sort of cooperation, in which each college, while maintaining and possibly emphasizing, its distinctive character, would gain the benefit of joint planning and action. Before I leave Mount Holyoke, I should like to see a beginning of this sort, against future eventualities in the liberal arts college." At that time Smith and Mount Holyoke were already sharing a visiting professor of comparative literature.[64] The machinery for regional cooperation had been oiled if not yet set in motion.

This "academic common market," as it has been called, expanded

---

* Actually, according to a survey by the *Amherst Student*, of the 1,427 married Amherst men from the classes of 1900 to 1972, who were alive enough to be surveyed in 1972, there were 838 Smith wives—58.7 percent— and 589 Mount Holyoke wives—41.2 percent.[63]

slowly, helped along by World War II and other emergencies;
by the scholarly imaginations which designed such ventures as the
cooperative agreement in 1950 among Amherst, Mount Holyoke,
and Smith librarians to purchase microfilms of all books printed
in English prior to 1550—a venture that became known as the
Hampshire Inter-Library Center (HILC) and is housed on the
University of Massachusetts campus; by the academic vision that
recognized the curricular possibilities in multiplying the course
offerings by five;* by the administrative creativity that recognized
the intellectual and psychological advantages that would accrue to
each faculty by the opening of the facilities and resources of the
other four; and by the Yankee shrewdness that perceived the
significant economies in sharing the cost of such very expensive
educational and research tools like the Five College Radio Astronomy Laboratory.

For such a sizable enterprise which involved multiplying problems as well as resources by five, there was remarkably little planning; no superstructure was imposed, no academic czar handed
down ukases. The forces of evolution seemed to be hard at work,
facilitating expansion as rapidly as events and budgets would
allow, but with a minimum of guidance—which was, of course,
part of the non-plan. The goal of the five-college cooperative
adventure, explained North Burn, its first professional coordinator
(since retired), in 1973, was to achieve "an educational whole
which is greater than the sum of the parts,"[65] but not at the
expense of institutional autonomy or identity, and it is highly
improbable that ten years from now one large institution, made
up of five units, each with its educational specialty, will have
evolved from the cooperative relationship among these four
private colleges and a state university.

There is no question that it has improved the academic picture
in central Massachusetts and may in fact keep these five institutions from going the way of the passenger pigeon and the Penn
Central. Benefits appear to accrue out of proportion to their cost
in time, money, or energy, making much the same impact on
academe that the theory of interchangeable parts made on rifle
manufacturing.

* Total available to a student at any one college by 1972–73 was 6,000.

However, all attempts at cooperation by institutions with long and proud independent histories—Bryn Mawr and Haverford, Wellesley and MIT, the Five Colleges—require increasing degrees of accommodation. On the negative side, the random evolutionary process may sacrifice meaningful cohesiveness to institutional autonomy. Expansion of facilities has not necessarily meant complementarity; joint calendars have not necessarily meant joint purposes; the sharing of computers has not necessarily implied the sharing of educational policies; and the common expenditure of time, money, and energy has not necessarily meant common commitment.

While the academic, as opposed to the fiscal, economy continues to expand, regional cooperation is where the action is. But so far, while there has been considerable progress, it has been largely of a mechanical nature, a simple computerization of students, faculty, courses, library books, telephone lines, calendars, and meal tickets.

In the critical area of academic departmental cooperation, where opportunities for increased excellence, both horizontal and vertical, appear almost unlimited, meaningful relationships have been torturously slow to form. Symposia abound. In the five-college arrangement legalized moonlighting has about doubled since 1967, and straight exchanges have about quadrupled; but joint appointments, which require considerably more depth of commitment, have been slower (two in 1967–68, and two in 1973–74); and where integrated departments existed, they were small, like Astronomy, lending themselves easily to integration, or they were newly created like Black Studies, imposed on the existing structure without affecting faculty sensibilities or damaging faculty protocols.

So far, no one institution has been required to give very much in any of these regional relationships, and there seems to be some reluctance to become inextricably involved. Real economies combined with real educational excellence might be achieved, for example, by limiting each institution to what it does best; however, there has been little exploration of such a possibility, and the wasteful duplication that Carey Thomas and Frederick Barnard deplored a century ago is still with us, even if decreasing. When this man-made academic economy reaches its maximum growth on this simple level, it remains to be seen whether these institutions will be capable of progressing to the next stages of cooperation, and whether they will choose academic excellence when or if it threatens independence and identity.[66]

3

The coordinate colleges, Barnard (coordinate to Columbia) and Radcliffe (coordinate to Harvard), remained, in the late 1960s when their Sisters were discussing coeducation, women's colleges in name only; in effect, both were already coeducational. Columbia men and Barnard women had been crossing Broadway in both directions and in increasing numbers almost since Barnard had moved out of the Madison Avenue brownstone, where the first classes were held, to join, in 1898, Columbia on Morningside Heights. Radcliffe women had been attending Harvard classes since World War II faculty and student shortages had forced an end to duplication of lectures, and they even had been admitted finally to the reading room of the Widener Library so long as they sat together behind pillars at one end of the room. (They were not, however, admitted immediately to the Lamont Undergraduate Library when it opened after the war because, explained the head librarian at the time, echoing President Eliot a century before, there were "far too many corridors and alcoves. Why, if we let girls in we should have to hire a force of patrolmen to watch the dark corners at enormous expense.")[67]

In the late 1960s, both Barnard and Radcliffe were on the verge of rewriting their marriage contracts in the light of the new social forces and economic factors affecting their unions. They had come to another fork in the road, and they faced the decision whether they could, or would, create out of past association some new and exciting educational relationship beneficial to both.

People don't change much, they only narrow their focus as they grow older; neither do institutions change, and it was apparent that the institutional tone set at the founding of both Radcliffe and Barnard nearly a century ago would not be altered; both of these institutions would remain, in greater and lesser degrees and in different styles, dependent for their existence and their tone on the producers of the show in the main tent.

In his visionary inaugural address as president of Harvard in

1869, Charles W. Eliot, the educator's educator of the nineteenth century, outlined a fresh approach to the university curriculum, endowing it with a new humanism and a new rationalism, at the same time establishing himself as a comer in higher education. Less laudable, perhaps, was the chord he struck for all future Harvard–Radcliffe relationships when he declared himself irrevocably opposed on moral and intellectual grounds to the admission of women to the nation's oldest and most prestigious university. The establishment, in 1878, of the "Annex" by a committee of women—all university-approved, all immaculately untainted by coeducation or woman's right—was essentially a compromise to remove from the university the pressures by Harvard daughters and sisters to change his mind and open the gates of the Yard.[68] And Radcliffe has, essentially, continued to be a compromise: tolerated, sometimes ignored, sometimes exploited, sometimes frankly discriminated against; at other times courted, and deferred to, but rarely dealt with as an equal. The relationship is awkward, but so hopelessly entangled that divorce seems out of the question.

As an institution, Harvard never lacked for women in its life, but these were social acquaintances, not professional associations. Women did not belong in the office, and Radcliffe did not belong in the classroom. "I have no prejudice in the matter of education of women," declared Harvard treasurer Edward W. Hooper in 1883 when faced with the prospect of Radcliffe women getting Harvard degrees, "and I am quite willing to see Yale or Columbia take any risks they like, but I feel bound to protect Harvard College from what seems to me to be a risky experiment."[*69]

Radcliffe was established on two premises, the inherent weaknesses of which argued against any assurance of institutional viability. The first was the provision in the original charter which contemplated the dismantling of the women's college as soon as Harvard admitted women, and if its author badly misjudged the character of the parent institution, the provision nevertheless accounted for a certain sense of precariousness at Radcliffe. The

---

* Radcliffe women did not in fact receive Harvard degrees until 1963; in 1894, when the Society for the Private Collegiate Instruction for Women was chartered as Radcliffe College, the university only agreed to offer an equivalency degree countersigned by the president of Harvard—an arrangement with almost unlimited potential for ambiguities.

second, and perhaps more damaging factor, was the failure to provide the women's institution with an independent faculty, the lack of which has left Radcliffe virtually powerless in Harvard's councils and virtually a supplicant dependent on Harvard largesse. Since President Eliot had ruled out coeducation, the only alternative was duplication of lectures at Radcliffe by Harvard faculty, but as Eliot informed a professor he was trying to hire in 1888: "There is no obligation to teach in 'the Annex.' Those professors who on general grounds take an interest in the education of women . . . feel some obligation but there are many professors who think it their duty *not* to teach there, in which opinion some of the Corporation and Overseers agree."[70]

There was, however, the attraction of extra compensation, and in 1888–89, 38 of the 93-member Harvard faculty, or a little more than a third, moonlighted at Radcliffe; a decade later, 105, or a little less than a third, of the 358-member faculty taught at the women's college.[71] These figures do not reveal, however, how many times Radcliffe students were stood up when the snow was too deep, the professor had a cold, or he simply decided to stay at Harvard to work on a book he was writing. There was no guarantee that the same 38 professors who taught at Radcliffe in 1888–89 would teach there in 1889–90, a situation that held potential for some curriculum inconsistency as well as the perpetuation of a sense of inferiority in the women's college—a sense that has not really been cast off during the first century of Radcliffe's existence. While complimenting what she called "the self-sacrificing zeal of many eminent Harvard professors," Carey Thomas of Bryn Mawr viewed the Harvard-Radcliffe arrangement for what it was: unnecessary and wasteful in a world where, by 1900, it was "almost everywhere possible for the professor interested in educating women to lighten his own labors by admitting them to the same classes with men."[72]

But time and motion economies were not the problem for the Harvard Puritans; women were. And duplication continued, the professors dashing the quarter mile to the Radcliffe Yard to repeat at 11 o'clock the lectures they had given at 9; messengers delivering books from the Harvard libraries twice a day to the young ladies waiting in the Radcliffe reading room.

World War II finally forced some changes, despite the male

chauvinism at Harvard.* In 1943, at the height of the demand for war-related research in educational institutions and of the shortages of faculty and students, Harvard and Radcliffe negotiated a new agreement: In exchange for 88 percent of Radcliffe tuition fees, the Harvard Faculty of Arts and Sciences would assume complete responsibility for the education of Radcliffe women through a program called "Joint Instruction"—a euphemism for coeducation. This agreement in effect opened the entire Harvard catalogue to Radcliffe students and afforded the women, no longer dependent on the whims of individual faculty members, a new degree of academic consistency and security. The arrangement continued with little modification for about two decades.

In the late 1960s, while Bryn Mawr and Mount Holyoke and Smith and Wellesley were toying with the idea of coeducation and Vassar actually tried it, Radcliffe chose to solve its financial difficulties** by increasing its dependence on Harvard, and in 1970–71 negotiated the agreement which became known, because of its half measures, as the "non-merger merger." Overall, the agreement was a halfway house between some semblance of autonomy and complete absorption; whether it would lead to the latter was to be reviewed in 1974–75.

The educational problems of the late 1960s were most often perceived in a financial framework, and the Harvard–Radcliffe agreement of 1970–71 was no exception. Provision was made for Radcliffe to turn over its deficit to Harvard ("to discard the queen of spades"[74] was the mischievous way the Radcliffe treasurer put it) in return for which Harvard would take over all Radcliffe tuition fees and all Radcliffe endowment *income* (but not endowment). Harvard would also be responsible for the operation of Radcliffe College (except for specified administrative functions such as the Radcliffe Institute, a program for women's continuing education to be described later), the Schlesinger Library, the office of Alumnae Career Services, some sports and recreation programs, and the offices of admissions and financial aid.

---

* President Nathan M. Pusey, on recognizing what the draft was doing to the number of men in Harvard graduate schools, is said to have commented: "We shall be left with the blind, the lame, and the women."[73]

** From a small surplus in 1960, Radcliffe went to a substantial deficit—$612,102—by 1970–71.

The academic theme that legitimized the financial aspects purported to "provide equal access and opportunities to men and women at all levels of academic endeavor"; and to prove its good faith, to demonstrate its intentions were honorable in the matter of commitment to the education of women, Harvard agreed to decrease the ratio of men to women in the undergraduate student body from 4:1 to 2.5:1 by 1975. Harvard began to absorb a few token women into the institutional structure. Radcliffe alumnae were even invited to vote for Harvard Overseers and admitted to the Harvard clubs, although not before the New York club voted the proposal down at least once.

The "non-merger merger" was fraught with problems: academic, administrative, and psychological. The important consideration was, however, observed Mary I. Bunting, during whose administration as president of Radcliffe the negotiations had been carried on: "We know that Radcliffe's financial situation would have forced even more difficult changes had we remained apart and that those changes would have reduced rather than expanded opportunities for our students."[75] It was an old story: marriage for economic security, the sort that can hardly help but result in complete absorption of the weaker by the stronger.

In December 1973, President Derek C. Bok of Harvard and Matina S. Horner of Radcliffe appointed a sixteen-member Committee to Consider Aspects of the Harvard–Radcliffe Relationship that Affect Administrative Arrangements, Admission, Financial Aid, and Educational Policy; chaired by Karl Strauch, professor of physics, the name was soon abbreviated to "the Strauch Committee." Following similar decisions by Princeton and Yale, this committee recommended in February 1975* "that an admission policy of equal access [by men and women] be instituted as soon as practical, that is for the admission of the class of 1980. . . ." Accompanying equal access to the institution itself was to be equal access to all other facilities of the university, from scholarships to squash courts. The new agreement looked forward to merger of the two admissions offices, a condition that has removed Radcliffe

---

* The committee's recommendations have since been approved or endorsed by the Harvard faculty, administration, overseers, corporation, alumni (although, as usual, less enthusiastically), the Radcliffe trustees, administration, and alumnae.

from the admissions and financial aid aspects of the Seven College Conference, and, ultimately and inevitably, absorption of Radcliffe by Harvard. By summer 1975, the first Radcliffe administrators had begun to be integrated into the Harvard administrative structure.

The Harvard–Radcliffe relationship over the past century places Harvard in the role of devising and relentlessly continuing a patently unequal partnership, in which the courtliness and deference of ancient chivalry degenerates into cynicism. And Radcliffe, like the women of medieval Europe, gratefully exchanged her autonomy for the economic security offered. Like similar relationships in the larger society, this one held out opportunity while at the same time it crippled emotionally.

Security has been an expensive item for Radcliffe: the fact that Harvard and Radcliffe students pay equal fees does not necessarily imply equal access to the university facilities. Radcliffe got, of course, the complete availability (since 1943, and substantial if arbitrary availability prior to that) of the Harvard faculty—a generally acknowledged leading intellectual resource of the nation—plus the accessibility of the Harvard curriculum, one of the most extensive both vertically and horizontally, in the nation. However, it has been accessibility and availability only. There has been little or no Radcliffe responsibility for academic policies and little or no Radcliffe input. Not Radcliffe, but the federal government—with its threats to cut off Agency for International Development and Department of Transportation contracts in 1970—began to change the make-up of the Harvard faculty, however slowly. There were no tenured women in 1970; by summer 1975 there were 9 tenured women among the 378 members of the tenured faculty; at that time there were still no women in Harvard's upper echelons (except Matina Horner): no women vice presidents, no women deans of schools, and except for Radcliffe deans, no women deans in the Faculty of Arts and Sciences.

In the spring of 1943, Harvard president James B. Conant appointed a twelve-man committee to redefine the goals of higher education, an investigation that resulted in publication in 1945 of *General Education in a Free Society*, the academically influential "Redbook" (so-called for its red cover). There was not a single Radcliffe name on the committee (Wilbur K. Jordan, one of the members, succeeded Ada L. Comstock as president of Radcliffe later that year, but he had not been elected at the time the committee was appointed). In the spring of 1975, Henry Rosovsky, dean of the Harvard Faculty of Arts and Sciences, appointed a nine-person committee to review the thirty-year-old Redbook. This time, there was one Radcliffe name on the committee, that of the president, Mrs. Horner. A psychologist by profession, Mrs. Horner was named to head a task force not on concentrations or pedagogical improvement or educational resources—the significant units concerned with curriculum and faculty—but the task force on advising and counseling.

At the same time Radcliffe has had to endure the continuing anti-female and anti-feminist ethos of the larger institution, carefully passed, like tribal lore, from administration to administration, from academic generation to academic generation, so that accessibility to a brilliant faculty has meant also accessibility to a faculty which the Department of Health, Education and Welfare (HEW) Office of Civil Rights, in its initial review of Harvard employment policies in 1970, found guilty of "a consistent pattern of paying women less than men for comparable work," of offering "unequal employment opportunity for women," and, in certain instances, of being "totally indifferent to the whole idea of affirmatively seeking female faculty."[76]

An April 1971 report by a Harvard faculty committee on the status of women in the Faculty of Arts and Sciences described how this attitude spilled into academic areas and affected student expectations: "The results of our questionnaire clearly indicate that . . . 26 percent of female respondents (as opposed to 11 percent of male respondents) answered that faculty members 'had told them or given them the impression that they were not serious students.' Moreover, 37 percent of the female respondents had been told, or had received the impression, that their sex was a drawback in their chosen careers. . . ."[77]

Accessibility to the vast number of course offerings in the Harvard catalogue has meant accessibility to a catalogue virtually devoid of mention of one-half the human race, a catalogue which in 1974–75, a decade after the advent of the new feminism, offered in its 653 pages of course listings just four courses in what might be considered women's studies: "Women and the American Ex-

perience" (Social Sciences 145); "Women in Chinese Society"
(Anthropology 245); "Psychological Study of Sex Differences"
and "Feminine Personality" (Psychology and Social Relations
1760 and 2450, respectively). A student could study Ethiopian history and religion, but could not enroll in a single course which
focused on one of the most sociologically, psychologically, and
economically significant figures, the black woman in America. A
student could study "The City in Literature" but could not find
a single course that focused on women in literature. To be fair,
however, it must be noted also, as one department chairman put it
acidly: his department offered no courses that focused "on canni-
bals, children, or veterans of foreign wars."*

Nor has accessibility to faculty and curriculum guaranteed anything like equal accessibility to some of the rewards often associated with academic effort. In 1888 one E. B. Pearson would have
been awarded the $100 Bowdoin Prize for an essay on "The
Roman Senate Under the Empire," except that it was discovered
in the nick of time that the author was an Annex student, and the
prize money was subsequently divided between two young men,
Miss Pearson accepting the humbler $30 prize which had been
established by Annex women for its students.[78] During the academic year 1973–74, two members of the Radcliffe administration investigated the awarding of prizes to Harvard and Radcliffe
undergraduates since the non-merger merger which was to have
expanded opportunities for Radcliffe women to compete (although at the time 24 Harvard prizes, because of bequest restrictions, necessarily remained available to men only, as 13 Radcliffe
awards remained open to women only). The investigators discovered that little had changed since Miss Pearson was denied the
fringe benefits of a Harvard education.

As a result of the non-merger merger, 29 prize funds were

---

* In February 1975, fourteen Harvard department chairmen were asked
whether the exclusion of women's studies was deliberate departmental policy;
whether there was any apparent interest in having such studies added and if
so, the source of the interest; whether there had been any attempt to incorporate women's studies into existing courses; and whether the chairman was
opposed, neutral, or favorable to the addition of women's studies in his
department. Eight chairmen answered. Their responses ranged from enthusi-
astic to lukewarm to hostile on the subject of women's studies, with the
center of gravity at lukewarm.

opened to women; as of commencement 1973, 25 of these had not been awarded to women. The amount of prize money awarded to undergraduate men ($15,466) was *sixteen* times that awarded to undergraduate women ($930) during the academic years 1971–72 and 1972–73 (the ratio of undergraduate men to women had in these years been more than 4:1 and was decreasing to 2.5:1). The amount of prize money that was *un*awarded ($3,000) even exceeded the amount awarded to women.

Twelve-year totals were compared for those prizes which had always been open to both men and women. It was found that undergraduate men were awarded $25,298, or six times the amount awarded to undergraduate women: $4,106. Although women made up 27 percent of the concentrators in English during this period, the $500 Bell Prize for an essay in American literature had not been awarded to a woman for the past twelve years.

Comparing all prizes awarded to undergraduate men and women in the past seven years, the total amount awarded to women was $18,969. The total amount awarded to men was $86,880.

The Strauch Committee recommended in its twelve-point program "a goal of awarding prizes and fellowships under a policy of equal access," which included some attempts to open restricted awards, to involve both men and women in the selection of winners, and wider publicity, all of which the Radcliffe investigators had found wanting. Also, they did not exclude outright discrimination.[79] One explanation for Radcliffe's poor showing, which was not spelled out by either the Radcliffe prize-money investigators or the Strauch Committee, was a prominent feature of Radcliffe's institutional relationships, characterized in 1894 by an editorial writer for the *Smith College Monthly* as typically feminine, and suffrage, education, and affirmative action plans have not been able to alter it:

It seems to me . . . we are painfully feminine in our dread of competition. The great number of prizes and honors openly given at men's colleges to the best of the ten or twelve men who are as openly working for them, has of course something to do with their fearless way of approaching the point; but this is not all. If there were a dozen prizes to be given to the girls of one class for different kinds of merit, I think it would be difficult to find a girl who would willingly acknowledge that she was "trying" for an honor. She would in all probability feel highly insulted at the suggestion. . . . We have literary societies, editorial and class elections, an Ivy Orator and a Junior Shakespeare essay prize. . . . The girls who honorably fail in trying for these positions are whispered about on many corners, but open sympathy is impossible even for a roommate. A college boy can say cheerfully, "Failed on that Alpha Delt business, didn't you, old man! but never mind, you'll make the Lit. Board next year easily enough, if you want it." That the report, "She was just dying for it, you know," should effectively kill a girl's chances for being class president, must seem to those who own to ambitions as unworthy as it is effeminate.[80]

Tales of discrimination in athletics at Harvard are hair-raising, although the Strauch Committee, admitting that facilities available to women "are sometimes less satisfactory than those for men," urged that high priorities be given "to the requirements of women in planning and construction of future improvements to the athletic plant, and that meanwhile efforts be expended to make existing facilities available on a more equal basis,"[81] a requirement that could very well be enforced by the federal government through Title IX of the Education Amendments of 1972 which bans discriminatory practices in a wide range of campus activities including athletics.

Traditionally, however, inequities have loomed large. While comparisons of dollar allotments can be misleading, there is nothing misleading about the fact that poverty has made Radcliffe women dependent on Harvard hand-me-down sweatsuits and shells. In the scheduling of use of facilities, women's teams appeared to have about the lowest priorities: women's varsities could be bumped from the swimming pool by a local swimming team that was not even affiliated with the university, or from the squash courts by faculty who wanted to play. And when the women's swimming team, two members of which were national record holders, complained because it had been roped off into two lanes under the diving board, the head of the Harvard Athletic department is reported to have responded: "OK, we'll give you equal access. We'll stage an open competition for use of the pool; lanes to go to the top thirty swimmers. We don't, after all, want to be discriminatory." Membership for women in university athletic eating clubs was not even considered, a situation which engendered, declared a 1974 report, *Athletic Opportunities for Women at Harvard and Radcliffe*, "bad feelings and impressions of second-class citizenship."[82]

But these are the obvious, out in the open where they can be studied, quantified, and waved in the face of the Harvard administration. Perhaps more injurious to Radcliffe's self-image is the unconscious perpetuation of stereotypes, the subliminal messages like the one that the Harvard-bred, urbane, kindly, courtly Radcliffe treasurer sends out when he explains the sale of Longfellow which before Joint Instruction had been the principal classroom for Radcliffe students: the building was sold in 1963 to Harvard, he notes, specifically to the School of Education to be its principal classroom building "because we thought, you know, it was to the interest of women to have the School of Education there in the Radcliffe Yard."[83] Or the Harvard coaches who find it hard to take women athletes seriously, who hesitate to push the Radcliffe girls because they're afraid the girls will quit.[84]

Mrs. Horace Mann, who was writing on academic matters at about the same time Charles William Eliot was presiding over Harvard, could hardly agree less with the Great Educator's assessment of women's moral and intellectual qualities, but she couldn't agree more with his assessment of coeducation's chances of success at Harvard. "Harvard College is not the place to try it in at present," she observed, due to "the traditional prejudice, the want of proper arrangements, the very low moral character of the college community."[85]

Columbia University has never been accused of treating its annex, Barnard, with anything approaching equality—Barnard, said one faculty member to explain Columbia's low regard for the women's institution, "educates undergraduates and it educates women, and it's difficult to know which is the greater cross to bear."[86] Nevertheless, Barnard's beginnings were somewhat more auspicious than Radcliffe's, and a somewhat more independent institutional tone was established and perpetuated.

It is hard to imagine Frederick A. P. Barnard, president of Columbia College from 1864 to 1889, who argued, through five presidential reports beginning in 1879, for coeducation at Columbia, prohibiting women, as Eliot of Harvard actually did prohibit them, from debating with men. Women, said Eliot in one of his more cynical pronouncements, had an "unfair advantage" because "the sympathies a woman speaker will excite invariably tend to influence judgment in her favor."[87]

Frederick Augustus Porter Barnard, out of solid Massachusetts Puritan stock, former president of the University of Mississippi, and, having turned little Columbia College into a university with national stature, no less an educator than Eliot, had a fundamental respect for women. Underlying all his arguments for coeducation is the simple assumption—moral imperative, if you will—that women are entitled to equal education; as he replied so pungently to a granddame of New York society who suggested education would discolor the peach: "I would favor no measure which would leave the slightest trace upon the delicacy of the bloom; but I would have the peach valuable for something more than its bloom merely."[88]

Women had been quietly bootlegging lectures at Columbia for years before Barnard opened, a mutually convenient arrangement that had worked smoothly enough until a Columbia trustee discovered his daughter engaged in the illegal academic traffic. Frederick Barnard's original intention had been to legitimize the trade and enroll women in Columbia classes as candidates for Columbia degrees; however, the Columbia board of trustees would have none of it, and he had to make do with a separate institution, an alternative made somewhat more acceptable by the prior establishment of Vassar, Smith, Wellesley, and, the year before when it was chartered as a college, Mount Holyoke. The Columbia annex opened, appropriately, as Barnard College, in a three-story brownstone at 343 Madison Avenue, New York City, in October 1889, with fourteen students who had passed the same examinations given to the young men entering Columbia.* .

* An early lack of self-confidence in the women's colleges required strict adherence to the standards of the men's colleges, and Barnard had announced that entrance examinations were identical with those given at Columbia. However, on the morning of the tests, it was discovered that the mathematics exam was not the same. The head of the Columbia mathematics department, who was not particularly friendly to women's education, had refused to release the Columbia examination papers and the examination had been written by someone else. The fact that the Barnard test was more difficult was beside the point; Barnard officials felt compelled to persuade the recalcitrant Columbia professor to provide the missing Columbia examination—which he ultimately did, although not without an argument.[89]

Structurally, Barnard was a different institution from Radcliffe. Unlike the Harvard annex, Barnard did not contemplate its own future dismantling, but was endowed from the first with a sense of permanence. It was a unit within a large university, but more important, Barnard absorbed institutional strength from its way of ordering education, specifically in its development of an independent faculty.

Duplication of Columbia lectures at Barnard, à la Harvard–Radcliffe, had been included in the original scheme; but it was only a short time before a young philosophy professor named Nicholas Murray Butler, later president of the university, recognized the unnecessary waste in such an arrangement, refused to repeat his lectures, and was instrumental in getting the Columbia bylaws changed so that women could take classes at Columbia, thereby setting the precedent early for future cross-registrations.

Barnard also began to hire its own faculty, a move which drastically reduced its degree of dependence on the older institution, although the actual decisions have always been subject to Columbia approval. And while Abbott Lawrence Lowell, who followed Eliot as president of Harvard, was described as "not cordial"[90] to the idea of women's education, Seth Low, who followed Frederick Barnard at Columbia, contributed to Barnard College, anonymously and out of his own pocket, the money to pay the salaries of three distinguished scholars to be added to the Barnard faculty, to be paid by Barnard[91] and to be shared with Columbia. It was a simple but calculated act of generosity which not only continued the institutional tone established by Frederick Barnard toward the education of women, but, more significant, gave this new women's college some considerable bargaining power within the larger university, making all the difference in its future relationship with Columbia.

By 1900, the tone of that relationship to Columbia had been firmly established: Where Radcliffe was entirely dependent, Barnard was, within certain limits, autonomous. Having its own administration, board of trustees and faculty—especially its own faculty, less star-studded perhaps than Harvard's or Columbia's, but independent—Barnard was integrated into the university structure as an independent institution responsible for the entire undergraduate education of women in the university (except those

at the School of General Studies, which admits undergraduate
women over the age of twenty-one, and those at Teachers College). And Barnard was represented in the larger institution's university councils, was party to its decisions, and shared in its management.

Having a faculty also afforded Barnard control over its curriculum: Barnard could add, subtract, experiment almost at will, and
if the fare was less extensive than that offered to Radcliffe students,
what there was could be tailored to suit Barnard's individual needs.
In addition, the Columbia catalogue was gradually opened to Barnard students.

There has never been any traffic jam at 116th Street and Broadway caused by Barnard and Columbia faculty and students exchanging classrooms; nevertheless, the options have been there,
always increasing, and limited largely only by individual imagination and by patience in cutting red tape.

Since Barnard is part of the university, Columbia maintains a
degree of supervision over the women's college, a supervision that
began, to Barnard's great advantage, as evidence of the academic
integrity of the new women's college and continues today as an
irritant. For Barnard, as a small undergraduate institution, there
are the usual anxieties and jealousies that go with living in the
shadow of an older, bigger, richer, and more famous institution
which, being oriented to graduate study and research, has little
time and patience for undergraduate concerns. There are student
complaints that Columbia faculty members are sexist in the classroom, and faculty complaints that the Columbia administration is
sexist in its policies: Patricia Albjerg Graham, former professor
of education and director of the education program at Barnard and
more recently dean of the Radcliffe Institute, reported in 1973
that although Columbia granted more doctorates to women than
any other university in the nation (19 percent of those completing
the Columbia Ph.D. program were women), only 3.5 percent of
the full professors at Columbia were women, and no top administrators except the president of Barnard were women.[92]

In January 1971, confronted by the same pressures that pushed
Vassar into coeducation, Radcliffe into deeper dependence on
Harvard, and the other Sisters into closer cooperative arrange-
ments with neighborhood institutions, Barnard and Columbia

were re-examining their relationship. Barnard, however, unlike Radcliffe, having some security in the possession of its own educational tools and buoyed by a new self-confidence born of the women's movement, was not about to be absorbed. Instead, the president of Barnard, Martha Peterson, and the president of Columbia, William McGill, put together a Joint Committee of Trustees to study the existing relations between the two institutions. Over the next two years this committee solicited recommendations from faculty, students, administration, alumnae, and alumni plus financial experts who were to untangle the finances of the two institutions and recommend future fiscal procedures. In early 1973, the committee report was approved by the full boards of trustees, and in 1974 a new agreement between Barnard and Columbia was signed. It was to be reviewed in the summer of 1976.

It provided, as official public relations had it, for "increased integration without assimiliation,"[93] and amounted structurally to something between the Harvard–Radcliffe arrangement and one of the cooperative relationships. Given Barnard's historical association with Columbia, the women's college is inevitably bound to some degree of dependence on the larger institution, although compared to the oppressiveness of the Harvard–Radcliffe relationship, the Columbia–Barnard alliance seems a free-wheeling affair. In addition, with its emphasis on increased student cross-registration, and faculty and administrative cooperation, it has characteristics of the Five-College community.

Basically, it is a financial agreement with academic overtones. Instead of handing over its income, its bills, and the task of balancing the two, which was what Radcliffe did, Barnard and Columbia agreed to put their financial alliance on a fee-for-service basis, the major provision of which was that Barnard would pay Columbia for courses, including faculty time, that Barnard women took at the larger institution, and Columbia would pay Barnard for courses, including faculty time, that Columbia men took at the women's college. In order that the exchange did not work to Barnard's disadvantage by putting Barnard faculty in an unequal competition for students with Columbia faculty, increased cooperative associations between academic departments were designed and encouraged, the result of which, in 1974–75, was that a few departments were still operating autonomously, a few had combined their functions so that there were some actual Columbia–Barnard departments, and most were somewhere in between.

Like the regional cooperatives, the Columbia–Barnard agreement provided economy through efficiency of operations at the same time that it enhanced academic offerings to students. Also, like the regional cooperatives, the agreement was still in an expansion stage, with plenty of room for increased cross-registration and increased faculty cooperation before the two institutions would be forced to face a new level of cooperation involving some institutional concession. And, like the regional cooperatives, it remained to be seen how strong the commitment to academic excellence would be.

4

While perhaps the most viable scheme for the late nineteenth century, the segregation of women's education conformed to the societal mold of ladylike retirement from the fray, a retirement that was economically unsound and only served to postpone the inevitable confrontation between the sexes. Holding advantages for both, however, it was encouraged by men and women alike.

Then in the 1960s, coeducation again began to be discussed, not so much because the women had been any better prepared to be coeducated but because the women themselves were demanding to be. This demand coincided with financial crunch so that meeting it seemed to offer economic salvation for the institutions.

The effects of the decisions for increased coeducational associations taken by the Sisters in the decade between the mid-sixties and mid-seventies* have varying significance for the economic as well as the academic and social futures of the Seven Sisters as institutions.

Financially, the institutions were surviving in the mid-seventies, their rescue due as much perhaps to tuition hikes and intensive capital campaigns—which seem, in their frequency, to tumble

* Vassar to go fully coeducational; Bryn Mawr, Mount Holyoke, Smith, and Wellesley to remain single-sex but to broaden their regional cooperative commitments; and Barnard and Radcliffe to increase their involvement with their coordinate institutions, Columbia and Harvard.

over one another—as to the increased presence of men on the campuses. But the picture was not a whole lot brighter in the mid-seventies than it had been when Yale began making passes at Vassar. Inflation and the energy crisis had eaten up whatever gains might have been made; tuition was at an all-time high (nearly double what it had been in 1964), threatening to price these private institutions out of the academic market; while competition for students—the major source of institutional operating income— had become much keener. The applicant pool had not doubled; instead of the Sisters fishing in one pond and the Ivy League in another, they were all now fishing in the same one.

Except in the Harvard–Radcliffe arrangement—in which the problem of duplication was solved early and to the complete advantage of one partner—the wastefulness implicit in duplication of resources that Frederick Barnard, Carey Thomas, and Sarah Blanding had deplored had not been done away with, although regional cooperatives may be a beginning. However, significant economies cannot be achieved without institutional concessions to interdependence for the good of the whole, and as long as Smith, Mount Holyoke, and Amherst, for example, continued to insist on offering essentially identical curriculums instead of concentrating on what each does best in terms of Five-College cooperation, wastefulness will account for academic as well as economic difficulties. All of these institutions have installed all manner of innovative housekeeping procedures in the name of economies; whether they are willing to attempt to apply some of the same principles to academic procedures is a question for the future.

The effects of the institutional decisions taken in the late 1960s and early 1970s by the Seven Sisters were expected to be felt first in the admissions offices, those ultrasensitive barometers of student vagaries of mood. Between 1969–70, when these institutions had fully entered the period of self-examination, and 1973–74, when the decisions had been made, no definite quantitative pattern emerges based on this specific set of decisions. All seven had begun to cast a wider net for students, and applications during this four-year period increased at Bryn Mawr, Radcliffe,* and Mount

---

* At least part of the Radcliffe increase undoubtedly reflects the enlargement of the student body by 61.3 percent as a result of the non-merger merger in 1970.

Holyoke; applications decreased at Barnard, Smith, and Wellesley. Vassar received 1,130 applications in 1969–70; by 1971–72, when the college was fully coeducational, it had 2,088, an increase of 958, or 84.7 percent; however, although following the establishment of coeducation the number of applications remained higher than before, it immediately began to decline, from the high of 2,088 in 1971–72 to 1,974 in 1973–74, or by 5.4 percent.[94]

One trend that has begun to emerge and bears watching for the future is a qualitative pattern change, a shift in student intellectual quality. Some of the Seven Sisters admissions officers have been concerned because the very top women students, whom the Sisters had traditionally attracted but who now for the first time could go wherever they chose, were choosing Princeton and Yale. The shift can be discerned to some degree by the numbers of National Merit Scholarship winners who have chosen these institutions. Between 1965–66 and 1973–74, the number of National Merit scholars in college increased 137 percent nationally; the increase in the number of National Merit scholars who chose Seven Sisters colleges did not even approach the national figure: Vassar's share rose 37.5 percent, Bryn Mawr's, 35.2 percent, Wellesley's, 8.8 percent, and Radcliffe's 2.7 percent; Barnard's, Smith's, and Mount Holyoke's shares decreased by 71.4 percent, 25 percent, and 4.7 percent respectively. At the same time the increase in numbers of National Merit scholars at the newly coeducational men's institutions at least approached the national increase and in some cases surpassed it: Dartmouth's share increased 90.1 percent, Princeton's, 85.2 percent, Yale's, 154 percent, and Williams', 261 percent.[95] And there were those among Seven Sisters faculty and administration who were wondering whether the quality of students at Seven Sisters institutions was deteriorating, not so much in terms of the national picture but in terms of their own history, and if so, these educators were asking, what were the implications for the quality of education for which these colleges traditionally had been noted? For the first century it had been a seller's market, the competition unusually keen among young women for the limited number of places.* By the 1970s, it had become a buyer's

---

* How keen is illustrated by a report in *The New York Times* of February 18, 1921: "Officials of Vassar College tonight announced that the registration list for the class entering in September 1925 has been closed, four years and

market, and although none of the seven had resorted to hard-sell tactics or recruitment by outside professionals, both of which were becoming increasingly common among institutions of higher education, Seven Sisters admission officers were stumping the country every fall searching for qualified young women, the emphasis, they were careful to point out, still on the word "qualified."

For most of the faculties (the Vassar faculty remained isolated in Poughkeepsie; the Harvard faculty remained isolated in its complacency), the intellectual communities had been expanded and the intellectual life enriched by the new arrangements, although the expansion was largely horizontal, not vertical, and the laboratories, libraries, and contacts necessary for the knowledge-expanding research—the lifeblood of the professionally dedicated and/or ambitious teacher—were only slightly more accessible than before.

Nor was there any marked improvement in the material rewards of teaching. Salaries by and large have attempted to keep pace with inflation, but in 1974–75 it was still almost $2,000 a year more financially rewarding to teach in a public university than in a private undergraduate institution. The average compensation for a full professor at the University of Massachusetts, Amherst, in 1974–75 was $28,200; at nearby Smith, $26,100; and at Mount Holyoke, $23,400.*

At Barnard, the Bryn Mawr–Haverford Two-College Community and the central Massachusetts Five Colleges Incorporated, the curriculum had been enriched enormously, and the number of

---

seven months in advance of entrance. Vassar admits about 320 freshmen each year and already 500 have regularly applied for admission in 1925. There are at present about 5,000 names on the advance enrollment lists, including children registered by parents at birth."[96]

* The real money for faculty in 1973–74 was to be earned at institutions like the City University of New York (average annual compensation ranged from $19,712 to $32,031) or the State University of New York (average annual compensation ranged from $17,826 to $22,548); whereas Seven Sisters average annual compensation for 1973–74 was $18,879 at Vassar, $18,697 at Wellesley, $18,175 at Smith, $17,906 at Bryn Mawr, and $17,654 at Barnard (compared to $23,272 across the street at Columbia); Mount Holyoke was not listed, and Harvard (Radcliffe) at $25,448 was up there with the public institutions. Even the salaries at public institutions do not approach the potential incomes of the future doctors and lawyers in the biology and political science classes.[97]

courses offered and the accessibility of faculty multiplied, beginning a trend that, if continued uninhibited, held a vast potential for improvement in the quality of education.

The increased presence of men, however, had done little to balance the sexual equation psychologically or socially which, under the pressures of the women's movement, had been one of the justifications for the essentially economic decisions of the late sixties and early seventies.

Classroom life had not noticeably changed with the increased presence of men. Even where men had clustered, they had not generally treated their fellow students and instructors to the cosmopolitan viewpoints, the urbanity and wit, the lively scenes and intellectual free-for-alls we were led to believe were standard fare at male and coeducational institutions where men were supposed to dominate. Female passivity, behind which women have been accused of hiding both their brilliance and their stupidity, continued to puzzle the psychologists and sociologists, and to distress faculty who found themselves frustrated by the classroom silences and lack of response.

Nor had the social milieu, another of the rationales for increased coeducation, altered in any significant way. Men and women were more accessible to each other; beer and wine were available in the student centers on the women's-college campuses, and there were weekend concerts, movies, and dances, all of which appeared to be popular and to reduce, at least a little, the much-despaired-of suitcase syndrome which has traditionally emptied out the women's colleges every weekend. But the high society bashes remained on the men's campuses, the invitations to football weekends and winter carnivals as coveted as ever, the women still ill-at-ease inviting men to junior proms and house parties at Smith and Wellesley.

All of which may indicate that accessibility might not be the point, that the factors required to balance the sexual equation may have very little to do with academic demography.

3

In loco parentis Repackaged.

1

"WOMAN SEEMS to be looking up to man and his development as the goal and ideal of womanhood," complained Dr. Edward Hammond Clarke, one of Boston's most prominent physicians, in his best seller of 1873, *Sex in Education*. "The new gospel of female development glorifies what she possesses in common with him, and tramples under her feet, as a source of weakness and badge of inferiority, the mechanism and functions peculiar to herself."[1]

Mothers, he warned, had better lock up their daughters. Whatever other harmful effects higher education might have on the female part of the American population, it was a simple, demonstrable, and alarming fact that the rigors of the college curriculum were at best dibilitating and more probably disastrous not only to the health of the women themselves, but also subsequently to the future of the race.

Clarke's premise, based on the widely held notion of women's constitutional fragility, only articulated with new authority the long-cherished social concept that women belonged in the home. Women did not question the logic of the assumption; rather, Mary Wollstonecraft had grumbled in 1792, women were "intoxicated by the adoration which men, under the influence of their senses pay them."[2] Women did not want equality, they were having too much fun.

Sex in Education, published at a time when there was a good deal of interest in women's health, was read in more American homes than its author had ever anticipated, with parents discussing it over brandy in gas-lit drawing rooms and mothers quoting it to their daughters behind closed doors.* Educators pondered its implications, sometimes in print, and scurried about the business of compiling statistics on the health of their coeds. Preachers made sermons of it. Editorial writers indulged their natural affinities for impassioned prose.

There were those who accused Dr. Clarke of mandarinism: He had graduated from Harvard College, been for many years professor of materia medica at Harvard Medical School, and was at the time of the book's publication an overseer of Harvard University. Some said he was using his eminence as a physician to support the reactionary social attitudes of the Great Educator. His use of science to reflect rather than to question social and moral biases was certainly a perversion of its meaning.

Dr. Clarke himself professed only the most *charitable* feelings toward the opposite sex, and claimed his little book had been prompted only by his deep concern for contemporary woman's health and for the unborn generations of Americans, should she persist in this foolish passion for higher education.**

---

* Bryn Mawr's Carey Thomas, who was thinking about college at the time Clarke's book was published and shortly afterwards entered Cornell, later recalled its impact: "We were haunted in those days by the clanging chains of that gloomy little specter, Dr. Edward H. Clarke's *Sex in Education*. With trepidation of spirit I made my mother read it, and was much cheered by her remark that as neither she, nor any of the women she knew, had ever seen girls or women of the kind described in Dr. Clarke's book, we might as well act as if they did not exist. Still we did not *know* whether colleges might not produce a crop of just such invalids. Doctors insisted that they would . . ."[3]

** ". . . [W]homsoever it oppressed," John Stuart Mill had written four years earlier, in 1869, in an essay 'The Subjection of Women,' "[power] always pretends to do so for their own good: Accordingly, when anything is forbidden to women, it is thought necessary to say, and desirable to believe, that they are incapable of doing it, and that they depart from their real path of success and happiness when they aspire to it. . . ."[4]

Whatever his rationale, Dr. Clarke's dire pronouncements and predictions had an immediate and lasting effect on American women. In the short run, they became the focal point for the great health debate of the 1870s: whether or not women had the stamina to undertake a college regimen as demanding as men's. In the long run, they contributed substantially to setting the tone for the women's colleges over the next century, an approach to educating the whole person that spilled over into motherly pampering and overprotectiveness. Gender having been removed from the academic curriculum, which was a straight across-the-board imitation of that in the men's colleges, it found a place in the extracurricular, and in the process served to perpetuate the image of woman as weak, docile, conformist—and ancillary.

In loco parentis was not a new idea in the last half of the nineteenth century; it had long been the standard university approach to students, and its point was articulated with particular sharpness in 1868 by President Martin Brewster Anderson of the University of Rochester: "No classes," he declared, "pass through my hands who are not on the eve of ruin from wayward natures, bad habits, or hereditary tendencies to evil. These men must be watched, borne with, and if possible saved to the world and their families."[5]

Thanks to Dr. Clarke's timely attack on the female constitution —which put the already defensive women's colleges up against the wall—the concept of *in loco parentis* forced the women's institutions to assume more than the traditional role of moral policeman, which largely had been the limit of non-academic interest of the men's colleges in their students, and to both directly and indirectly encourage and discourage certain attitudes and activities among the young ladies.

There are many today who mourn the disappearance of *in loco parentis*. The fact is it has not really disappeared at all, but only has been skillfully repackaged.

Dr. Clarke did not squander his arguments against woman's higher education by discrediting her intelligence, by pointing out her lack of opportunities to use such an education, or by calling attention to the moral pitfalls of coeducation, as many of his contemporaries did. These were certainly important considerations, and they were publicly and extravagantly debated throughout the second half of the nineteenth century. But these considerations never carried the weight that physiology did—and does—when women's role is discussed. Physiology was, and continues to be, with or without the pill, the one unalterable, unarguable fact of women's existence, Henry Adams' inertia of sex. Dr. Clarke, appropriately for a physician, delivered his attack from his fortress of physiological expertise, describing in intimate detail woman's special physiological unfitness for undertaking the strenuous regimen demanded by the college curriculum.

"Woman," he began, "in the interest of the race, is dowered with a set of organs peculiar to herself, whose complexity, delicacy, sympathies, and force are among the marvels of creation. If properly nurtured and cared for, they are a source of strength and power to her."

However, he warned, "if neglected and mismanaged, they retaliate upon their possessor with weakness and disease, as well of the mind as of the body."[6]

Unfortunately, the critical stage in the development of this complex and delicate reproductive apparatus coincided with the period of woman's educational life, and, Dr. Clarke reasoned, "The same system never does two things well at the same time. The muscles and brain cannot *functionate* in their best way at the same moment."[7] Energy was diverted from ovarian development to the learning of Latin and mathematics only at the expense of the entire reproductive system—and, it follows, humanity.

"There have been instances," the doctor warned, as somberly as if he were describing terminal cancer, "of females in whom the special mechanism we are speaking of remained germinal,—undeveloped. . . . They graduated from school or college excellent scholars, but with undeveloped ovaries. Later they married, and were sterile."[8]

Nature, he explained, "has reserved the catamenial week for the process of ovulation, and for the development and perfection of the reproductive system. . . . A careless management of this function, at any period of life during its existence, is apt to be followed by consequences that may be serious; but a neglect of it during the epoch of development, that is, from the age of fourteen to eighteen or twenty, not only produces great evil at the time of the neglect, but leaves a large legacy of evil to the future. . . . Disturbances of the delicate mechanism . . . induced during the catamenial weeks of that critical age by constrained positions, muscular effort, brain work, and all the forms of mental and physical excitement, germinate a host of ills . . . known to physicians and to the sufferers as amenorrhoea, menorrhagia, dysmenorrhoea, hysteria, anemia, chorea."[9] Some of these ills victimized women for life, others might be shaken off in time; occasionally they caused sterility.

If this were not enough to keep women supine for approximately one fourth of her youth, a second physiological demand made upon her body, declared Dr. Clarke, was the rate of interstitial change: "The replacing of one microscopic cell by another . . . With every act of life, the movement of a finger, the pulsation of a heart, the uttering of a word, the coining of a thought, the thrill of an emotion, there is destruction of a certain number of cells. . . . As fast as one cell is destroyed, another is generated" throughout one's life.

Now, during the period of development, "the cells of muscle, organ, and brain that are spent in the activities of life, such as digesting, growing, studying, playing, working, and the like, are replaced by others of better quality and larger number."

Although both sexes shared this growth process, its duration was compressed—and therefore more physiologically demanding —for a girl: "In the four years from fourteen to eighteen," Dr. Clarke explained, "she accomplishes an amount of physiological cell change and growth which Nature does not require of a boy in less than twice that number of years." One need not waste one's entire cell development to leap ahead to Dr. Clarke's conclusion: "that a girl upon whom Nature, for a limited period and for a definite purpose, imposes so great a physiological task, will not have as much power left for the tasks of the school, as the boy."[10]

Unfortunately, American higher education, whether carried on in coeducational institutions or in the new women's colleges such as Vassar—which by definition resembled men's institutions—was "arranged . . . to meet the requirements of the masculine organization,"[11] using age and proficiency but not sex as factors in classification. "Girls lose health, strength, blood, and nerve, by a regimen that ignores the periodical tides and reproductive apparatus of their organization. . . . The sustained regimen, regular recitation, erect posture, daily walk, persistent exercise, and unintermitted labor that toughens a boy, and makes a man of him, can only be partially applied to a girl."[12] The doctor documented his prognosis with the case studies of six young women who had come to his office with serious female complaints, all attributable, he was certain, to overstrain either as students or as working women during the crucial stage of development.

The doctor conceded he would not arbitrarily deny all education to all women. For those who insisted on it, he would substitute for identical education what he called "appropriate"[13] education: fewer hours of study per day and "remission and sometimes intermission"[14] of studies and exercise every fourth week for as many days as the individual required.

In passing—but only in passing—he was forced to admit that not all female ailments could be traced to women's educational life; he would even acknowledge that not all educated women were pathological specimens. He could, however, assure every girl and her mother that "The number of these graduates who have been permanently disabled to a greater or lesser degree by these causes is so great, as to excite the gravest alarm, and to demand the serious attention of the community. If, he warned, "these causes should continue for the next half-century, and increase in the same ratio as they have for the last fifty years, it requires no great prophet to tell that the wives who are to be mothers in our republic must be drawn from transatlantic homes."[15]

That did it! Woman's stamina had frequently been questioned before whenever her education had been discussed, and her lack of it had frequently been used as a convenient rationale for denying her access. Rarely, however, had it been attacked so vehemently by one with such superior scientific credentials. *Sex in Education* offered those whose notions of womanhood, for whatever reasons, coincided with Clarke's a focal point for opposing women's higher education, and support was not long coming.

The physician attached to an unnamed New England women's institution reported: "The college attempted the same course of studies as prevailed in the best colleges for men. The women were quick-minded, ambitious, and determined to excel; they worked well, and were in no way inferior to men of the same ages. The result was that within the year more than one-half of all were in my hands for derangements of the sexual organs."[16]

Sex in Education appeared to be a stunning blow to the movement, just then beginning to gain momentum, for women's higher education: Mount Holyoke Female Seminary, nearing its fiftieth birthday, was contemplating charter as a full-fledged college; Vassar was eight years old; Smith and Wellesley were blueprints. And now the appearance of what was considered hard data that pandered to the reactionaries. How reject the testimony of a physician, the priest in every home?

"Every woman," cried Caroline H. Dall, long a crusader for education and professional employment for women, "who takes up her pen to reject its conclusions knows very well that it will penetrate hundreds of households where her protest cannot follow; . . . upon the major part of the community our words will fall with no authority, or experience invite no confidence."[17]

How indeed! The opposition rallied quickly and effectively. Prominent men as well as women—authors, professors, physicians—joined in vigorous rebuttal to Dr. Clarke's procedure and conclusions.

It was corsets and cant, not calculus (or Kant), that were destroying the female constitution: food, fashions, and false values, not physics.

The first casualties were the doctor's facts. One of the case studies he had cited to support his arguments had been described as a fourteen-year-old Vassar student whose periodic headaches and fainting spells in the gymnasium had been ignored by the college staff; the girl had progressed rapidly from dysmenorrhoea to amenorrhoea and nervous hysteria, graduating from Vassar "with fair honors and a poor physique."[18]

Dr. Alida C. Avery, resident physician and professor of physiology and hygiene at Vassar—a beautiful but stern-looking woman who customarily dressed in black and wore a large cross on a chain at her waist—challenged Dr. Clarke's data, her indignation apparent in every sentence. In the first place, she declared, Vassar did not admit girls under fifteen. In the second place, the symptoms the doctor had described never could have been ignored at Vassar. On the contrary. Aware that the eyes of the nation were focused on the experiment at Vassar, college authorities took

every precaution to protect the students' health. The first catalogue had announced that "Great care will be taken in the sanitary
regulations of the College. . . . Good health is, in the first place,
essential to success in study; and subsequently, whatever attainments may have been made at school or college, if health has been
sacrificed to secure them, will be valueless as the means of a useful
or happy life. . . ."

Girls were forbidden, Dr. Avery informed Dr. Clarke, "to take
gymnastics at all during the first two days of their period; and, if
there is the least tendency toward menorrhagia, dysmenorrhoea,
or other like irregularity, to forgo those exercises entirely. They
are also forbidden to ride horseback then; and, moreover, are
strongly advised not to dance, nor *run* up and down stairs, nor do
anything else that gives sudden and successive (even though not
violent) shocks to the trunk."[19]

Reverend Olympia Brown, a robust product of Antioch's
undergraduate and theological schools in the 1860s, who could
walk ten miles a day with ease, in addition to keeping lecture and
preaching engagements, called Dr. Clarke's polemic "absurd." All
the time *she* was at Antioch, she "never heard of a young lady in
the college requiring a physician's advice."[20]

Testimony from Oberlin[21] and the University of Michigan, both
coeducational, was similar. "About eighty of the students are of
the sex which some call 'weaker,' " wrote Reverend C. H. Brigham
of Michigan, "but which here, at any rate, is shown to be equal in
endurance, in courage, in perseverance, in devotion to study, and
in cheerful confidence, to the strong and stalwart men. The health
of the women who are here now is in almost every instance
excellent."[22]

Writing in the *Woman's Journal* in November 1873, Thomas
Wentworth Higginson—Civil War soldier, clergyman, respected
man of letters, and incidentally, a fellow student with Clarke at
Harvard College in the early 1840s—discredited the doctor's
methodology. One swallow did not make a summer, and six cases
from a physician's notebook did not prove the universal physiological frailty of the female constitution. Had Clarke been less
hasty and more thorough (as became a scientist of his caliber),
investigating, for example, the physiology of American women
against their social, ethnic, geographical, and educational back-

grounds, he might have discovered some serious problems inherent in the American educational system. However, concluded Higginson, Dr. Clarke "seems to have entered on his inquiry in the spirit of an advocate, not of a judge."[23]

There was no doubt among Dr. Clarke's critics that the state of the American woman's health—whether she was educated or illiterate—was a problem of significant proportions, and the enormous popularity of *Sex in Education*, focusing national attention on female physiology, offered a timely opportunity for exposure of psychological and social causes.

It was the double standard, not mismanagement of her reproductive apparatus, that was debilitating women, said Julia Ward Howe, who is perhaps better remembered for authoring "The Battle Hymn of the Republic" than for her contributions to letters and social reform. Boys had, she explained, "the healthful hope held out to them of being able to pursue their own objects, and to choose and follow the business or profession of their choice. Girls have the dispiriting prospect of a secondary and derivative existence, with only so much room allowed them as may not cramp the full sweep of the other sex. . . . 'We are only women, and it does not matter,' passes from mother to daughter."[24]

To which Mrs. Dall added humiliating detail, at the same time informing Clarke what real overstrain was: "Women, and even young girls at school, take their studies *in addition* to their home cares. If the boys are preparing for college, they do not have to take care of the baby, make the beds, or help serve the meals. . . . So far women have written in the nursery or the dining-room, often with one foot on the cradle."[25]

The American woman's life-style was the despair of many. "If Dr. Clarke," wrote Mrs. Horace Mann, "had assailed the abuses of society,—children's parties, fashionable dress in its feature of bare neck and limbs, thin shoes, sudden change of costume, late hours, and a thousand hardships and exposures to which the less favored classes of society are subjected,—he would have done better service than by discouraging women's systematic education, and throwing obstacles in the path of their culture."[26]

Popular author Mrs. E. N. Duffey agreed: "The follies and dissipations of fashionable society"—the late hours, the "pernicious" sexual stimulation of nightly dancing, and the popular sensational literature—were turning her into a "sexual monster unfit for wife-hood and motherhood."[27]

Her costume completed the destruction: the confinement of the corset, to which was added ten to twenty pounds of skirt below and an extravagant chignon above (not to mention the milliner's ingenious beautifying but constrictive devices in between) and, declared Dr. Mercy B. Jackson,* one of America's earliest women homeopathic physicians, "constant strain is imposed on the muscles to keep the balance." More important, she declared, the medical colleges, refusing admission to women, denied all women the necessary medical care. "For a long period," she said, "women have been treated by men who, having no corresponding organs, could not possibly understand their diseases, and they have been left uncured, only palliated, and often made worse by this great error."[28]

Of course physiology *was* a problem, but it had nothing to do with Dr. Clarke's depressing cosmic law of periodicity. It had, rather, to do with poor diet, poor respiration, and lassitude, the doctor's critics retorted.

These were not new ideas. Mary Wollstonecraft, a century before, had complained of women's "wearisome confinement . . . at school. Not allowed, perhaps, to step out of one broad walk in a superb garden, and obliged to pace with steady deportment stupidly backwards and forwards, holding up their heads, and turning out their toes, with shoulders braced back, instead of bounding, as nature directs to complete her own design, in the various attitudes so conducive to health. The pure animal spirits, which make both mind and body shoot out, and unfold the tender blossoms of hope are turned sour."[29]

Mount Holyoke's Mary Lyon had included calisthenics in the list of studies published in a preliminary pamphlet in 1835. Recognizing the value of regular exercise but lacking both a proper gymnasium and a properly trained teacher of physical training, Miss Lyon required her earliest students to carry wood and coal, to wash, iron, cook, sweep, do dishes, and clean, as much for their value as physical exercise as for institutional economy, although

---

* Dr. Jackson had graduated from the New England Female Medical College at age fifty-eight and was adjunct professor of children's diseases at Boston University School of Medicine but had been denied admission to the American Institute of Homeopathy on the basis of her sex.

it certainly contributed to the financial well-being of the struggling young seminary. The girls also did simple calisthenics based on dance steps of the time, were required to walk a mile every day, and although no formal instruction in hygiene was offered, they were given advice "in regard to bathing and care of the health."[30]

However, except for a few pioneers like Miss Lyon, Catherine Beecher who invented a system of calisthenics for the girls in her school at Hartford, and Dio Lewis who emphasized physical culture in his Home School at Lexington, Massachuetts, the American educational system virtually ignored the physical well-being of its students, boys and girls alike. Children were closely confined for long hours in poorly ventilated rooms and offered the cheapest, starchiest food; to this regimen was added for girls, for whom athletics and even strenuous outdoor play were not considered respectable, a life of general physical inaction.

The publication of *Sex in Education* served unintentionally to unite *not* those who would cloister women but those who would establish modern health practices. Women, declared Dr. Clarke's opponents, required more, not less exercise—of the healthful rather than the spine-curving variety, which was all too available to young girls who prematurely had to carry heavy loads in what was prettily called "helping their mothers." Programs of regular exercise under expert instruction—some faddish, some sound: ranging from voice training and chest-expansion exercises to golf and bowling—were devised and promoted as the cure for women's delicacy.

If Dr. Clarke had intended the calamitous predictions of *Sex in Education* to decrease the number of women college students, he misjudged his readers. A few mothers did withdraw their daughters from school, and a few students shortened their courses of study, but it was too late to have any serious effects on enrollments. For every six study-damaged girls taken from Dr. Clarke's office files, any college president of an institution to which women had been admitted could find sixty robust specimens.

Nevertheless, *Sex in Education* had a significant impact on women's higher education, not at all that intended by its author. Social attitudes and customs may not have altered much, and fashion crept only very slowly toward simplicity and comfort.

However, as a result of the vigorous and widespread debate, co-educational and the newly developing women's colleges, self-consciously perhaps but not the less enthusiastically, focused an extraordinary amount of attention on the health of their students. It was one thing to have an intellectual grasp of sexual equality; it was quite another to confront the reality; the colleges were understandably nervous.

L. Clark Seelye, Smith's first president, thought it appropriate to include some reassurances to parents in his inaugural address of July 1875, two months before the institution opened. "Women's health is endangered far more by balls and parties than by schools," he told the audience. "For one ruined by over-study, we can point to a hundred ruined by dainties and dances. Give our schools and colleges all the light they need about hygiene and physiology, but let us not indulge the folly of supposing that mental strength can only come through physical weakness, or that woman must suffer as the penalty of the highest intellectual enjoyment the life-long torment of a diseased body." Smith girls, President Seelye was confident, "will be benefitted physically, as mentally, by their work."[31]

Sound nutrition was emphasized. And at Wellesley, *Harper's Magazine* reported in August 1876, "Nothing that can contribute to the cheerfulness of the rooms or to the sanitary condition of the establishment has been neglected. The natural advantages of the situation and the soil have been supplemented by the most careful attention to the scientific principles, and the most thorough application of the best modern methods. While pure air is constantly being supplied to the interior, the impure air is as constantly being withdrawn. A resident physician gives personal attention to hygienic discipline, as well as to the wants of the sick; and it is safe to believe that whatever physical evils may have crept in to the systems of female education as commonly administered, all such will be to a great extent avoided here."[32]

If gymnasiums were not the first buildings erected on the new campuses, they were included in the original plans and followed shortly, their availability prominently advertised in the college catalogues. Vassar girls organized baseball clubs, played basketball and golf; Wellesley girls exercised with dumbbells and Indian clubs; Barnard girls, whose earliest facilities in the Madison Avenue brownstone did not include a gym, dressed up in heavy dark bloomers and flat-soled slippers to work out at the nearby Berkeley gymnasium. At Mount Holyoke tennis, boating, and walks to the top of Mount Nonotuck had all but replaced the earlier domestic work, and what was left had been considerably lightened by the introduction of steam heat and the hiring of cooks and outside help for housecleaning and dishwashing.

Physical examinations were mandatory, and in an age of increasing popularity of elective systems, the colleges *required* students to take courses in physiology and hygiene; these were usually taught by the resident physicians, an uncommonly tough breed of determined veterans of the male-dominated medical colleges and uncommonly equipped to discredit whatever notions of feminine frailty might linger to constrain a young girl.

The immediate results of this concentration on women's health were gratifying to the new institutions. President Seelye of Smith proudly described the first graduating class (1879): "The health of the students had not been impaired. All of them were as well and most of them stronger than when they entered college. There had been neither death nor serious illness among them, nor had they grown apparently less womanly or less winsome as the result of higher education."[33] (In fact, of the seventeen members of that first class, two died in their mid-thirties, and the date of one woman's death is unknown; of the remaining fourteen, three survived into their eighties, eight survived into their seventies, two survived into their sixties, and one into her fifties.)[34]

In 1885, a Special Committee of the Association of Collegiate Alumnae, in a survey of women graduates from member institutions (Boston, Cornell, Kansas, MIT, Michigan, Oberlin, Smith, Syracuse, Vassar, Wellesley, Wesleyan, and Wisconsin), found them equally robust. On the basis of replies from 705 women, the committee was able to demonstrate that "the seeking of a college education on the part of women does not in itself necessarily entail a loss of health or serious impairment of the vital forces."

The statistics showed that about one fourth of the alumnae had married, and "of the whole number of children borne by them, the greater part are living and in good health." During college, only 20 percent showed any decline in health, 60 percent showed no change at all, and 20 percent showed improvement.

The alumnae actually had better health records than the working girls of Boston with whom the Special Committee compared them.

As far as the committee was concerned, the great health debate was over, won by the advocates of higher education for women. "The graduates, as a body, entered college in good health," its report declared, "passed through the course of study prescribed without material change in health, and since graduation . . . do not seem to have become unfitted to meet the responsibilities or bear their proportionate share of the burdens of life."[35]

Vestiges of this early concern for bodily health lingered, however, long after *Sex in Education* had gone out of print. The requirement that students take a certain number of hours of physical education (as distinguished from participation in intercollegiate sports, which is quite another matter, having less to do with physical health than with social attitudes toward competition [intercollegiate sports will be dealt with later]), during their college careers—for which they usually received no academic credit—lasted nearly a century.

Some of these mandatory hours were spent in specifically body-building courses. For some years Smith required freshmen to take a posture-corrective course called Body Mechanics, and Barnard freshmen of the mid-1950s were required to take a course in relaxation on the theory that chins, chests, and grades rose in direct proportion to the degree of nervous tension present. Other hours were spent in developing the skills necessary for participation in whatever sports were fashionable at the time among genteel young ladies: croquet, crew, tennis, and golf, in the early days, to which were added basketball and field hockey. Today the offerings are virtually unlimited and include such previously male-dominated sports as squash, lacrosse, and track, a development physical education instructors are inclined to attribute to the contemporary women's movement.

The emphasis was on health through physical recreation. A young lady's fortune being dependent largely on her face, nothing so strenuous or rough as to threaten cosmetic damage was offered. The point was, by improving skills through instruction, to prepare young women whose lives were and probably would continue to be basically intellectually oriented and therefore sedentary, to combine a sound body with a sound mind. With the advent of the

institutionally disruptive sixties and the subsequent disappearance
of certain academic requirements and social regulations, the physical education requirements (except for the ever-present mandatory
swimming test) also began to be abandoned or at least to undergo
modification. There is still, however, concern for the physical
well-being of the students, and institutional encouragement,
through diversity of offerings and instructional expertise, of
voluntary enrollment in physical education courses.

This solicitude for women's health was unique. Such interest
was never shown in men's physical well-being. The University of
Wisconsin provided medical care for women ten years before
such care was provided for men, and Harvard's first gymnasium
was opened not for exercise but to give the young gentlemen a
place to let off steam, thereby reducing, it was hoped, the number
of pranks.

Since they were radical experiments, the women's colleges had
understandably been put on the defensive. Matthew Vassar had
seen the problem clearly. "I think," he told his architect in 1862,
three years before Vassar opened, "the success of our College
depends much upon the reputation it can maintain for the *health*
of its Pupils—if thru' bad ventilation sickness should occur it
would be ascribed by the public at *Once* to the unhealthy locality
of the College and not to the imperfect ventilation."[36]

2

It was only a short step from poor ventilation to prayers, from
sanitizing the body to sanitizing the whole person. To survive,
the women's colleges had had to recognize the "specialties in the
feminine constitution," recalled John Howard Raymond of Vassar
some years after the college opened. "Young women away from
home," he observed, "should be surrounded with more effective
social safeguards; . . . special sanitary provisions should be made
for them; . . . they should be furnished with ampler means of personal and domestic comfort than are usually thought necessary
for young men."[37]

Raymond might have added it was not so much the "specialties
in the feminine constitution" that had to be catered to but parental
anxieties about the "specialties in the feminine constitution" that

had to be calmed, a task that assumed dimensions all out of proportion to the problem, education not being considered the necessity—and sometimes not even the desirability—for women that it was considered for men.*

This oversolicitude for women's physical well-being was translated into an institutional life-style quite different from that of the predominantly men's institutions. There, *in loco parentis* was largely a matter of policing the rowdies' manners and morals by the clergymen scholars who made up the faculties. At the women's colleges, *in loco parentis* assumed, in addition to the disciplinary functions, the responsibility for active standard setting, sometimes directly by regulation, sometimes indirectly by subtle encouragement or discouragement of specific activities, so that the curriculum was stretched to include far more than the strictly academic —an expansiveness Dean Virginia Gildersleeve of Barnard later characterized as a *usurpation* of the parental obligation which made college education for women "a daring personal and a very expensive process."[39]

However, aspiring from the first to be truly national colleges, the Sisters had, of course, to be residential, a feature that required institutional responsibility for the whole person, particularly in the case of young women. So that just as the parent is responsible for the child's physical, mental, and spiritual growth, the women's institution assumed the responsibility for its daughters' entire maturing process during the critical, socially formative years in which it had charge. Much of this control was exercised directly in the early days, through a series of complicated and constraining social rules, through a faculty whose work load included character development in addition to physics and French, and through administrators hired specifically to supervise the young women's behavior, the intent being to turn out academically something better but certainly socially nothing less than the products of the "female seminaries" and finishing schools.

Over the first century, the rules were gradually lightened as the

---

* This situation has not changed as much as one might think: Radcliffe's president, Matina S. Horner, reported in February 1975 that Radcliffe parents, unable to meet tuition payments during economic recession, were refusing to accept loans that might, they feared, become negative dowries, jeopardizing the futures of otherwise marriageable daughters.[38]

moral certainties of the nineteenth century were abandoned by the larger society; the faculty turned almost exclusively to academics; and the stern social arbiters were replaced ultimately by centralized housekeeping and deans of students with advanced degrees. But the institutional psyche had changed far less than one might expect. Although a Mount Holyoke student could get an abortion on demand in 1975, its cost a normal part of the college insurance package,[40] nevertheless the parental tone was still very much in evidence on all Seven Sisters campuses.

The outward and visible sign of this non-academic side of the women's-college communities was—and is—a careful attention to physical setting. First, there is a sense of isolation about them: Even Barnard, packed into upper Manhattan, has a measure of physical integrity, located as it is across Broadway from Columbia; and Radcliffe, cheek-by-jowl with Harvard and once described by LeBaron R. Briggs—its second president—as "composed chiefly of a few back yards and an undersized apple tree,"[41] seems to be at least partly self-contained. Of course Wellesley, carved out of the rolling hills beside Lake Waban, exudes a feeling of remoteness, although it is only fifteen miles from metropolitan Boston. Aside from the romantic desires of the founders for the serenity of mind and spirit that accompanies natural landscape beauty, remoteness was a convenient public relations gesture a century ago, effectively removing high-spirited adolescents, away from home for the first time, from potentially injurious dissipations of the too-worldly metropolitan areas, and at the same time relieving parental anxieties; the walls of Castle Adamant were virtually impenetrable.

The Castle Adamant image, however, is no longer appropriate. What was rural a century ago is hardly suburban today, and the subway has brought central Boston within minutes of Harvard Square. Today, campus security is an increasingly significant problem, and campus newspapers recount crime statistics as serious if not as numerous and frequent as those in the daily metropolitan press, the institutional response to which has been a disproportionate preoccupation with security. This preoccupation, while necessary, seems strangely out of character in the formerly serene academic communities where a locked door or a locked bicycle was grounds for suspicion of paranoia. However, Wellesley sponsored a self-defense class during the 1975 winter term, out of necessity; Radcliffe formed a Committee on Violent Crime, and installed extra lighting and emergency telephones with which to summon police; Vassar initiated a nighttime student escort service; Barnard and Columbia volunteers, in the new spirit of "increased integration without assimilation," operated a Rape Crisis Center in connection with St. Luke's Hospital; and on all the formerly open campuses, there have been disproportionate budgetary increases for modern security equipment and professionalized security services. The point was brought home sharply to the Vassar community by its president, Alan Simpson, who, during a widespread epidemic of vandalism at Vassar during 1975, warned at a special convocation: "When we get down to planning the budget of 1976–77, with an estimated $730,000 deficit inherited from 1975–76, we should be prepared to weigh the costs of electronic surveillance against the costs of a student service or the costs of an academic program."[42]

If the women's institutions were to appeal to the large middle class, with its tradition of self-conscious gentility, personal grooming was as essential as remoteness. Writers for the national magazines of the late nineteenth century, which took frequent and detailed editorial note of this new development in higher education, devoted more space to describing the architecture of the colleges (most of it some form of collegiate Gothic which today mingles with modern cement-block and brick attempts to blend old and new with a minimum of dissonance) and the elegance of interior appointments than to describing their academic adventures. At Wellesley—which still looks less like a college campus than a Hollywood notion of a college campus—Henry Fowle Durant, to ensure gracious living, had given monogrammed Wedgwood china for use in the dining halls, although the gesture proved futile. The china was soon nicked into uselessness by hard wear, and something plainer and more durable had to be found. Even today, the decorator touch is apparent on these campuses, and male Dartmouth exchange students at Smith, down from the New Hampshire woods for a semester or two, have felt some obligation to keep at least the public rooms of Sessions Annex neat and clean.

The elegance of the physical settings provided appropriate backdrops to the institutional attention to social niceties. Barnard girls *always* wore hats to cross Broadway, and Wellesley alumnae of the early 1940s recall the appearance of visiting alumna Madame Chiang Kai-Shek in slacks, which at the time were strictly forbidden on campus; an event to which President Mildred McAfee later responded: "I suggest limiting the campus appearance of slacks to those students who think they look as smart in them as Madame Chiang did."[43] Fighting a losing battle against World War II economies and egalitarianism combined, the neat sweaters and skirts, Peter Pan collars and pearls of the 1940s were soon replaced by what was considered a democratizing costume: blue jeans, a Seven Sisters fashion that survives today in varying degrees of neatness and cleanliness.

Dress standards were only part of the regimen of Seven Sisters' "gracious living"—those code words uttered as frequently in derision as respect. The concept involved all those middle-class social customs, from modulated voices to after-dinner demitasse, which the parents of daughters had come to expect from educational institutions, confusing as they sometimes did the responsibilities of the liberal arts college with those of the finishing school; and the colleges responded, recognizing as they did the social imperatives for educating the whole person.

Today, much of the enthusiasm for gracious living has disappeared. Anti-establishmentarian revolts of the late 1960s combined with the high cost of maintaining frills have lessened its impact. For example, centralized dining—a noisy, tray-banging affair, hardly adaptable to candlelight—has replaced separate dormitory dining rooms at Vassar, and the other six have made certain modifications in the same direction. Still, traces remain, the contemporary ambivalence evident in the daily afternoon Vassar tea ceremony: duffle bags parked on the delicate Victorian chairs in the elegant parlors of Main, and blue-jeaned young men and women draped over the sofas drinking tea from real tea cups served out of white china teapots.

Reputation-making a century ago demanded also rule-making. It was essential that the women's institutions return to their parents young ladies who were in every way none the worse for intellectual wear. "It is just as important," Matthew Vassar told a charter member of his board of trustees in 1861, "that we have our

Scholars under our own control as the Colonel of a Brigade when going into battle . . . an essential element of our Institution is the perfect *Control* of the pupils during the period of their instruction in the College, anything short of this is a yielding up of our immediate guardianship, while the responsibility remains,—happen what may to these young thoughtless creatures in a moral point of view the College must incur the Odium."[44]

The colonel of the Vassar brigade was the lady principal, an institution which survived at Vassar until 1915 when she was replaced by a Board of Wardens and a somewhat liberalized set of rules. Her lieutenants were the faculty, constituted at least partly in those days, of clergymen and involved not only intellectually in the college community but often equally in the emotional and spiritual development of students. The president's chief executive officer, the lady principal was guide, model, and confidante of students, trusted handmaiden of nervous mothers, advisor to the president for non-academic affairs, and the ultimate institutional arbiter of good taste and morality for all. The first incumbent was Hannah W. Lyman, recruited from a girls' seminary in Montreal and described by an early graduate as ". . . resplendent . . . tall and large of frame, though rather spare, with wonderful snow-white curls framing the rarely fair and beautiful strong face. Her dress was of silver-grey silk, her shoulders were draped with an exquisite white shawl; a white cap of finest lace, with a streamer of rose-pink ribbon on either side. . . . I think she wore white kid gloves." Her interpretation of her heavy responsibilities left untouched no area of a young lady's life. She presided regally at the dinner table and at chapel, assigned chaperones for shopping trips to Poughkeepsie, judged equally rigidly the propriety of a young lady's callers and the mode of her dress; earliest Vassar girls, all of whom lived together in Main, were even required to report each Monday to their corridor-teachers such minutiae as the number of times they had bathed the previous week (twice was mandatory).[45]

Gradually this heavy-handed despotism was abandoned. Although boarding students at Radcliffe—where supervision was less intrusive, the women's college being an adjunct of a major university in a metropolitan area—had to have their landlords approved by a committee of ladies from the Annex corporation and under no circumstances could they board in families where Harvard students lived, the institutions came increasingly to realize that young women, while high-spirited and warm-blooded, were not in fact the irresponsible children they had been supposed to be—Matthew Vassar's "young thoughtless creatures." And thirty-four years after Vassar opened, Carey Thomas could boast that Bryn Mawr students were at least socially self-governing. They could come and go as they saw fit; no silly regulations stifled their intellectual freedom—a situation that did not go unnoticed by President Eliot of Harvard, who predicted on a visit to Bryn Mawr, no doubt with some relish: "If this continues, I will give you two years, and no more in which to close Bryn Mawr College."[46] Bryn Mawr, of course, did not close; neither did her Sisters. And by 1930, William Allan Neilson was relaxed enough to tell Smith students in one of his regular chapel talks:

You are here to grow into women. We do not believe you can do so without having a large measure of freedom to control your own time and your own actions—a large possibility of going wrong. And the strength of mind that is demanded of the administration of an institution like this is to stand by while the risk of going wrong is in operation and to keep hands off. The art of government here as elsewhere is knowing at what point a student ought to be temporarily saved from herself by compulsion. I say "temporarily," because compulsion can never save her from herself permanently. She alone can do that—but from time to time one has to intervene to prevent irreparable damage.[47]

A fringe benefit of woman's increased independence following the suffrage campaigns, plus the greater responsibilities thrust on her and opportunities opened to her by World War I* was the decided trend away from authority and toward guidance, and the installation in women's colleges of the house mother: the "cultured" but not overly intellectual older gentlewoman—often a widow—who, in her soft sweaters, pearls, and tweeds, was there to exude tea and sympathy to students and social security to anxious parents. She was housekeeper, hostess, confidante, guide, and policeman—the emphasis always on guide, although in local

* The impact on women as a sex of external events over which they had little control—wars, depressions, and so on—has never been properly explored.

dormitory matters the ultimate responsibility and authority were hers. She was every middle-class mother; the reliability of her unschooled common sense the very antithesis of the faculty woman whose scholarly pursuits may have led her into eccentricity, the house mother served as role model to generations, the institutional symbol of social stability.

Another war, another round of feminism, combined with financial difficulties which tend to have a disproportionate influence on both academic and social policies, and another role model has emerged. The house mothers at Smith, for example (who commanded, for full-time responsibility $3,600 a year plus room and board) were replaced—as the old family retainers had been replaced by automatic dishwashers and self-starting ovens in middle-class homes—by centralized housekeeping systems and thirty-five "head residents," who received in 1974–75, for part-time responsibility, $300 to $500 a year plus room and board. Labeled "wardens" at Bryn Mawr, "resident directors" at Barnard, "heads of house" at Wellesley, but responsible everywhere for liaison, the head residents are usually young enough to establish a rapport with students, from whom they are often indistinguishable in appearance. Some may even be seniors, others may be graduate students, either at Smith or neighboring institutions; still others may be setting out on careers; some may be married, with husbands studying or working at nearby institutions and pitching in on dormitory chores.*

Rules have been liberalized, as they have been in the larger society. By 1900 Vassar had eliminated the 10 P.M. bedtime rule; by 1921 juniors and seniors were allowed to go to the movies unchaperoned even when they went out with men, and could motor unchaperoned with men—during daylight hours—but of course the driver had to be approved by the warden. The fol-

---

* Radcliffe, being co-residential with Harvard, is an exception. Here, in an institutional attempt to integrate the academic and the social, to create small cohesive intellectual communities within a larger community whose size and diversity defy cohesiveness, distinguished professors serve terms as masters of the various residential houses to which tutors, advisors, and university staff as well as students are assigned. The houses individually sponsor social events, seminars, lectures, concerts, and plays—the variety of activity, academic or social, limited only by the collective house imagination.

lowing year daytime signing out for absence from college was officially ended at Wellesley; to mollify students who wanted to stay overnight in Boston and at the same time maintain some measure of control of student behavior off-campus, the college bought a house on Commonwealth Avenue where students might weekend in town. By 1923 a Radcliffe girl might walk up from Harvard Square with another girl or even a man, after tea, but not from Central Square or Boston. When visiting mothers and sisters began to embarrass students by lighting cigarettes on the dormitory steps, smoking rooms were designated in college buildings, and another barrier fell.* In 1929, the evening motoring hour was extended to 10 P.M. at Vassar, and parental permission for unchaperoned motoring was no longer required; thirty years later, all classes except freshmen had unlimited night leaves; dormitories remained open until midnight; juniors and seniors had unlimited 2:30 A.M. late permissions; and seniors were allowed to have cars at college all year. By 1962, the life of a Radcliffe girl was circumscribed at only two points: she had to pass her exams and she could not entertain men in her room; she had no compulsory classes or curfews, a situation seen by a Harvard faculty member as "a type of challenge a great many people would have trouble handling in their truly adult years."[49]

A decade later, of course, she *could* entertain men in her rooms (although she still had to pass her exams). The heat from the discussion has dissipated, and the issue of parietals—collegiate jargon of the late 1960s for the hours when dormitories were open to visitors—has been settled; they are open twenty-four hours a day, not only at Radcliffe but at Barnard, Bryn Mawr, Mount Holyoke, Smith, Vassar, and Wellesley. If there are any limitations, they are for security and not social reasons.

In addition, all seven have resident men in varying proportions, and as one Vassar alumna put it, "Saturday night has turned into Tuesday."[50] At Vassar, of course, dormitories are fully coeducational, as is the institution; Radcliffe and Harvard dormitories are, in the local jargon, "co-residential"; Bryn Mawr

---

* The response of Smith's William Allan Neilson to the problem of smoking has become a college legend. "Smoking," he said in one of his regular chapel talks, "is a dirty, expensive, and unhygienic habit, to which I am devoted."[48]

and Barnard maintain dormitory exchanges with Haverford and Columbia respectively; Smith, Mount Holyoke, and Wellesley continue the Twelve-College Exchange Program which still draws at least a sprinkling of temporary resident men from Dartmouth, Williams, Trinity, Wesleyan, Bowdoin, and Amherst, although fewer since these last installed their own women. All seven do maintain, however, some area where women may live who do not choose to share the plumbing with the opposite sex, preserving at least the illusion of free choice.

Fears of administrators, parents, and alumnae, a few of whom actually stopped contributions when their institutions formally installed such modern conveniences as gynecological services, largely have not been realized. While the women's colleges may have lost some of their monastic tone, they have not become supermarkets. As Alan Simpson wrote in his presidential report, 1964–70, to Vassar trustees and alumnae, "Five years from now posterity will wonder what the fuss was all about."[51]

Some observers, particularly older faculty, regard contemporary attitudes toward sex as carnal. However, the promiscuity predicted in what was perhaps overbilled as the sexual revolution of the 1960s and later did not materialize, and the father of a Wellesley student who publicly charged the college, in Spring 1976, with teaching "sexual immorality" and promiscuity elicited shock, anger, and dismay at the charge but much less sympathy than one might have anticipated among other parents.[52] There is of course experimentation, some of it bizarre, and there is some casual bedhopping—for all of which there are ample role models in the larger society. Every corridor in every dormitory has its standard tales of the moveable feast, the shifting room arrangements when boy friends visit—by the day, week, even the month. And of course, there are the obvious campus queens, for whom the role models also exist in the larger society. In mid-summer 1975, the *Washington Post* published an article on the advantages and disadvantages of the various forms of contraception on the market at that time; more interesting than the information offered was the fact that in matters of personal taste, the writer quoted not married women or men, but students, who appeared to respond as casually as if they were comparing laundry soaps.[53]

It seems that the young, rather than being liberated from Victorian morality—which never really existed—have been liberated from the *hypocrisy* of Victorian morality, and their frankness has been misinterpreted as nonchalance. It is an openness that sometimes makes their elders uncomfortable, and the other standard anecdote on campus is the uneasiness of the visiting parent or older alumna who is confronted in the shower room by the honesty of the opposite sex.

Redbook's 1975 study of female sexuality notwithstanding, over the past half century there seems not to have been significant substantive change on the sexual scene. In an early study of American sexual behavior in 1928, G. V. Hamilton found that 59 out of 100 men and 47 out of 100 women, all middle-class New Yorkers under forty, had had either premarital or extramarital intercourse.[54] A decade later, Lewis M. Terman, in a sampling of 1,250 upper- and middle-class urban and semi-urban Californians, reported that while persons born before 1890 were less than 50 percent likely to have had premarital sexual experiences, the incidence rose with each decade until among those born in 1910 or later only 13.6 percent of the men had never had premarital experiences, and only 31.7 percent of the women remained virgins at marriage. The key, however, was commitment, and overall, the highest percentage of premarital experiences were between people who eventually married.[55] In a survey of undergraduate sexual behavior at Stanford in 1970–71, only half as many seniors approved of casual sexual relationships as approved of serious sexual commitment.[56] A Harvard–Radcliffe study of co-residency, comparing a group of women who lived in segregated dormitories in 1969 with a similar group in 1971–72 who had lived in co-residential dormitories for two years, reported that "full sexual relationships are somewhat more frequent in the integrated group . . . Casual encounters, however, were about the same for both groups, and all but one woman in *each* group felt these had been a mistake. Contrary to some people's predictions, sexual promiscuity in attitude and behavior was not different between the two groups."

Overall, the Harvard–Radcliffe study concluded that co-residency was beneficial: "The emotional task of late adolescence is to learn to make close, intimate, loving relationships, and to find one's own style and sense of self as a separate individual with personality and gender. Being in proximity with people of both sexes encourages each person to work on these issues for herself. In these areas, the co-residential experience offers greater opportunity for maturing, and as a group the young women in this study who lived in coed dormitories were more mature in these dimensions than their segregated sisters of two years before."[57]

Some concerns remain; it is not totally the picture painted in the alumnae quarterlies. A lack of knowledge in the area of human sexuality is one problem. Students today are not likely to prepare, as Margaret Mead reported she and her flapper friends at Barnard prepared—in true academic fashion—a five-page typed list of home remedies for pregnancy which they gave to a sixteen-year-old acquaintance discovered in bed with a man.[58] Students today, however, by and large, college physicians say, have not progressed intellectually in this field as far as they have emotionally and morally, and not a few continue to rely on what they learned at Girl Scout Camp.

Another, deeper concern of institution and student is pressure. Institutional pressures mistakenly perceived by young women as promoting promiscuity by prescribing contraception or offering advice on sexual matters. Frankness perceived as preoccupation: the Radcliffe student who charged the college health service had offered her "birth control pills to console me for my sore throat, the morning-after pill to cure the 'flu, and pregnancy counseling to remove any number of stomach aches." Peer pressures, perhaps the most irresistible and potentially damaging of all. Parental pressures, both for and against premarital chastity. And, of course, the young woman's own internal pressures to try her wings at womanhood at the same time she is experimenting with and proving her intellectual powers.[59]

For young men, who are not immune from these, there are also other pressures. Caroline W. Bynum, associate professor of church history at the Harvard Divinity School, wrote:

Many men in our society are threatened by successful, forceful women; it is, after all, extremely damaging to self-image to be bested by someone whom you assume, however subconsciously, to be inferior. This threat is especially strong for males between the ages of 20 and 30, who are meeting a competition from women for jobs and professional school admission that their fathers never dreamed of. But the ethos of women's liberation not only produces this competition; it also suggests that a man who settles for a supportive woman rather than an equal is an emotional and moral coward with a 1950s life-style. If he absorbs this attitude, the young man of 25 may thus feel expected to establish an open and honest relationship with the woman who terrifies him most.[60]

Despite the gradual phasing out of unconditional institutional authority, however, Seven Sisters' students have not been left to cope with the complexities of contemporary life on their own.

The social milieu of the women's colleges is hardly unique, but only reflects the larger society where, it's been said, we all live in a technocracy, reduced by overspecialization to slaves of the machine, men and women only in the strictest physiological sense of the words. As a corollary, the contemporary academic, not only in the women's colleges but elsewhere, preoccupied with imparting increasingly specialized information and conducting research into increasingly narrow fields has been remarkably professionalized, with his or her responsibilities gradually removed from the social and moral areas of the curriculum and confined to the strictly scholarly. So, too, the non-academic side of the women's colleges has been professionalized, divided and subdivided like biology, the non-scholarly duties of the old clergymen scholars and lady principals redistributed among several functionaries. And just as the molecular biologist may not enjoy perfect communication with the geneticist, the redistribution has had a somewhat fractionating effect on the community as a whole. Nevertheless, the overall tone of the women's college as surrogate parent remains.

What Hannah Lyman was hired to do more than a century ago at Vassar has been redistributed through an elaborate counseling system with three more or less equal branches: the college chaplain, the college physician, and the dean of residence, an arrangement that sometimes casts religion, medical science, and social psychology in overlapping roles of guide, model, confidante of students, handmaiden of nervous mothers, advisor to the president for non-academic affairs, and ultimate arbiter of good taste and middle-class morality.

The college chaplain may be part clergyman, part social worker, part personal counselor. Today his studied casualness of dress and youthfulness may make him almost indistinguishable from the male exchange students.*

The college physicians are still somewhat in the style of Alida Avery and her like: an uncommonly tough breed of veterans of the male-dominated medical colleges. They may also be specialists in adolescent medicine, a discipline that involves considerably more than the treatment of mononucleosis and the setting of bones broken in skiing accidents; it includes a large dose of psychology—usually sponsorship of courses in the fundamentals of sexual relationships, with emphasis on the nuts and bolts aspects but not excluding the emotional, moral, and ethical considerations. He or she—usually but not always she—has the resources of a psychiatrist and a gynecologist within reach if not on the permanent staff, and, as one of these women put it, "we fuss."

There was a time when the position of dean of residence was reserved for older faculty members who were about one fence from pasture. Today, the dean of residence is trained in administration and psychology and heads an informal counseling structure made up of the head residents in each house plus a fairly recent phenomenon called peer counselors or student advisors: young women scattered through the dormitories trained, in a deft legitimization of peer pressures, to discuss at certain elementary levels such potentially problematic subjects as drugs, birth control, venereal disease, abortion referral, roommate problems, course offerings, faculty idiosyncracies, and, with newcomers, the shortest path to the library. They are also trained to recognize the point at which their training stopped and to know where to refer a problem they are not equipped to cope with.

The essence of this system is that it's voluntary, and nobody counts how many baths a student takes a week or appears to notice with whom she shares her room. However, part of the responsibility and training of all these functionaries is to be discreetly aware of what's going on, to know when a student hasn't

---

* Wellesley finally broke the tradition of male chaplains for the academic term 1974–75 when a young woman graduate of Wellesley and the Harvard Divinity School took over while the college chaplain was on sabbatical leave. Vassar a few years ago enjoyed the part-time services of a woman rabbinical student.

been down to breakfast for three days and to recognize the point at which she as advisor may inject herself.

The purpose of the system, with its interlocks, overlaps, and backstops, has not really changed since Matthew Vassar hired Hannah Lyman to command the Vassar brigade: to return the young women to their families none the worse for intellectual wear, and it is an agile young woman who can sidestep the implications of control. While the control is certainly less pervasive and intrusive under a chic young dean of residence with her ready smile and capacity for understanding than under the rigid discipline of a Hannah Lyman, the achievement of social independence has not kept pace with the achievement of intellectual independence, and a sense of sheltering, of protectiveness, of direction, linger to underscore and perhaps prolong the sense of little-girlhood.[61]

3

It is part of the official public relations of the single-sex college to zero in on the obvious absence of discriminatoin on the basis of sex in the area of extra-curricular activities and the consequently enlarged opportunities for women at women's institutions to participate freely and effectively—opportunities which purport to offer the organizational experience necessary if women are to assume positions of leadership. As Mildred McAfee, former president of Wellesley, once wrote: "Many a town has reason to be grateful for the experience of residents who learned, in college, to run a community chest drive, to govern a residential group, to organize a college church, to direct theatrical productions, to edit a publication, run a radio station or perform other functions of a democratic residential community."[62]

At Mount Holyoke, the editor of the college newspaper and her staff are women. Period. In contrast, at Radcliffe, although women have been staff members of the *Harvard Crimson* for two decades, and three women had, prior to 1975, been elected managing editor (the first one in 1966), a woman, as of 1975, had never been president, the top position on the publication which was founded in 1873, and the masthead remained heavily male (about 72 percent). Nor had there ever been any women heads of the *Harvard Advocate* or the *Harvard Lampoon.* When a Radcliffe junior took over as president of the *Harvard Independent* (a new publication, maverick in style and outlook) in January 1975, she was the first woman ever to head any Harvard student publication.[63] (*The Harvard Law Review* elected its first woman president in February 1976.)

Wellesley girls run the Shakespeare Society and the Wellesley College Theater. They always have. At Radcliffe, the Harvard Dramatic Club, which is about 70 percent male, got its second woman president in fifteen years in 1974.

In the women's colleges, women *are* the student government. At the University of Chicago in 1924, when three of the four male class presidents had to resign for one reason or another, "petticoat government"—succession by the female vice presidents—was averted by holding new elections. It could never, by definition, happen at Smith.

The cliché is that men assert their presence out of all proportion to their numbers and tend to dominate campus life. An analysis of campus offices nationally, published by the American Association of University Women in 1970, reported that women on coeducational campuses were most frequently found in primarily non-elective, or appointive, offices, positions requiring writing or detail work, while men were most likely to hold the elective—and most powerful and influential—political offices; men ran the student government and captained the debating team; women wrote the yearbook and edited the literary magazine.[64]

The report of the faculty committee that weighed the pros and cons of coeducation for Smith, published in April 1971, suggested that a potential threat to the first-class status of women there existed even in the presence of small numbers of male exchange students. The committee cited the fact that when departmental representatives were elected to participate in curriculum discussions, three of these representatives were men, although they had been at Smith for only a few weeks and would remain for a year at the outside.

And John R. Coleman, president of Haverford, observed regarding the merger of the Bryn Mawr and Haverford newspapers into the *Bryn Mawr–Haverford News*—which was part of the Two-College Community arrangement:

I think back to the reservations of Miss McBride [president of Bryn Mawr, 1942–70] when the papers were merged. At the time I thought she was dead wrong and that one ought to laud automatically all cooperative ventures. But as I read the papers in the past couple of years, I'm no longer sure. I think Bryn Mawr has had a short deal. I do not think that your news has been covered nearly as completely as ours.[65]

That's the cliché: the inevitable triumph of male aggressiveness. More to the point, however, may be female passiveness, deference if you will, which is a prominent feature not only of the women's-college academic life but also of the organized extracurricular life—and by a simple effort of transference, of the larger society—a characteristic that the Sisters institutionally, in their choices of what to support, what not to support, and how to do it, have done more to perpetuate than to alter.

It is true that the extracurricular fare has always been extensive. Encouraged by the institutions, Smith, Bryn Mawr, Mount Holyoke, Vassar, Wellesley, Barnard, and Radcliffe girls organized themselves early into mutual interest groups emphatically open to all—an egalitarianism intended to offset the social competition that traditionally has been a prominent feature on the fraternity- and sorority-dominated university campuses. The first Vassar catalogue, 1865–66, reported that an "Organization has been formed among the students for mutual improvement," i.e., "recitations, readings, music, and other literary or aesthetic recreations."[66] The fifth Vassar catalogue reported, in addition to the above, the organization of a Philaethean Society which was to stage several dramatic productions a year, a music club, a French club, the Society for Religious Inquiry, and the Floral Society for "exercise and improvement in ornamental gardening." By 1898, no fewer than thirteen such organizations had flowered on campus. The cult of the extracurricular reached its peak in the 1950s, when ninety-six activities, including eleven musical organizations, cluttered a Vassar *Student Handbook*. Students wrote literary pieces for the college journals, went to concerts and lectures featuring the very best, especially imported talent (Matthew Arnold, Mark Twain, Charles Dickens, Jane Addams, Joseph Jefferson, and the Webbs were the stars of the lecture circuit in the 1880s, for example), took an interest in student

government, and demonstrated a commitment to "Christian"
ideals which in the nineteenth century meant largely missionary
societies and settlement houses. Social issues of the time also included women's suffrage and related feminist issues, but para-
doxically, the women's colleges were rarely, at least as institutions,
concerned with these—but more of that later. Traditions, essentially light-hearted, developed: Ice carnivals, float nights, hoop
rolls, step sings, lantern nights, and Vassar's Daisy Chain was
predecessor to Atlantic City.

If there was a sense of busy work about it, it was a veritable
feast on which a young woman could dine uninhibited by the
dominating presence of the opposite sex. However, lacking this
presence, it seemed unrealistic to contend that the conditions in
the women's college in any way resembled those a student would
encounter after graduation, that editing the *Sophian* was practice
for serious journalism, or that running for office at Bryn Mawr
had any relation to running for mayor of Cleveland or even to
the political aspects of business and professional organizations.
The extracurricular *was* practice for the future, but in quite another sense. The development of the extracurricular on Seven
Sisters campuses has amounted, over the past century, to little
more than an expansion to a new level of sophistication of the
old childhood game of "playing house," by the same old players.
It *was* practice for adulthood, for a specific sort of adulthood
during which the large majority of alumnae would continue—
not as leaders in the larger society, but as the *wives* of leaders or
the leaders of other women—the lives of creative leisure they
had begun at Wellesley and Vassar.

Nowhere is this more evident than in the activity common to
all the Sisters and known as student government. For decades the
women's colleges considered the institution of student government one of their proudest achievements. "If Bryn Mawr has a
soul," wrote Harris L. Wofford in his first *President's Report*
1970–73, "an important ingredient is the spirit and practice of
self-government.[67] And Smith girls, President Herbert Davis
(1940–49) is supposed to have muttered, "can hardly have a
simple conversation with a friend without electing a chairman,
a treasurer, and a secretary."[68]

Student government is not peculiar either to the Seven Sisters or to other American colleges and universities. However, of all the extracurricular activities, it has always been one of the most prominently displayed features of the women's-college ambience, the implication being that women could get no training for citizenship in a coeducational institution where men traditionally held all the offices. Although few others have elevated it to the exalted position it enjoys on Seven Sisters campuses, nine out of ten American institutions of higher learning traditionally have supported some form of student government wielding varying degrees of power. Its origins can be found in the unendowed medieval European universities, which depended wholly on students' fees for their existence. There, a disproportionate amount of authority was conferred on the students, who actually controlled some universities, electing the rector, hiring the faculty, and issuing academic regulations. (This indirect power over the institution, this consumerism, still exists, thanks to the free elective system, in the sense that student interest determines the viability of the academic curriculum, but it was never formalized in the endowed and state-financed American institutions as it had been in Europe.) American student government began, in a small way, not at Harvard, but at William and Mary immediately following the Revolution when students were given authority over certain disciplinary matters and later devised an honor system. The structure was refined early in the nineteenth century at the University of Virginia where Thomas Jefferson required students to practice for their later roles as statesmen. Jefferson's system, which delegated authority over most student activities, including the honor system, to students, served as a model for American student government in general, which gradually spread to other collegiate institutions.

The formal organizations, largely student initiated, were established in the earliest years of the Seven Sisters, not then as training ground for participation in democratic government—women *could* not participate at the time—but as a result of rapidly rising enrollments which necessitated regulation of increasingly complex group living. These associations go by a variety of names but share common purposes, adequately stated in 1927 by Vassar president Henry Noble McCracken: "The young men of the junior and senior classes in college have passed the legal age for voting, while the young women have passed the legal age for consent to their most important life decision [marriage] . . . they are certainly old enough to be trusted with some measure of responsibility." In addition, there was the educational value, the opportunity "too great to be lost," for a social laboratory right on the college campus, in which "by participation in their own government, students can learn something about law and obedience."[69] But there was no nonsense about Vassar women assuming positions of any importance.

The annals of these organizations are filled with proud joustings against the local academic establishment: The Self-Government Association of Bryn Mawr and the honor system versus Carey Thomas and the proctor system; the Vassar Students' Association and voluntary class attendance versus the Vassar faculty and administration and compulsory class attendance. (In both cases, the students eventually won.) With the advice and consent of the faculty and administration, the student organizations legislated such social issues as smoking, drinking, noise, curfews, and chaperones; and they passed sentence on errant students for infractions: temporary suspension for slipping gin into the lemonade; early sign-ins for too many bicycle parking tickets.

But real governance of the institutions eluded them; the power was largely illusory. They had little impact on decision-making, and little influence on curricular and faculty policies, except indirectly through the pocketbook. Basically, they were impotent; they derived what little control they had of social conditions not from the consent of the governed but from the consent of the governor. David Riesman and Christopher Jencks in *The Academic Revolution* compared student governments in general to colonial governments dependent for authority on the administration back in Whitehall—and not always able to command the respect of the "natives."

Over the past decade, significant changes have been made in college governance, but these have been the result of pressures from external forces and not, largely, institutionally self-motivated. Beginning in the early 1960s, political revolution and natural social evolution met in a kind of clash of academic biorhythms. At about the same time students were gaining added control over themselves as social beings, the full political impact of the twentieth-century black and women's movements struck halls of learning everywhere and, culminating in the upheavals of the late sixties and early seventies, resulted in, among other things, some new degree of academic autonomy for students throughout the world.

A new sense of purpose seemed to emerge; at the Seven Sisters, developments generally followed the outlines written by the larger academic society. A new college journalism surfaced which concerned itself less with the literary than with the social and political. Women began to take a new interest in intercollegiate sports competition. An untypical preoccupation with ethnicity that had begun with the introduction of large numbers of black students to the institutions, but was not long limited to blacks, replaced the French clubs and floral societies and persisted in the politicalization of campuses. In this line, Barnard, for example, listed nine such organizations in 1973–74, including the Asian Women's Coalition, the Chinese Students' Club, the Latin American Students Association, the Student Struggle for Soviet Jewry, in addition to the seed organization, the Barnard Organization of Soul Sisters (BOSS).

Students began to contribute, under strict controls, to actual governance of the colleges. They had discovered the potential in real politics: They had sat-in and prayed-in with the Civil Rights movement, they had learned more about politics in the brief abortive presidential campaign of Senator Eugene McCarthy than they could ever learn in a student senate, and they had discovered their own enormous potential for power in their Indochinese war protests. Interest in what had been at best, according to Riesman and Jencks, a "charade,"[70] dwindled noticeably. Students would have, they declared, no less than self-determination.

Formal student government still exists on Seven Sisters campuses, but it is a shadow of its former self, with widespread apathy the most common symptom of its powerlessness. That's just not where it's at. In 1974, Judicial Board, Mount Holyoke's traditional arbiter of social policy in the student government structure, was voted out of existence. There were no longer any significant social or personal regulations to enforce; students were not interested in running for offices which meant little more than presiding over meetings at which there was nothing to discuss.

At Bryn Mawr, in the spring of 1975, there was considerable doubt whether the Self-Government Association could muster a quorum to vote on a new constitution. (Enough voters did eventually show up, and the constitution was duly ratified, but it was a near thing.)[71] Uncontested offices are becoming commonplace.

However, students have gotten a foot in the door of institutional government. Student representation, usually but not always including voting representation, has been legislated for college governance committees and, in some institutions, for the boards of trustees. If not a student, there may be a "young" trustee, a member of the graduating class, often the outgoing head of student government. In 1965, the search committee that chose Ruth M. Adams president of Wellesley was made up of seven members of the board of trustees and a non-voting advisory committee of five tenured faculty. Reflecting the broadened base of college governance, the search committee that chose Barbara W. Newell successor to Miss Adams six years later was made up of eighteen voting members: nine trustees, *four* faculty, and *five* students.[72]

Which *is* where it's at. Some of these students are elected, others are appointed, reserving some establishment control; all student representatives are in a minority, and total control is not likely to be passed to students. Nevertheless, there is student input, if not decision- and policy-making, on matters of faculty and administration appointments, reappointments, promotions, tenure, curriculum, admissions, financial aid, even how the college invests its money.*

---

* This is considerably more than even some junior faculty have achieved. At Smith, for example, among the standing faculty committees for 1974–75, the influential College Planning and Resources Committee included two trustees, the president of the Alumnae Association, four members of the administration including the president, five senior faculty, and *two* students but *no junior* faculty; the Committee on Committees includes the president, four senior faculty, *four* students, and *one* junior faculty. Across the Connecticut River, at Mount Holyoke, the Academic Policy Committee, one of the most powerful factions on campus since academics is the soul of the institution, listed for 1974–75—the second year of student representation on this particular committee, the first year of student *voting* representation— the dean of the faculty, the registrar, the director of admissions, the dean of students, the dean of studies, six senior faculty, *two* students, and *one* junior faculty.[73]

While some of these student gains were achieved with resort to confrontation politics—albeit reasonably ladylike—administrators now officially view this expansion of student influence on college policy as a healthy development, giving the institution the benefit of the younger and often liberalizing perspective, at the same time recognizing the student's maturity, her stake in academic matters, and offering her some minimal control of her expensive education.

That is one side of the coin: institutional support and positive encouragement for the cultural and intellectual interest groups engaged in some mutually attractive projects, and for the establishment and continuation of student government, even with its increased implications for college governance. The focus is on the group, on the value of community, a laudable aim no doubt, but hardly designed to produce innovation or leadership so much as docility and conformity, characteristics traditionally assigned to females.

The flip side is the historical *lack* of institutional support and some subtle but nonetheless real *dis*couragement of competitive activities which encourage individual initiative, resourcefulness, and aggressiveness.

Competition, said the editor of the *Smith College Monthly* in 1893, "is likely to become an end in itself instead of a means to an end . . . and that, in the conditions under which alone it is practicable, it is likely to be disastrously wasteful. The waste of excitement and the expense of emotion are unfortunately large throughout life, and nothing seems to be gained by extending the area exposed to them."[74]

Three quarters of a century later, a Connecticut judge in a 1971 decision denying the right of women to participate on a cross-country team declared: "Athletic competition builds character in our boys. We do not need that kind of character in our girls, the women of tomorrow."[75]

Over the past decade, partly as a result of the contemporary women's movement, intercollegiate sports have become a fact of life on Seven Sisters campuses, but the heartiness of the institutional welcome leaves something to be desired, a certain timidity persists, and the prevailing attitude continues to be approximately what William Allan Neilson, perhaps Smith's most beloved president (1917–39), is supposed to have declared it: The best thing about a women's college is that it never lost a football game.[76]

Enjoyment of sports may be sex-blind, a fairly universal condition to which the Sisters undoubtedly contributed by their early defensive preoccupation with setting strict health standards, part of which included vigorous sports programs. Competition in sports, however, is not. Formalized sports competition began, of course, with the Olympic Games which were essentially a spin-off of combat drill and stressed the manly arts of war; women were not even allowed on the playing fields as spectators. The sports ethic has changed little in the ensuing two thousand years.

As professionals, women have been barred outright from certain major sports and discriminated against, especially financially, in others. Generally, the conditions on the college campus are no different from those in the larger society; not only separate but patently unequal. Institutional pennies are pinched to support the rare woman on an athletic scholarship while male athletes are supported in high style. In 1974, Pennsylvania State University's $3.6 million athletic budget, which included fourteen men's sports and eleven women's, allocated $40,000 for women's athletics; this discrepancy was not an uncommon one and, beholden to football or not, such an enormous difference spells discrimination which is not atypical at large universities. There are horror stories from both Barnard and Radcliffe of second-class citizenship and second-hand equipment, a situation which the enforcement of Title IX of the Education Act Amendments of 1972 (barring sex discrimination by institutions that receive federal money) may in time alleviate; in fact, the threat of federal intervention and the possibility of withdrawal of federal funds has had the salubrious effect of doubling, tripling, even quadrupling or better, women's athletic budgets at several large institutions, and even Harvard has seen fit to make some minimal adjustments in Radcliffe's situation.

At the Seven Sisters, discrimination obviously has not been against women; it has instead been against competitive athletics in general. Sports remained a health measure, a pleasant recreation, a socially useful instructional period, a physical education requirement, or a study break. Competition was not part of the package, and teams were what the girls cheered on Saturday afternoons at Harvard stadium.

It is of course true that most young women arrived at college without a strong athletic orientation. The soccer players and the duck-duck-goose players having been separated by the second or third grade, women lacked the expertise and specific goals, and interest, unencouraged, was casual at best. The institutions, however, did little to sharpen their interest. They had copied verbatim the academic curriculum of the men's colleges, but had reacted strongly against the use—which, it is true, held a vast potential for abuse—of the competitive sports arena as a viable function of the educational experience for women.

Middle-class gentility dictated this attitude: Women had been taught from childhood to hide their aggressiveness behind their croquet mallets, lest bulging muscles detract from femininity and ultimately from marriageability, the only respectable option. In addition, as Neilson of Smith did say, in 1929, "The women's colleges have an enormous advantage in their freedom from the incubus of the intercollegiate athletic contest. They pay, on the whole, more attention to the health and exercise of the individual student than the men's colleges do, and they have a healthy but not exaggerated interest in intramural competition. But athletics do not constitute the serious distraction which is all too manifest to teachers in men's colleges." Furthermore—and it is Neilson the fund-raiser and Neilson the former Harvard professor speaking now—"the alumnae let athletics alone."[77]

And so, during the first two decades of this century, while alumni were feverishly building football stadiums at the universities—a condition that did on occasion make the educational institutions overly beholden to that sport*—the women's colleges were holding polite intramurals and annual field days. By 1940, they had lost some of their enthusiasm even for these, and appeared to be more interested in the socially useful sports: tennis, golf, skiing.

Now feminine self-assertiveness, at least to a limited, ladylike

---

* Yale, out to raise a record $370 million in the mid–1970s, reported some reluctance to contribute on the part of certain wealthy alumni who were using economic pressures to express their dissatisfaction with the scarcity of athletes in the student body; in fact, Yale's director of institutional development and capital support disclosed that one benefactor said he was writing a $2 million bequest to Yale out of his will because "a certain quarterback didn't get admitted."[78]

degree, has become more socially tolerable if not actually worthy of encouragement, a development that surfaced on Seven Sisters campuses—as it did on other campuses across the country—in demands for intercollegiate sports.

The demand was heard in administrative circles with some skepticism. Academics was the excuse: At highly challenging, intellectually oriented institutions, the commitment, which had to be to academics, could not be diverted or divided—although Harvard, Yale, Princeton, Dartmouth, Williams, Amherst, and Cornell had traditionally been at least somewhat institutionally schizophrenic without apparent serious injury to either class rankings or academic reputations; and if the commitment to sports was not so intense as that of Ohio State or UCLA, the Ivy League institutions could be assured a minimum of institutional support and encouragement.

The demand for intercollegiates at Seven Sisters institutions was met, finally, a sport at a time as student interest dictated, and swimming meets, regattas, and even fencing tournaments are now part of the Seven Sisters athletic furniture; field hockey and women's basketball games are standard fare; increasingly popular are such traditionally male sports as lacrosse, squash, and water polo. In a 1974 statistical survey of six New England "neighborhood" colleges with which Wellesley students were then competing (Mount Holyoke, Trinity, Brown, Smith, Wheaton, and Wellesley itself), the *Wellesley News* reported that participation in intercollegiates average 14 percent of the students, with a high of 25 percent at Trinity (coeducational) and a low of 7 percent at Smith.[79] In spite of discrimination in the rowing tanks and forced dependence on Harvard's hand-me-down shells and oars, Radcliffe's crew has been successful in national competition.

Except at Radcliffe, where the presence of Harvard has served many purposes over the century, and at Vassar which is newly coeducational and where the power structure has urged improvement of intramural and intercollegiate sports "if Vassar is to appeal to a broad spectrum of qualified male applicants,"[80] intercollegiate sports are more tolerated, however, than actually sponsored at Seven Sisters institutions.

Funding is minimal. The Big Ten they're not. The Wellesley swimming coach had to pass the hat, literally, in the spring of

1975, to send two swimmers, who had qualified in the New England championships, to Arizona to compete in the National Championships.[81] The total Wellesley Sports Association budget for 1974–75 was $3,000 which was expected to support thirteen sports —entry fees, membership dues, officials, equipment, occasional food and lodging—plus $1,000 to reimburse faculty for traveling expenses.

Lacking money and ready transportation, a situation calculated, as one coach put it, "'to dampen the spirits of the most dedicated," students have had to economize and extemporize, with teams traveling in student and faculty automobiles and sleeping six to a bed.

Some of the Seven rushed out to join the fledging Association for Intercollegiate Athletics for Women (AIAW), established in 1971 as the feminist answer—albeit a low-key answer—to the blatantly sexist National Collegiate Athletic Association (NCAA);* others did not because both the dues and the high degree of organization seemed prohibitive. Despite increasing national interest in such items as sports training camps for women athletes and intensifying competition for skilled women athletes on coeducational campuses, the Sisters intend to stay out of the businesss of athletic scholarships, with its indecorous, unladylike pressures and potential for corruption, a decision that may in time further reduce competitive sports opportunities for non-participants.

Competition is usually regional, with team travel limited at Mount Holyoke, for example, to two-hour trips. It is also low-key; Smith and Mount Holyoke at one time shared a diving coach, a situation that raised some sticky questions at Smith–Mount Holyoke swimming meets.

The college catalogues bury—when they do not altogether ignore—information about intercollegiate sports. Athletic prizes range from scarce to non-existent, though finally, in time for the 1975 commencement, Radcliffe established two athletic awards for women. And when the university coaches arrived in Washington in the summer of 1975 to protest the sports regulations in-

* An NCAA representative at an AIAW convention in January 1975 was asked: "What plans does the NCAA have for small women's colleges such as Wellesley"; he answered none, and asked if Wellesley was a school in this country. The NCAA official line has been that enforcement of Title IX regulations in sports will end intercollegiates.[82]

cluded in Title IX, not a women's-college official troubled to join them.

The major rationales for the low grade of institutional commitment to intercollegiate sports are three: the limited funds of the small, private liberal arts college; the negative examples provided by men's and coeducational institutions which, in the eyes of the women's-college administrators, have allowed the tail to wag the dog; and academic priorities. At the Seven Sisters, intercollegiate sports are kept "in the right perspective," which is the Bryn Mawr way of saying that the hockey team is fine, dear, so long as it doesn't eat into anthropology. But the subliminal signals indicate an additional factor: that it's all right to be a male jock, far less acceptable to be a female one.

4

"The dilemmas confronting women in extracurricular activities," observed Riesman and Jencks in *The Academic Revolution*, "are, of course, mainly a reflection of larger dilemmas confronting all American women."[83]

Is the American woman a mature and independent adult capable of assuming responsibility, of pulling her weight in the larger society? Or is she a little girl, still playing house?

Riesman and Jencks put the situation in a single-sex college versus coeducational institution context:

It could theoretically be argued that an exclusively female college forces girls to take charge and discover their talents, whereas a coeducational college encourages them to play subsidiary roles. Some women's college papers lend credence to this thesis. . . . In general, however, the girls who run newspapers at women's colleges appear even less willing to be combative or entrepreneurial than those in coeducational colleges. They create papers that, instead of liberating their staffs from conventional definitions of femininity, seem to reinforce them. On coeducational campuses on the other hand, the newspaper is more often a mix of masculine and feminine staff, skills, and attitudes. Girls often rise to the top of these papers, and despite the pseudo-professionalism and front-page posing into which their male colleagues sometimes push them, they usually get a broader view of themselves and their powers than they would on a girls' college paper.[84]

All of which is undoubtedly true, but begs the point of women's-college responsibility for attempting to help change a situation which may have less to do with the presence of male students on campus than with the institutional tendencies to perpetuate the traditional feminine characteristics through overextension of *in loco parentis* in all those direct and less direct ways. One result of this is to signal to women that it's all right to make one's ladylike way up the League of Women Voters ladder (which has more features of an escalator than a ladder), but less acceptable to deal with the serious competition of the professional world.

At least one medical school dean has noticed that women students in general, most of whom have entered with better academic records than male students, have not done as well as the men under the heightened stresses of medical school, a situation he attributed to the fact that men generally are more experienced in and inured to stress in their personal lives, having endured more in such areas as competitive sports, street fights, and so on, than women who generally have been sheltered prior to entering medical school.

If women are to be pampered, protected, and persuaded to postpone confrontation with stress for the first two decades of their lives—not so much through the absence of men as through the presence of patronization—can they in fact be *expected* to assume the roles of mature adults? The potential for sexist mischief in such arrangements is almost unlimited.

Perhaps, a hundred years later, Dr. Clarke has indeed had his way with us.

4

"If the earth had waited for a precedent, it never would have turned on its axis!"

—MARIA MITCHELL, *Professor of astronomy*, Vassar College, 1865–88, to her diary.

1

"So FAR AS the mere imparting of information is concerned," declared Alfred North Whitehead of Harvard and Cambridge universities in 1929, "no university has had any justification for existence since the popularization of printing in the fifteenth century."[1]

It is an easy exercise in transference from Whitehead's plea for imaginative methodology in higher education to the curricular implications, some forty years later, of some remarks made by David B. Truman, president of Mount Holyoke, at a convocation in the fall of 1973. "What must women's education be?" he asked.

It should confront the destructive stereotypes and their symptoms as explicitly as possible; it should encourage independence, initiative, autonomy and involvement; it should discourage the inclination to deal with anxiety and self-doubt by withdrawal; it should encourage the widest possible range of opportunities for testing and assessing competence, and not merely academic competence; and it must provide assurance, not indulgence but assurance, that the effort to break the stereotypes, to achieve real choice, and to compete with anyone of comparable talent is possible as well as desirable, however difficult.[2]

Or, as Kate Millett had put it more succinctly at the Wellesley commencement in 1971, "to deserve the name, a woman's college must serve women like a zealot."[3]

Although the Seven Sisters are certainly as thoroughly special-interest institutions as the theocentric medieval university, neither pedagogical imagination nor feminist zeal have been prominent characteristics of these women's colleges during the first century of their existence. If the rationale for their establishment—to prove women the intellectual equals of men—had a smell of unorthodoxy about it in the latter half of the nineteenth century, the academic curriculum, when it was finally devised, did not. The women's colleges have always been, and continue to be, importers of curricular ideas, and Mary Wollstonecraft's *Thoughts on the Education of Daughters* (1787) in which she did "confront the destructive stereotypes and their symptoms" may have been the last white paper to address seriously the meaning and application of women's education, a condition that not only created a lopsided—and, of course, unfavorable—balance of trade, but also revealed a certain academic timidity (can one go so far as to say a peculiarly feminine motive to avoid success?) that belies their common reputation for academic excellence, leaves the institutions wanting as role models, and may do more to *dis*courage than to *en*courage those qualities of "independence, initiative, autonomy, and involvement" which Mr. Truman would have women develop.

Academic imitation of the men's institutions was a prominent feature of the Sisters in the earliest days, although not everyone considered it an advantage, and Maria Mitchell, Vassar's first professor of astronomy, sighed wearily to her diary in 1866: "Our faculty meetings always try me in this respect: we do things that other colleges have done before. We wait and ask for precedent. If the earth had waited for a precedent, it never would have turned on its axis!"[4] Nevertheless, the early women's-college catalogues are virtually indistinguishable from those of the men's colleges. Vassar and Amherst students of 1866 were both offered, in approximately the same proportions, the ancient and modern languages and literatures including English, mathematics, natural philosophy, chemistry, natural history, political science and history, mental and moral philosophy; it was a curriculum designed, said the first Vassar *Catalogue*, "for those who seek a thorough, liberal education," embracing those studies "which experience has shown to be most effective for enlarging, disciplining, and refining the mind."[5] It was also designed to perpetuate the status quo, utilizing as it did the history and philosophy texts which only underlined the second classness of women. (Interestingly, the women's colleges tended initially to put a good deal of stress on the study of astronomy, and on the early acquisition of an observatory; whether for scientific, symbolic, or poetic reasons is not always clear.)

Selective in their choice of students from the beginning, the Seven Sisters immediately achieved reputations for excellence in terms of the purely academic. The common academic standards and quality remain uncommonly high, the result of which has had the happy circular effect of perpetuating uncommonly high selectivity of young women and a virtually uninterrupted chain of uncommonly intelligent student bodies. All of which has been uncommonly reassuring to the Smith and Wellesley and Bryn Mawr graduates that their B.A.'s were often worth somewhat more both financially and socially than the diplomas of women from Brand X.

This academic imitation was, of course, inherent in their establishment. Apples and oranges not being comparable, if the institutions were to prove beyond doubt the intellectual equality of men and women, it would hardly do to offer different courses at Vassar and Amherst. Ditto, if, as Vassar's first *Catalogue* stated, the goal was "to accomplish for young women what colleges of the first class accomplish for young men; that is to furnish them the means of a thorough, well-proportioned, and liberal education."[6]

Imitation was also inevitable in the institutional need for academic and social approval, a need that would not be satisfied through additional academic innovation; or, as John Howard Raymond of Vassar put it, "Whatever theories might require, it was idle to adopt a scheme which would not attract a liberal patronage from the well-to-do classes of the community."[7] Furthermore, the young women themselves, aware of their vulnerability and determined to prove themselves, "refuse," wrote Bryn Mawr's Carey Thomas in 1900, "to regard as satisfactory any modification whatsoever of the usual academic courses."[8]

And so, concluded an early critic of women's education in 1918,

"The growth of the curriculum of the woman's college has been marked by no particular originality; that is, the woman's college cannot be pointed out as the source of any single tendency in the American college today." However, she added, underscoring their policy of consumerism, "Their great increase in size and wealth points toward the conserving power of safe imitation."[9]

The tone had been firmly set; over the second half century, it was not to be altered substantially. If resistance to change is a prominent feature of academe in general, its prominence is multiplied in the women's college. This "safe imitation," a reluctance to risk, continued, and curriculum innovation at the Sisters has generally, with some exceptions, meant little more than the redistribution of knowledge across the various disciplines; the repackaging of it into smaller and smaller boxes as it becomes more specialized; the abandonment of certain requirements, and the concomitant enlargement of opportunities for electives and independent scholarships. All of these are obviously important, but hardly the sort of pioneering one might expect from special-interest institutions; they tended instead to follow the outlines laid down at Amherst, Dartmouth, and Yale. All of which only serves to emphasize further the Sisters' willingness to rely on outsiders to define them, an abdication of responsibility that goes beyond an early lack of enthusiasm for women's studies in the curriculum—although this is part of it—and includes the entire psychological, social, and intellectual direction of the academic areas.

2

One consequence of academic timidity at Seven Sisters institutions has been to invest the curriculum with an antiseptic quality, as if truth—whether sociological, economic, psychological, historical, or biological—were sexless. Truth is sexless in the same way that Western history is objective; that is, *de facto* white, male, and Protestant Christian.

"Was I aware of what women had done in the past?" asked a 1965 Smith alumna some years later. "Not really, and that's the most serious gap in my education. . . . I took all those history courses. Why wasn't I interested in how women got the vote?

Why wasn't I interested in the conflict between the abolitionists and the feminists over the question of the women's movement? Why didn't I focus more on women authors in my English courses?"[10]

If sex was an important factor in the non-academic side of the women's-college curriculum where the physical, moral, and psychological development (i.e., safety) of young women must be carefully considered, it was virtually ignored on the academic side for nearly a century, until finally the contemporary women's movement raised the consciousness of us all. Prior to that, however, it never occurred to the faculty—most of whom, male or female, were products of the male-dominated graduate schools—to bring it up among students, of whom the brightest might go on to male-dominated graduate schools.

The obvious chart of faculty interests is research and publication, on which promotion and salary largely hinge, despite the Sisters' prominently advertised commitment to undergraduate teaching, and traditionally these interests rarely included nineteenth-century feminism or women authors.* Many of the women faculty, prior to being hired by Seven Sisters institutions, had experienced academic discrimination at first hand, as undergraduates, graduate students, and job applicants. Once hired, however, with, theoretically, all the resources of a leading women's institution at their disposal, they failed either to utilize these resources or to explore the status of their sex—whether for lack of encouragement, interest, or imagination is not always clear. As leaders of the contemporary women's movement discovered, it does not require too many pulled threads to make holes in the social fabric; still, the women's-college faculties were content to settle for academic respectability and security, thus perpetuating the traditional institutional conservatism. There was, after all, little professional mileage—either in one's own institution or in one's discipline—to be got out of exploring, in whatever scholarly ways, the roles and needs of the second sex; the potential prestige lay, until the last few years, in the reinvestigation of Wordsworth's poetry, the Italian Fascists, retailing in the Soviet Union, Bertrand Russell's philoso-

---

* Interestingly, Robert E. Riegal, professor of history at Dartmouth, was awarded a grant by the John Simon Guggenheim Foundation in 1960 for "Studies in the History of American Feminism."

phy of morals, and Sir Gawain and the Green Knight, the last-named a popular academic staple in the field of Gothic myth.

The major charitable foundations—the main support of academic research—are, and always have been, overwhelmingly male-dominated* and have been more interested in sponsoring research on social change in Bolivian tin-mining towns and the foreign policy of Byzantine emperors than they have in the broad areas of women's studies. Until the 1970s, when women's studies became at least respectable if not chic, grants for such research were rare, and Seven Sisters names among the grantees even rarer. During the thirty years from 1944 to 1974, the John Simon Guggenheim Foundation, a particularly lucrative source of support for academic research, made grants for nineteen (out of several thousand) studies in what might loosely be considered women's fields, excluding fiction and poetry but including biography; of these nineteen, *one* award was made to a Seven Sisters faculty member.**

For the three academic years 1973–1974, 1974–1975, and 1975–76, the Ford Foundation sponsored a program of faculty research specifically geared to the field of women's studies. Of the forty-

---

* For whatever reasons, foundations in general have not been overstaffed with women. Of the private foundations, the Ford Foundation had 2 women (15 men) on its board of trustees in 1973, an increase from none in 1950; the Rockefeller Foundation also had 2 women on its board of trustees in 1973 (19 men), also an increase from none in 1950; the Carnegie Corporation of New York had 3 women on the board of trustees in 1973 (14 men), again, an increase of 2 from 1950; and the John Simon Guggenheim Foundation has yet to appoint a woman, other than Mrs. Simon Guggenheim, to the board of trustees or the selection committees, although there has been some representation on the Educational Advisory Boards. Women fare slightly better in government-sponsored foundations: The National Endowment for the Humanities had 4 women, 22 men on the National Council on the Humanities in 1973, 67 women and 324 men on the advisory panels; the National Endowment for the Arts had 7 women (including chairman Nancy Hanks) and 20 men on the National Council for the Arts in 1973, 37 women and 152 men on the advisory panels; the National Science Foundation in 1973 had 23 men and 1 woman on the National Science Board (equivalent to a board of trustees), down 1 woman from 1950, but on the advisory panels in 1973 there were 355 men and 36 women compared to 101 men and *no* women in 1950.[11]

** To Patricia Albjerg Graham, Barnard professor of education and director of the education program, later director of the Radcliffe Institute, in 1972, for a history of women in higher education.

four fellowships awarded, one went to a Seven Sisters faculty member.*[12]

While the field holds a vast potential for frivolous research, it holds an equally vast potential for serious, substantive work.

The Project on the Status and Education of Women, an arm of the Association of American Colleges, published in May 1975 *A Survey of Research Concerns on Women's Issues* containing roughly thirty-three pages worth of programs and projects, all overripe for systematic analysis, in the fields of history, economics, sociology, psychology, law, biology, and physiology.

Now that contemporary feminism has made this variety of research academically more acceptable—and financially and politically more rewarding—some Seven Sisters institutions have in fact become involved in it. By fall 1974, major research was being carried on at the Radcliffe Institute in the fields of health care careers for women, family planning, and women's career patterns in general, all supported by grants from public and private establishments. A year later, a Radcliffe-sponsored series of biographies of women was in the works. At Wellesley, under the sponsorship of the Carnegie Corporation of New York, the Federation of Organizations for Professional Women, and the college, a national center for Research on Women in Higher Education and the Professions had opened to explore women's educational, professional, and social needs. At about the same time Mount Holyoke, with grants from the Carnegie Corporation, the Andrew W. Mellon Foundation, and gifts from IBM, General Motors, and the Monsanto Fund, launched an experimental "Program on Administration in Complex Organizations," a multi-disciplinary course, the purpose of which was to increase women's understanding of—and, theoretically, their upward mobility in—such organizations. And at Smith, Jill Ker Conway, the seventh—and first woman—president, was talking, even before her inauguration in October 1975, of mobilizing the college resources for serious research on issues of crucial importance to women, a utilization of the academic she considered essential to the solution of social problems.[13]

It had required, however, a full century for the women's col-

---

* To Judith D. R. Porter, assistant professor of sociology at Bryn Mawr, for a study of "Cross-cultural sex role stereotypes of young children."

leges to become academically aware of women and, in fact, the bulk of foundation grants in the field of women's programs and research still appear to be going to institutions other than the acknowledged leaders in women's education: to, for example, MIT, for a workshop on women in science and technology; to the University of California at Berkeley, for research on women in American history; to the Claremont Colleges, for internship programs to train women as administrators for academic positions; to Sarah Lawrence for a program of graduate training in American history. And so on.*

It is hardly surprising, then, that when the boomlet for curricular attention to women's studies developed, it did so not in the women's colleges but in the coeducational institutions. Beginning in 1965, at the Free University of Seattle, courses by, for, and about women spread through the West and Midwest, much the way coeducation itself had done a century before. At the Seven Sisters, which had learned to deal with the woman question by ignoring it, thereby helping to make the statement of women's inferiority self-fulfilling, the deans were somewhat taken by surprise and, having lived at least academically without the question for nearly a hundred years, their enthusiasm for women's studies was at something less than fever pitch.

There were, of course, always "women's studies" in the women's college curriculum—women's studies in the sense that certain courses were considered appropriate to the genteel woman's post-graduate role. Carey Thomas of Bryn Mawr deplored the trend three quarters of a century ago:

Except practice on the piano and violin and banjo and other musical instruments, which we might have believed that women would wish in a college course (although most happily they do not) let us ask ourselves what other subjects peculiar to women could be introduced in a college curriculum? I have never heard more than three suggested: infant psychology, to which there is no special objection, as an elec-

---

* In any survey of foundation grants, it is impossible not to notice the conspicuousness of the name of Harvard. In one query to a foundation for information on awards to Seven Sisters institutions, the secretary supplied all except the list of awards to Harvard (Radcliffe), explaining wearily, the "list is very long." However, in the area of research on women, Harvard's name is equally conspicuous by its absence.

tive . . . (I believe, however, that as many men as women will be foolish enough—I am expressing my own point of view—to elect it, and, after all, as many college men will become fathers as college women will become mothers); chemistry with special reference to cooking; and food values and domestic science generally, which is already introduced in some coeducational colleges and will never, in my opinion, be largely elected because it lacks the wider outlook of the more general sciences and belongs in the technical school; and physiology with special reference to motherhood and wifehood, which is never likely to be elected voluntarily by women college students who do not know whether they will marry; nor is it, in my opinion, desirable that it should be elected. It would certainly lead to much unhappiness in married life if such courses were elected by women and not by the men they marry also. These subjects, even if we grant (which I do not) that they are especially desirable for women to study in college, would not constitute a woman's curriculum. They would simply form three electives out of many to be introduced as occasion serves into such colleges as are open to women.[14]

Young women could not train to be nurses at Vassar, nor could they take home economics at Bryn Mawr. Nevertheless, the women's colleges did attempt to broaden some related studies to fit the liberal arts framework, and came up with such courses as child study in the psychology department (a double-barreled offering, appealing as it did to both future teachers and future homemakers), social welfare and social work in the economics department, marriage and the family in the sociology department (where roles as wives and mothers stressed adjustment and roles as husbands and fathers were ignored). Vassar, which was actually brassy enough in the 1940s to offer preprofessional course work to aspiring engineers, experimented briefly also with an interdepartmental concentration or major misnamed Euthenics which was designed to offer "theory and technique in certain fields of knowledge fundamental to the betterment of living," and included the appropriate courses in the departments of hygiene, physiology, anthropology, economics, psychology, zoology, and political science. Altogether, they constituted the institutional attempts to legitimize academically woman's role as companion/homemaker; but there was no nonsense about the ambiguities and ambivalences and complexities with which a woman must cope if she was to fulfill her biological destiny as well as the professional ambitions for which her superior education had equipped her; there was little attempt to "confront the destructive stereotypes."

Nor was the hard-core curriculum so calculated. It wasn't so very long ago that one could spend four years at Smith—or Bryn Mawr or Wellesley or Mount Holyoke—and never, literally *never* hear the name Elizabeth Cady Stanton spoken. Or Lucy Stone. Or Carrie Chapman Catt. John Stuart Mill was a staple of the Smith syllabus—*On Liberty* and *Principles of Political Economy* but not *The Subjection of Women.* William Lloyd Garrison and Theodore Parker were heroes, but whoever heard of Lucretia Mott or Susan B. Anthony? And no one ever mentioned that the law discriminated against women in some subtle and some not-so-subtle ways. Whatever liberalization the West Point curriculum has undergrone in recent years, it was and is mandatory for future military officers to learn the dynamics of military leadership. Women, however, were taught very little about the complexities of membership in the sex at Vassar or Wellesley or Radcliffe.

During the decade from 1965 to 1975, at a peak of the contemporary women's movement, 885 American colleges and universities offered 4,658 courses in women's studies, their academic value varying from institution to institution and from department to department within an institution; 112 of these same colleges expanded their offerings into full programs, some of which included the granting of bachelors and masters degrees, and at least one program led to a doctorate. This rapid popularization of women's studies and the accompanying research, while hardly a panacea, did serve women, however, in much the same way Black Studies programs served blacks: bolstering self-confidence, correcting some of the historical inaccuracies, and demonstrating alternatives to traditional life-styles.

Nevertheless, the women's colleges were not anxious to incorporate women's studies into the curriculum. Some of the arguments they used were analogous to those they had used to discredit Black Studies programs. Too expensive, they said. Divisive. Separatist. A prejudiced perspective. Women's studies only removed women's affairs from the mainstream (whatever that is). Frivolous. Faddish. Academically unsound. Intellectually illegitimate: subjective methods of research and instruction conflicted with traditional objective and systematic standards. Political polemics. A reluctance to see the institution identified with a cause, making anything except an intellectual commitment to its students. And besides, they argued with finality, what would you do with a women's-studies major after you finished it?

The arguments ended in a draw. In a departure from the Black Studies pattern, the establishmentarians were generally able to avoid offering a major or creating an entire women's studies department. The reformers among the faculty members (male and female, all ages, but mostly female and young) and students succeeded in creating and winning at least temporary approval for courses about women and scattering them through the various disciplines, and the academic consciousness was at least raised to the point where an effort—self-conscious at first perhaps—was made to include the missing links of history, many of which happen to be female. (Even at Harvard, where the female profile may be the lowest and where department chairmen, when queried, ranged from antagonistic to lukewarm, there was a general tendency to leave the question of individual women's studies courses up to individual faculty members.) Where it's appropriate, efforts have been made to weave women's roles, achievements, failures, attitudes, and problems into existing courses.

But again, it required a century for the women's colleges to respond to women's special problems and postures. And when they finally did, it was only under the pressures of external forces, with the results that, again and again, imitation substituted for ingenuity and invention, and seemingly haphazard placement substituted for unity, all of which at worst raised questions of the Sisters' institutional seriousness about its sexuality (even Vassar still claims to maintain its historical commitment to women's education), and at best raised questions of institutional judgment about the length of time this acknowledged transitional phase may require, before full curricular equality is reached.

3

One of the current crucial concerns of women is re-entry into the job market from the outer space of family life, without being destroyed at the threshold by atmospheric friction. One of the pieces of re-entry equipment being utilized more and more frequently to make the passage smoother is what is known as "continuing education." By 1974, institutions in all but four states offered special education courses for the mature woman—the woman with special educational, psychological, and logistical requirements but with a sharpened sense of purpose, usually but not always a recognizable talent, and often, in these days of enormous strain on the institutional financial aid resources, the money to pay her tuition. In 1974, 410,000 adult women were enrolled in continuing education programs in the United States, ranging in academic styles from Deanza College (in the highly fertile but rapidly urbanizing Santa Clara Valley of California), where academically high-risk minority women were increasingly successfully acquiring knowledge and skills of various, often marketable, kinds, to the prestigious Radcliffe Institute where professional women were offered Harvard's substantial resources and the opportunity to investigate some sophisticated individual projects. The forty-seven-year-old matron among the freshmen in History 11 no longer appears out of place.

The concept itself is not a particularly new one. Richard G. Gettell grappled with it in a small way at his inauguration as president of Mount Holyoke in 1957. Concerned about women's intellectual stagnation during the time- and energy-consuming child-bearing and child-raising years, he urged the women's colleges to "press further their efforts at designing refresher material for their graduates," suggesting the distribution of bibliographies of current reading in their former students' fields of concentration and in recent general cultural progress, intellectually more stimulating alumnae meetings and publications, summer institutes—programs not "elementary and dilettantish as are some ventures in adult education, but . . . at a high level, suitable for the intellectual equality of the best graduates."[15]

Official sanction of academe's responsibility to cope with the discontinuities of women's lives goes back to the October 11, 1963 report of the President's Commission on the Status of Women which recommended, among other things, that colleges, universities, and vocational schools expand opportunities for mature women to continue their education beyond high schools through increased curricular flexibility and financial aid, re-examination of traditional admission and graduation requirements (such as physical education and residence requirements) along with transfer credits and course prerequisites, plus expansion of educational services such as counseling.

Higher education continued to be, however, "prejudiced against older students," declared the Carnegie Commission on Higher Education nearly eight years later, in January 1971, and urged "that opportunities be created for persons to re-enter higher education throughout their active careers in regular daytime classes, nighttime classes, summer courses, and special short-term programs, with degrees and certificates available as appropriate."[16]

There were at the time a few continuing education projects for women already in existence. One of them was the decade-old experiment at Radcliffe.

In 1960, Mary I. Bunting, soon to be the only Seven Sisters administrator to serve on one of the President's Commission's six committees (she was chairman of the Committee on Education) was inaugurated as president of Radcliffe College. A professional woman,* Mrs. Bunting was also a wife and mother, and she had as one of her major concerns the dearth of educational, and therefore professional, opportunities for the married woman. "We have assumed," she wrote shortly after arriving at Radcliffe, "that if she marries early she is not interested in continuing her education. The possibility that the choice could be a question of timing rather than goals has not received serious attention. Insofar as institutions of higher education have made it impossible for her to continue, they must at least share the responsibility for her 'drop out.' "[17]

A biologist by training, Mrs. Bunting decided on an experimental approach to the problem, establishing the Radcliffe Institute for Independent Study as a laboratory in which to investigate the problems and potential of "mature" women. Academically reared in the Vassar–Harvard–Radcliffe tradition of elitism, Mrs. Bunting chose as her white mice, women who were already well educated and on their way to establishment as professionals. Were there such women, she asked, who had been handicapped by lack of time, unavailability of resources or "more subtle forms of isola-

---

* An alumna of Vassar ('31), she had taught at Bennington, Goucher, and Wellesley, had been a research assistant at Yale, and the dean of Douglass College from 1955 to 1959, and, in 1964, the first woman appointed to the Atomic Energy Commission.

tion" who had projects on which they wanted to work? "Could we release them to be productive? Would they then be in a position to move ahead on their own? Would the fact that we valued what they did with their trained minds help to change people's expectations? Working in the gray area between college aspirations and proven performance, we wished to find out whether there are roadblocks which, if removed, would enable qualified but stymied women to become professionally successful."[18] Part-time fellowships were offered to selected women in the Boston area, along with an office or studio or laboratory (the classic room of her own), access to Harvard University's resources, including faculty and curriculum, and, perhaps most important, recognition (read encouragement).

The first questions were answered with the flood of applications that were received at the announcement of the fellowship program on November 20, 1960: 200 from doctors, dentists, lawyers, psychiatrists, psychologists, sculptors, painters, musicians, writers, historians, economists, educators; "the need," declared the Institute in classic understatement, "in fact, might be greater than had been foreseen." Twenty scholars, ranging in age from twenty-eight to sixty-one and in professional status from the Ph.D. to no college at all (7 Ph.D.'s, 2 M.D.'s, 1 LL.B., 1 B.DS. who also had an M.A., 7 master's degrees, 1 artist with a B.A. and an art school diploma, and a poet with no college at all), were selected to begin work July 1, 1961; the Institute acquired a sixteen-room yellow clapboard house on Mount Auburn Street in Cambridge, and turned bedrooms into studies to provide that precious privacy. Each scholar was engaged in some independent project which appeared to require only the removal of the "roadblocks."

Within the first decade, the Institute (which has since assumed various other responsibilities including the Radcliffe Seminars—a program of non-credit liberal arts courses established in 1950—and various projects of major research into women's professional and vocational milieu) had 187 alumnae, of which 138 had been granted fellowship renewals. By 1973, the Institute had awarded 448 fellowships to 268 individuals in the Program for Independent Study, plus 76 special grants through a program for women physicians financed by the Josiah Macy, Jr. Foundation, and plus 169 grants in a special program for women enrolled in part-time graduate study financed by the Charles E. Merrill Trust. In 1975, the Institute received a $323,000 Carnegie Foundation grant to establish a program of part-time fellowships for non-tenured women in the Boston area; the point was to allow junior faculty the opportunity to do the research necessary to compete for tenured positions.

Mrs. Bunting's experiment appears to be a success. The program has provided these women with "some degree of continuity in their professional activity," it has "tried to increase the choices open to women who want to have careers," it has increased their professional visibility, and thus smoothed the way into positions of increased responsibility. Based on the prerequisite of a certain minimum of professional and/or intellectual sophistication of its fellows, the Radcliffe Institute is, of course, elitism, but it is elitism at its best, assuming professional competence and confidence as its major goals.[19]

This very elitism, however, while it must be served, and while the Harvard–Radcliffe resources may even be its best servants, limits the scope of the institute. What are the options for the other several hundred thousand women who wish to continue their education?

At about the same time Mrs. Bunting was persuading the Radcliffe trustees to support her plan for a program of independent study for women, similar developments were taking place at Sarah Lawrence College, then a small women's liberal arts institution in Bronxville, New York, which had some tradition of experiment and innovation (it has since gone coeducational). Esther Raushenbush, then dean of the college, had concluded from conversations with mothers who were putting their last child into college that many of these older women would have appreciated similar opportunities for education. Having previously discovered that there was "no magic in ages 18 to 22 for students in higher education," Mrs. Raushenbush later wrote, and having previously admitted a few older women to undergraduate study, the obvious next step, which Mrs. Raushenbush eagerly took, was to create some special program of continuing education. In 1960, two special classes were opened for former Sarah Lawrence students, now mature women returning to complete their studies for degrees. The following year, women who had interrupted their education at other institutions were admitted to the special classes which, being composed largely of their peers, afforded the older women support while they revived rusty study skills and mental discipline, prerequisites to entering regular Sarah Lawrence courses. In January 1962, Sarah Lawrence, with support from the Carnegie Foundation of New York and with Mrs. Raushenbush as director (she later resigned to become president of the college), opened a Center for Continuing Education with its own special classes, admissions procedures, administration, and counseling services. The response to its announcement, like that to the opening of the Radcliffe Institute, was overwhelming, indicating once again the enormity of the need.

A decade later, recognizing the increased demand for the alterations in educational patterns in the light of the changes in women's "life designs," and recognizing the potential for continued change* the Sarah Lawrence Center for Continuing Education had established a three-tiered program: (1) to provide an undergraduate liberal arts program for women (although occasionally men were enrolled) who had not completed their undergraduate studies and who had been away from formal education for an appreciable time; (2) to provide, in conjunction with universities and colleges in the New York area, a new design for graduate study for professions traditionally open to women (elementary education, guidance, social work, library science) who could then follow them in the communities in which they lived, and (3) to create new programs, two of which (a program in Preparation for College Teaching leading to a Master's degree, and a program in training women for a profession in medical genetics) materialized.

The typical Center student, as described in official public relations, is the wife of an executive or professional man, usually in her thirties, with her children in school. She is a college drop-out but has taken, on a hit-or-miss basis, a few courses since she left college: "As she describes it, the college was relatively meaningless to her when she was first an undergraduate. She didn't really

* "We do not know fully yet, but will have to learn," Mrs. Raushenbush wrote in 1972, "how drastic those changes are bound to be; how fully working women, women in the professions, women in graduate schools, women as working mothers at all economic levels will, within the generation now coming to maturity, develop new relations to work, to study, to family."

extend herself in her studies, and marriage was not only attractive in itself but was an excuse to drop out. Now she is deeply involved in her community, in the Parent-Teacher Association, the League of Women Voters, ecological organizations. She is concerned with the kind of education her children are getting, the kind of world her children are going to grow old in. She also feels, and feels deeply, that she must make something of herself as an individual and be effective in her community and that to do this she needs more education."

There are also the career-oriented students: "The ballet dancer who has come to realize that she will never be another Pavlova and has concluded that dance is not enough to fill the rest of her life; the widow with a full-time job and two children away at college, who works two evenings a week in order to spend two mornings at the Center pursuing her own education; the student who was a high school drop-out, but has since gone on to found her own market research company, to pass high school equivalency exams and to enroll at the Center on her way to becoming a psycho-analyst; the Registered Nurse whose original love of medicine has now crystallized in a determination to go to medical school; the student whose early education was in refugee camps in Germany after World War II and who is now aiming for a career in psychiatry."

The first older women admitted to Sarah Lawrence were considered a "high-risk" group, largely because they were untried. Ten years later their cumulative records indicated "that any lingering doubts should be dispelled." Like continuing education programs elsewhere, the Sarah Lawrence Center had demonstrated both the need and the validity of educating the mature women, "that older minds can learn as effectively as younger ones; and that education for its own sake is of value whether or not the student concentrates in a particular discipline or prepares for a profession."

The Sarah Lawrence continuing education program is not elitist in the sense that the Radcliffe Institute, with its prerequisite of professionalism, is; it does, however, require commitment toward working for a degree, and candidates are accepted only after extensive interviews with the administration; official literature refers to students as "highly qualified"; most, although exceptions are sometimes made, students have some credits toward a college degree.[20]

Conforming to educational patterns established over the past century, it is the public sector of higher education that has assumed responsibility for the masses of women who would continue their education. About the time Mrs. Bunting and Mrs. Raushenbush were putting together their plans for Radcliffe and Sarah Lawrence, Dr. Virginia L. Senders, a lecturer in the psychology department at the University of Minnesota, and Elizabeth L. Cless, assistant to the dean of the General Extension Division of the university, were devising and seeking support for what has become known as the Minnesota Plan for the Continuing Education of Women. While, as the plan's first report, 1960–65, states, "adults who seek continuing education are a self-selected lot," the Minnesota Plan has no elitist overtones (no admission requirements, not even a high school diploma), but seeks to return to "the nation's paid and unpaid manpower pool a group of intelligent, educated women whose talents might otherwise be underused during their mature years; and second, to increase the personal happiness of many women by exposing them to new interests, by helping them to find new objectives, and by making the goals of the more distant future an integral part of their present lives," for which all the resources of a large university were made available plus some special counseling facilities (including skills workshops) tailored to fit the particular educational, vocational, financial, and psychological requirements of the "mature" woman (including inexpensive child care services) who had gained little except weight during the intellectually fallow years of child-bearing. In addition, a series of special seminars (including a number of women's studies) were created to update and to reacquaint the older student with the developments in science, the social sciences, and humanities which had occurred while she was space-walking.[21]

These three—the Radcliffe Institute, the Sarah Lawrence Continuing Education program, the Minnesota Plan—demonstrate what can be achieved through application of a little imagination and elbow grease. Imitated or adapted by other institutions, they represent three rather different approaches to the concept of the continuing education of women, perhaps one of the hottest items in higher education today, certainly one of those in greatest demand and, in spite of the large numbers of enrolled, still a virtually untapped market. Some observers have pointed out that if college administrators were not so preoccupied with finding anachronistic solutions to their increasing financial woes, they might discern in this fairly recent applicant pool a whole new source of paying guests.

Where do the Seven Sisters stand on this contemporary development in the education of women?

They have not been highly visible, although women in the socio-economic levels they have traditionally served had won their freedom from lives of narrow domesticity long before those women who are crowding the classrooms at the University of Minnesota. Even at Radcliffe, the Radcliffe Institute is a separate establishment from Radcliffe College, the latter having followed the practice of admitting older women as A.B. degree candidates occasionally and "by accident."[22] Only in the spring of 1975 did the institute get around to exploring the possibility of modifying the undergraduate regimen in such areas as admissions (although employers' recommendations could be substituted for teachers', candidates were still required to take College Board examinations) and curriculum (part-time study, except in extraordinary circumstances, was not considered). Smith embarked on its second century with an announcement, among others, of the Ada Comstock Scholars Program, named for Ada L. Comstock—Smith '97, professor of English, dean of the college, later dean and president of Radcliffe—and described as "the extension of our liberal arts commitment to qualified scholars having a wide range of ages and experience."[23] The others admit older students in varying numbers. As leading luminaries in the area of women's education, they have done relatively little in a positive fashion to bring their specialty, an academically rigorous liberal arts program, to women beyond the age of twenty-two.

While the Sisters do not require physical education credits for fifty-year-olds, the institutions continue to exhibit a certain rigidity, an inability to consider seriously the needs of mature women apart from those of young, residential undergraduates. Little has changed in Northampton or Poughkeepsie or South Hadley since 1962 when the Carnegie Corporation of New York was already complaining that "Despite the obvious and much talked about needs of opportunities for lifelong learning, most educational activities are still designed for young people who have nothing else to do. The present system is badly suited to those who must fit their learning into a busy life.[24]

Those programs that do exist, aside from the Radcliffe Institute, are small, informal almost to the point of vagueness, revolving around filling the requirements for the Bachelor's degree, or in the case of Bryn Mawr. which operates a small program to prepare older students for medical school, filling requirements for admission to professional school. Special counseling facilities range from rare to non-existent; there are no courses designed to help the older student update her frame of reference or to revive rusted study skills, and campus scheduling is geared to the residential undergraduate so that merely obtaining a book from the library reserve shelf becomes a major offensive for a woman with family and household responsibilities. There is a negativism about it, a general institutional lethargy expressed by a Vassar dean who said: "We're not out advertising to get more. We're coping with those who come to us."

All of which only serves to underline the fact that the leading women's colleges in the United States have not been leading in this area of women's education.

4

Women's studies and continuing education programs have won considerable if not unanimous favor in the academic marketplace, and the Seven Sisters have begun, with varying degrees of enthusiasm, to add them to their curricular portfolios. As adaptations of definitions that others have written, however, they lack not only originality but also significance for the academic world, and serve not to treat but to continue institutional lethargy, the cause for which lies elsewhere.

"Your speech generates no heat,"[25] complained Woodrow Wilson in 1887, describing his experiences as an associate professor of history at Bryn Mawr.

"I remember when I came from City College to Barnard,"

recalled Mary Mothersill, chairman of the Barnard philosophy department nearly a century later, in the winter of 1974, "I had a kind of culture shock because classes at City were all boys at that time and they were very rough sort of aggressive students and there was a great deal of sort of rancorous discussion in class. And when I came to Barnard the first class I had was a senior seminar and the Barnard students handed in some papers and I gave them back and I said, 'you know, these papers are so lousy, they're so badly written, they're so awful that I didn't even take the trouble to grade them,' which was sort of a normal thing to say at City. . . . I would say that kind of thing to City College students and they would say, 'that's only because you're anti-Semitic, or you're incompetent,' or something, and I would say, 'if I'm incompetent, you're even worse.' "

But the Barnard girls were different. "I remember that first class, their response was they simply averted their eyes and were so offended and insulted. They wouldn't talk to me at all. I would ask them questions and they would just look away. So finally, after an hour, I said, 'Look, I'm sorry, I apologize, I didn't mean to be rude. Forgive me, let's start all over again.' So that first year was very tough."[26]

A not untypical story; a story, moreover that seems to have no beginning and no end. Smith's William Allan Neilson was prone to scold women undergraduates publicly for their docility, and it is not uncommon today to hear a woman faculty member recall her own passivity as a student at the same time as she describes her students' unwillingness to engage her intellectually.

Students do not disagree. On the contrary. "We sat in lecture classes, taking notes on the professors' wisdom," recalled Liz Schneider, Bryn Mawr '63, in an essay "Bryn Mawr and the Failure of Feminism." "Rarely did we venture a differing opinion, fearing to be found wrong. We only felt confident in our ability to read extensively, digest the various facts and ideas, and organize them into lengthy, well-documented essays. . . . We all commented on the recklessness of Haverford students who boldly challenged their professors whenever they disagreed or didn't understand. They seemed to feel that they had every right to an opinion and some even felt that they had to have an opinion to satisfy their own egos. . . . We didn't have the confidence to trust ourselves. We continued to be passive recipients just as we had been raised to be."[27]

This tendency of women students to hide their talent, to fail to develop a critical intelligence, a tendency that limits classroom intellectual spontaneity and puts illogical and self-defeating restraints on the relations between instructor and student, manifests itself in several ways: a deference to men in classrooms and laboratories; a predilection for the lecture system as opposed to the seminar which presupposes dialogue (a predilection that has provoked a number of not-very-funny academic jokes regarding women's preoccupation with elaborate note-taking, including notes on the instructor's deliberate offering of misinformation which, so they say, the women dutifully record without even dropping a stitch of their knitting); and a reluctance on the part of women to pull out all the intellectual stops. All of which results in, among other things, not only the conspicuous ability of women to get better grades than men by handing back on examinations and in term papers what the instructors handed out in class, but in the incomplete development of their analytical and critical capacities, a stifling of mental growth that may have as much to do with the academic woman's much-maligned research and publishing record as any other explanation that has been offered.

The commonly accepted cure at the women's colleges was to add men to the classes, whether through full coeducation, increased accessibility in coordinate education, or the cooperative education exemplified by Five Colleges Incorporated, a remedy which, like the belated addition of women's studies to the curriculum, treated the symptoms and not the cause, and left the institution to malinger.

Serious substantive curriculum innovation, which held some potential for altering the feminine stereotype, was not so well received. An informal custom, which had its roots in the traditional work-study program at Antioch College, was grafted on to a strict liberal arts curriculum when political science professor Raymond Moley sent his Barnard students of the 1920s into the courts and government agencies of New York City in an attempt to connect political theory and practice. This was made academically legitimate when members of the Mount Holyoke political science department, beginning in 1949, pioneered the political internship, a term of intensive applied education, in which students signed on with a political campaign or a government office— elected or appointed, local, national, or international. The pragmatic approach to learning of this program appeared to hold potential for kicking the docility inherent in the lecture habit not only in the field of political science but also in other fields. The program has been widely imitated. Under certain conditions, its imitators have been willing to grant students academic credit; Mount Holyoke, however, refused to give academic credit for the first twenty-five years of the program's life; finally, in spring 1975, the faculty voted to give some credit, to be designated "internship credit" and *not* to count toward the degree, an attitude that indicates not only an institutional ambivalence toward its own program but toward altering the patterns of women's education.

Actually, the causes of the malaise lie deeper within the institutional psyche: in the parallel unwillingness of the Seven Sisters themselves to engage in the academic dialogue with their peers; in their reluctance to challenge the guardians of the academic traditions as symbolized by the Harvards and Yales; their abject humility (even the addition of women's studies was an import)— a petticoat mentality with all the anachronistic characteristics of Victorian modesty and inferiority that the word implies. They were the unwitting victims of their own ethos.

As the student depends upon the authority of the instructor, the women's institution relies upon the authority of Harvard and Amherst to define its purposes, listening respectfully, absorbing uncritically, reserving its little enthusiasms for alumnae clubs and house organs; it is as if the serious affairs of this world were still being discussed and decided over cigars and brandy while the women adjourn to the drawing room for embroidery and gossip.

Failing in their slavish imitation of men's institutions (not so very dissimilar to the university-building Africans trapped by their perceptions of Oxford and Cambridge) to reassess in any meaningful way this academic underpinning of social conservatism, the Sisters have been of little real consequence in defining either their own special area, women's education (one might argue plausibly that they have hardly made it their own) or any area in the larger academic community. With some exceptions (Bryn Mawr's former president Katherine E. McBride, 1942–70, whose stature as an educator secured for her a place as one of two women on the recent nineteen-member Carnegie Commission on Higher Education, comes immediately to mind) Seven Sisters leadership has tended to leave the academic debates out of which innovation may emerge and the academic white papers in which academic policy is defined to the Eliots, the Conants, the Boks, the Goheens, the Brewsters, the James Perkinses* and their ilk.

The women's colleges preferred to remain, like their students, essentially passive, content to listen, to receive, reluctant to venture. As a student at Cornell in the 1870s, Carey Thomas, one of the early coeds, was disappointed in the quality of the other women students; although they "felt themselves to be pioneers striking out in the new field of women in institutions of higher learning, they were unaware," reports her biographer, "that their responsibility went beyond doing their academic work adequately and committing no indiscretion likely to bring criticism upon their sex."28 Institutionalized, this timidity has resulted in a historical failure of the Seven Sisters to assume responsibility for serious women's education, which in turn has helped to perpetuate the ancillary role of women.

For example, which of the presidents of a Seven Sisters institution, all of whom have been and continue to be articulate, scholarly, and thoughtful, have offered their ideas on women's education to the larger academic world, though their experience must have given them some expertise and perspective in the field? In 1975 Macmillan Company published *Guidelines for Creating Positive Sexual and Racial Images in Educational Materials*, which was designed as an aid to textbook writers and to which Matina Horner of Radcliffe wrote the preface. But for a profession that lives off the printed word, the output has not been spectacular.

A survey of the *Education Index* (which catalogued 223 educa-

---

* An Arthur M. Schlesinger, Jr. report has it that Perkins, as vice president of the Carnegie Corporation, later president of Cornell, was so highly visible as an academic leader that President John F. Kennedy voiced his irritation at hearing the name Perkins in the recommendations of his aides for every high-level government job opening, whether or not it demanded Perkins' particular expertise. Later, Clark Kerr, of the University of California, became the name to advance. It should happen to Alan Simpson!

tional periodicals in 1975, exclusive of alumnae and alumni magazines and other such parochial campus publications) from 1960
through March 1975, indicates that of the hundreds of articles
published on women as college students, women as educators,
women's studies, and so on, two were written by Seven Sisters
presidents during that fifteen-year period: Radcliffe's Mary I.
Bunting (with others) on "Academic Freedom and Incentive for
Women," in the *Educational Record* for fall 1970, and Smith's
Thomas C. Mendenhall on "Women's Education and the Educated
Woman," in *School and Society* for November 19, 1960, the latter
actually a reprint of his inaugural address in which he lamented
that "The realities of equality for women are still far from coin-
ciding with the law or the idea,"[29] but broke no new ground. In
addition, Jill K. Conway, at that time a vice president of the University of Toronto and president-elect of Smith College, contributed
to the Fall 1974 issue of *Daedalus* (which was dedicated to the
"uncertain future" of American higher education), a critical
analysis of the direction women's concerns had taken in higher
education in the areas of curriculum and affirmative action, but
offered little in the way of corrective measures.

Who, then, has written those hundreds of papers on women's
concerns? Congresswomen, HEW officials and the Office of Education officials, staff members of the Educational Testing Service,
faculty and administration from Harvard, Yale,* the University
of Maryland, Arizona State College, Jackson (Mississippi) State
College, the University of Wisconsin, of California, of Missouri,
Ohio State, Purdue, and on and on.

Of books, except for memoirs, there has not been a single one on
women's education published by the president of a Seven Sisters
institution, although some presidents have published within their
particular disciplines. Smith's William Allan Neilson and Vassar's
Henry Noble McCracken, contemporaries cut from the same pat-

---

* Elga Wasserman, who as director of the office of women's education was
one of Yale's small administrative concessions to the arrival of women on
campus, wrote on "Coeducation at Yale" for the *Educational Record*: " 'But
I love it here.'—Coeducation Comes to Dartmouth" appeared in the Spring
1974 issue of the *Journal of the National Association for Women Deans,
Administrators and Counselors*; Vassar has yet to offer its official experience
with coeducation to the academic world.

tern of college-president-as-scholar, were particularly prolific; and Alan Simpson, while president of Vassar and in collaboration with his wife, edited a book of letters by Thomas Carlyle's wife, Jane. Others published, largely within their own fields, both before and after their administrations: Margaret Clapp, for example, was a Pulitzer Prize winner for her biography of John Bigelow before she was named president of Wellesley.

In the broader area of education in general, the record is similar. Although the educational periodicals address, as one of their major functions, all those curricular questions of concern to all institutions of higher education—liberal arts versus vocationalism, the pros and cons of various grading systems, requirements versus electives, interdepartmental studies versus strictly defined disciplines, teaching versus research, methodology, the whole gamut— their writers come from Harvard and Dartmouth and Yale and Williams, from Notre Dame and SUNY and the University of California; the leaders of women's education in America, administration and faculty both, have been largely silent.

Take, for example, just a few leading periodicals. From 1969 through 1974, *one* faculty member of a Seven Sisters institution (Roger W. Holmes of the Mount Holyoke philosophy department) wrote a curriculum-related article for the April 1969 issue of *Journal of Higher Education*, which is published by the American Association for Higher Education, on "A Proposal for the Undergraduate College: a School of Language"; no administrative officer of a Seven Sisters institution was published in the *Journal* during this period. *Liberal Education*, published by the Association of American Colleges, between 1970 and 1974 published *no* articles by Seven Sisters faculty or administration. (A borderline case is "How Five Colleges Operate" by North Burn, five-college coordinator in October 1973). A Seven Sisters president on the American Council on Education (ACE) appears to be part of the council's quota system; yet Seven Sisters faculty and administration are rarely published in the ACE Journal, *Educational Record*; from 1969 through 1974, one Seven Sisters faculty member (a Wellesley professor of economics on institutional finances) was published by the *Record*. Wellesley's Barbara Newell had been published in the Winter 1970 issue when she was acting vice president for student affairs at the University of Michigan, as had Bryn Mawr's

Harris L. Wofford when he was president of SUNY, Old West-bury. *Change*, a relatively recent addition to the list of higher-education periodicals, dedicated its Summer 1975 issue to "The State of the Humanities," which included four articles on the hu-manities, an editorial, and extracts from a symposium sponsored jointly by *Change* and the Rockefeller Foundation in which twenty-three prominent educators participated. Not one Seven Sisters name appears among them.

Over the past century, it has not been Smith or Bryn Mawr or Wellesley that has attempted to adapt academic concerns to con-temporary social and technological change. It has been Swarth-more and Amherst and Harvard: Swarthmore, whose exploration of the state of the independent liberal arts college—*Critique of a College*—was published in 1967; Amherst, whose study of under-graduate life (curriculum, financial aid, admissions, fraternities, athletics, religion) begun in 1941 was published—having been interrupted by the war years—in 1955, redefined and readjusted certain areas of the liberal arts, particularly in relation to the applicability of the small independent liberal arts college; and Har-vard, several of whose presidents have been nationally influential (Eliot, with his free elective system, and other items, set the tone of American higher education for nearly a century); Harvard, once more, whose *General Education in a Free Society*, the influ-ential "Redbook," attempted to come to terms with the relation-ship between the pursuit and uses of general and specialized knowledge and between the role of the university, outlining in the process a system of general education that was widely copied. Again, Harvard, recognizing the profound changes* that had occurred since publication of the Redbook in 1945, undertook in 1975 a broad reevaluation of its entire educational system, which was to result in a replacement of the Redbook.[31] No comparable white papers have issued from any of the Seven Sisters.

---

* "The 'exponential growth' of knowledge and its increasingly important role in the organization of society; the expanded research function of the University and the growing orientation of faculty members toward their disciplines and professional activities; the mounting pressures upon students to undertake technical and professional studies at the earliest possible time; and, most recently, a countering impulse to devalue the ethic of individual achievement while stressing instead (in some cases) a strong commitment to social service."[30]

Privately, in their nightly bull sessions, women students are as articulate, as mentally agile, and as determined to make their ideas felt as any male student; privately, the same can be said of their faculty and administrators who lavish their individual and collective academic wisdom on alumnae clubs and house organs, but rarely do they offer it in any public forum.

Do they fear to be wrong? Or do they fear to be right?

It is a little as if, like their women students, as institutions the Seven Sisters believed they could not afford to be seriously academic and intellectual as well as acceptable, and while students and faculty are hardly dilettantes, they are also not so deeply involved in their academics as to be either threatened or threatening.

Therefore, as the faculty have come to expect a lesser degree of formal intellectual commitment from their women students than they might expect from men, society has come to expect a lesser degree of commitment from the women's colleges than they expect from the men's, or the male-dominated.

Which is what each has gotten.

If women are ever to be emancipated from traditional attitudes of self-denigration, and from the conditioning of their mental and emotional faculties which results in docility and humility and conformity, so they can develop some sense of autonomy, self-confidence, and individualism, must not their leaders, their special institutions, show them the way?

5

"Her education ... has merely allowed her to get all dressed up with no place to go."

—Eunice Fuller Barnard in
The New York Times, May 1, 1932.

1

THE ADVOCATES of coeducation are fond of arguing that a liberal arts education (originally grammar, rhetoric, logic, music, astronomy, geometry, and mathematics, to which the biological, physical, and social sciences were later added), which is predicated on a continuous and healthy tension between breadth and depth of knowledge and constituted the broad curricular outline initially adopted by the women's colleges, has no gender. "Language, literature, science, philosophy, history, art are the same for women as for men," explained L. Clark Seelye, Smith's first president, to answer a charge that women's colleges were in fact only imitations. "The leading studies of a college course cannot be considered as masculine or feminine, but as intellectual, and must be regulated by those principles which determine the growth of all intellectual life."[1]

While what is in effect a finite body of knowledge may not with impunity be altered to suit either men or women (although there are those who argue that the method of presentation might be), the concept of liberal arts does carry implications of class, and with those implications of class, implications for gender.

Derived originally from social and educational patterns of ancient Athens (where the lowest classes learned to perform the most menial tasks, and the upper classes, liberated from the day-to-day chores and routine, were trained to think, to plan, to lead, perpetuated through the medieval universities by the scholarly priests who made up the faculties, and imported from the continent by the earliest immigrants whose social theories were essentially conservative, the liberal arts brand of education was generally reserved to the higher classes of American society.

For the graduates of the men's colleges (linear descendants through John Harvard's modeling of the institution that bears his name after his own alma mater—Emmanuel College, Cambridge—and the elitist British universities) the mandarinism inherent in the liberal arts curriculum assumed validity from its purposes. Originally these purposes were the providing of a superior, essentially contemplative classical education for clergymen. Later, they were expanded to provide the nation's future leaders in government, politics, business, the sciences, and the professions with what Cardinal Newman called the "philosophical habit,"[2] and with some sense of historical perspective by which to judge the significance of contemporary events—plus, as we are so sharply reminded in this post-Watergate era (and as we have been reminded so often in history), a sense of moral perspective. For some champions of the liberal arts, the last is the overriding consideration.

As the demand for higher education developed nationally (predictably, since education is a major underlying assumption of a democratic society), public institutions brought the science and technology of agriculture and industry to the masses. The liberal arts institutions, most of which were small and independent (the emphasis on independent), were to provide for the few—Nathan Pusey's "individuals of exceptional ability who, having received the necessary exacting training, are encouraged to go beyond average attainments":[3] those on whom the future quality of civilization depended.*

---

* In practice, each segment of this heterogeneous system has reinforced the other, with the public institutions aiding the local communities through vocational training and technological research, while the independent liberal arts institutions have added to the body of knowledge through theoretical research and have set standards of academic quality. Even more important, perhaps, the independent institutions, while vulnerable to alumni caprice,

Although the Seven Sisters and the public institutions (the latter with origins in the Morrill Land Act of 1862 and an emphasis on raising standards of living at the local level through vocationalism—an egalitarian ethos) had their greatest flowering at about the same time, the kinship ends there. The Sisters (most of whose founders—all except Mount Holyoke's Mary Lyon who had had to struggle financially for her own education as a teacher—came from a privileged stratum of society where economics permitted women a large degree of leisure and social pressures dictated how it would be used) looked to the sisters and daughters of elitist Harvard, Yale, and Amherst men for the bulk of their students and to the men's institutions themselves for curricular respectability, necessarily committing their resources to liberal arts, at the same time endowing "vocational" courses, with their overtones of materialism, with just a hint of unsavoriness—an unsavorness that still lingers.

"To be liberally educated," explained Mildred H. McAfee, Wellesley's seventh president (1936–49), in 1937,

is a privilege accorded to a small minority of our population. . . . An ideal society would give to every member the chance to enjoy the adventure of thought, the security of perspective. Until we attain that ideal, these assets of the liberally educated man will be the gift of good fortune to a few. It will be only the favored few who can afford to devote their youth to developing their power to think and to cultivating their understanding of the world of time and space and values in which their thought occurs. The liberal-arts college concentrates the opportunity for that developmental process. . . .

The tradition of the women's colleges facilitates the emphasis on deliberately created educative opportunities. They have not had to spend the time of undergraduates on activities which were designed to produce an immediate income rather than to enlarge the world in which the student would thereafter live. They have been dealing with women—a group which in the American scene has been traditionally

---

traditionally have stood free of the political pressures and inevitable vested interests of the state legislatures, a freedom which allowed the exercise of moral leadership in the face of political excesses, thereby contributing much to the preservation of both. Today the lines are less clear-cut and, for good or ill, having accepted, even solicited, various and proliferating government supports, educators increasingly are being brought into line, sometimes forcibly, with government policies.

free from economic responsibilities. With numerous exceptions, their characteristic clientele has been of an economic level which made it possible to emphasize work of educative significance whether or not it had remunerative value.[4]

There being realistically, however, little question of Harvard and Yale men voluntarily sharing the privileges and responsibilities of civilization's leadership with *women* in the latter half of the nineteenth century (or any time thereafter), the Seven Sisters docilely adapted the academic elitism of the men's institutions to suit what purposes were left (purposes which had been born in intellectual radicalism, but having stopped short of the social, economic, and professional radicalism necessary for significant societal change, served to cancel out the original adventurous spirit of the enterprise) and they remained content to turn out finely educated women, responsible citizens, who would fill the socially acceptable roles of teacher, philanthropist, social worker, and/or the informed wife and companion of a real leader. Women's education, declared Eunice Fuller Barnard in 1932, "merely allowed her to get all dressed up, with no place to go."[5]

When Seven Sisters faculty and administration talk about curriculum, they tend to focus on the issue of liberal arts versus vocationalism. That issue is beside the point. The problem appears to lie not in the liberal arts formula itself, with all its implications of elitism—elitism in the best sense of the word.* Rather, the source of the trouble resides within the institutional psyche which encouraged and applauded single-minded devotion to academics during the undergraduate years but lacked the sense of mission inherent in traditional concepts of liberal arts. "In spite of widening opportunities," President Ellen Fitz Pendleton of Wellesley told the men and women gathered to celebrate Mount Holyoke's

---

* I didn't know," explained Barbara Tuchman, Radcliffe '33, on being presented with a Radcliffe Alumnae Recognition Award in 1975, "that it was unAmerican or very reprehensible to refer to or even think of the word 'elite.' . . . I thought that that's what the university *was* and that's what we were here for. I thought that to be at this institution and take advantage of the extraordinary riches and resources that the generations and the centuries had built up to offer to people like myself was a marvelous opportunity and that my purpose would be to make use of it in some way that would return to society something useful. I thought that that's what being an elite was."[6]

seventy-fifth birthday in 1912, "with the exception of the comparatively few women who enter professional life, the career of women is bound to be narrowly specialized. . . . Women, therefore, more than men, need to be equipped with liberal training furnished by the study of pure science, of humanities, and the arts."[7] Or, as President Mendenhall of Smith put it sixty-odd years later in one of his most frequently quoted statements, "At Smith you receive the kind of liberal arts education that will make your mind an interesting place to live in for the rest of your life."[8]

A 1974 study of departmental attitudes at Wellesley by a sociology student unearthed a wide range of approaches to the liberal arts, including complaints about a contemporary Wellesley preoccupation with professional considerations and a statement by the chairman of the theater studies department that it was "the intention . . . not to produce working professions [sic] (though there have been some) but to cultivate an understanding and enjoyment of the theatre."[9] Would a similar study at Dartmouth or Princeton or Haverford reveal such an attitude?

Betty Friedan, Smith '42, was editor of one of the campus newspapers during her undergraduate years. She later recalled:

I would be invited as editor of the paper to meetings with other college editors. Kingman Brewster was editor of the Yale paper then and was host for one of these things. There was something in the way the men like Kingman Brewster were expected to do big things in society and that expectation propelled them to do it. I don't think this could possibly have been true at Smith. . . . The expectations of producing a thousand leaders a year couldn't come out of Smith. The Smith education was geared to produce very intelligent wives of executives and other prominent men, who would do traditional community service.[10]

"Universities," declared Harvard's Derek C. Bok in his 1975 presidential report to the board of overseers, "have a major opportunity and responsibility to set about the task of training a corps of able people to occupy influential positions in public life."[11] Bok then went on to outline a scheme for continuing professional education for public service, implying, self-consciously perhaps but none the less emphatically, his own university's historical commitment to elitism and his own university's historical claim to the establishment of such a program. Is this the vocabulary of Bryn Mawr or Vassar?

Founded not to provide leadership for a society but to provide intellectual exercise for the heretofore academically disenfranchised, the women's colleges continued to celebrate their institutional triumphs in a Gertrude Stein (Radcliffe '97)* or a Margaret Mead (Barnard '23) but generally left both the rights and responsibilities for leadership to their betters.

The ambivalence is illustrated sharply in the institutions' self-definitions: For years the Smith *Alumnae Quarterly* carried a regular feature (since discontinued) called "Reflected Glory," which reported achievements of Smith husbands; in Mount Holyoke's official public relations for 1974–75, Ella Grasso's (Mount Holyoke '40, M.A. '42) successful campaign for the governorship of Connecticut shared the spotlight with Nancy MacGinnes' (Mount Holyoke '55) marriage to the Secretary of State. Official Harvard public relations, however, took no such notice of that particular accomplishment of Henry Kissinger (Harvard '50, M.A. '52, Ph.D. '54).

Given the relative societal positions of the sexes, plus the reluctance of the Sisters to assume their rightful positions of leadership, it was, perhaps, inevitable that those women's colleges would adopt the body of the men's-college curriculum but not its heart and soul, its underlying purposes. In 1967, Daniel Defoe proposed, among other socially beneficial *Projects* such as banks, highways, and "Friendly Societies" of seamen and widows, "an Academy for Women," where the second sex might study, in addition to the usual purely decorative subjects, some history and languages, less for her own intellectual profit or for the beneficial effects on the larger society (this latter is rarely a consideration when women's education is discussed), than for her worth as an informed companion to men. The direction of women's education has changed little over the ensuing three centuries. The academic was made servant to the status quo, which had to be, in the end, a perversion of all that higher education stood for.

---

* "Like almost everyone else I wanted to be a writer," Gertrude Stein later observed on her experience at Radcliffe, "but nobody encouraged me much."[12]

2

In 1853, the writer, clergyman, and Civil War hero-to-be, Thomas W. Higginson, in an essay "Woman and Her Wishes," quoted an eminent Boston schoolteacher whom he had known as a firm friend of women's education: "'That boy on yonder bench may be a Washington or a Marshall. . . . That fair-haired girl may be' [what?—not a Guion or a Roland, an Edgeworth or a Somerville?—no, but] 'the future *mother* of a Washington or Marshall.' "[13]

At the time, Mount Holyoke was still a female seminary, thirty-five years short of charter as a college, and Matthew Vassar, although beginning to show some interest in a small Poughkeepsie school operated by his niece, still intended to lavish his fortune on a new hospital for Poughkeepsie.

A half century later, all seven of the Sisters had opened and were doing a landslide business, their major problem their ability to keep pace with the demand for their services. Little, however, had changed societally, and sociologist David Riesman much later recalled the situation of his mother who had graduated first in the class of 1903 from Bryn Mawr and been offered the coveted European fellowship, enabling her to study abroad:

My mother was confronted with the dilemma that the post-feminist generation also encountered, for it had not occurred to her to seek a career, academic or otherwise; she was under no compulsion to marry immediately, but she was expected to wait for callers from the small covey of eligible men, one of whom, a Philadelphia physician . . . had made a shy but persistent presence felt. She declined the fellowship, while treasuring the honor and resenting her lot. She and her friends had discovered the excitement of ideas and books in college; and a very few of these women did go on to pursue careers, for example, in settlement house work, never marrying, while more of those I later had a chance to meet ended up as gracious housewives. . . . She postponed marriage to the doctor for five years, while she read novels . . . [and] absorbed high culture in other spheres. She knew painting and painters . . . music and musicians. . . .

My mother was not alone in her outlook; many of her blue-stocking friends had a similar insatiable hunger for culture; it is possible that, lacking any function in a society that made full use of their talents, the voracity for culture served as a kind of substitute.[14]

Add another fifty years, and still nothing has changed, with Rosemary Park, president of Barnard from 1962 to 1967, telling her board of trustees in her 1962–64 report: ". . . the women's college has not yet succeeded in making any great contributions toward clarifying the interestingly structured modern feminine existence . . . too many parents and daughters decided that college was a good safe place to have the girl until she was ready to take over a home. Learning, even though substantially the same in its requirements as at the men's colleges, had a tendency to become an ornament rather than an integral part of the personality."[15]

Lacking the sense of single-minded purpose and mission transmitted by the educators of men, the educators of women failed to deal realistically with the potential for conflict inherent within the sex ("She is a kind of prototype of contemporary intellectual women," said sociologist Jessie Bernard of anthropologist Ruth Benedict, Vassar '09. "Like them, she wanted nothing more than she wanted love, marriage, and motherhood, and like them, she found these were not enough."),[16] coming down hard on the side of the traditional concepts of womanhood which had long ago declared for wifehood and motherhood or, if one were unwise or unfortunate, for a career. One could BE one's sex, or one could ignore it; there were no compromises.

The former was, of course, the more desirable option, its desirability a hangover from the earliest days when some of the most respected physicians were predicting that the higher education of women, with its dire consequences of declining fertility, meant certain racial suicide. Add to this the accusations that segregation of girls at this vulnerable age invited lesbianism, and it is hardly a wonder that the Sisters as institutions were meticulous, not to say defensive, in putting before the public the fact that education did not detract from women's traditional worth. In survey after survey of alumnae (traditionally, the marriage rate has been one of the most available alumnae statistics), the Sisters were grateful to be able to demonstrate that their graduates, most of them anyway, ultimately did marry, that they produced the requisite numbers of children, that their divorce rate was within tolerable limits, and that they considered careers distinctly secondary to family obligations and household responsibilities, however dull and lonely the latter might be. And in 1929, one finds Mount Holyoke's Mary Emma Woolley—feminist and statesman (the only U.S. woman delegate to the Geneva Conference on reduction and limitation of armaments in 1932) as well as college president—carefully explaining that contrary to popular notions, higher education did not unfit a woman for marriage and that she had the wedding invitations from Mount Holyoke graduates to prove it.[17] In the mid-1970s, with the advent of the so-called sexual revolution and the contemporary lessening in the centrifugal force of the family, one can still find concern that Seven Sisters students, some of them the best and the brightest, may in fact fail to reproduce themselves.

Marriage has been also, of course, the most financially rewarding option for women. "In defiance of the axiom that he who works, eats," argued Emily Jane Putnam in *The Lady* in 1910, "the lady who works has less to eat than the lady who does not. There is no profession open to her that is nearly as lucrative as marriage, and the more lucrative the marriage the less work it involves. The economic prizes are therefore awarded in such a way as directly to discourage productive activity on the part of the lady. If a brother and sister are equally qualified for, let us say, the practice of medicine, the brother has, besides the scientific motive, the economic motive. The ardent pursuit of his profession will if successful make him a rich man. His sister on the other hand will never earn absolutely as much money as he, and relatively her earnings will be negligible in comparison with her income if she should marry a millionaire. But if she be known to have committed herself to the study of medicine, her chance of marrying a millionaire is practically eliminated."[18]

Neither of these conditions—the social or the economic—has been forcefully challenged by the women's colleges, although both are major factors that undermine notions of equality between the sexes. The Sisters devised no new patterns, broke no new ground, but only preached the old gospel and sent their graduates out to adapt to the same societal molds their mothers and grandmothers had fit.

It has always been a source of pride in the women's colleges (as opposed to the coeducational institutions where women in influential positions are rarities) that the top administrative positions have been filled consistently by women who serve as role models to their students. However, just as the curriculum failed to unravel the complexities in the fulfillment of women's physiological and professional ambitions, these traditional examples of professional fulfillment did not make the situation much clearer.

Who are they?

Of the forty-nine presidents (or deans in the early days of Barnard and Radcliffe), the ratio of men to women has not been so lopsided as might be expected in institutions committed to the education of women: twenty-one men to twenty-eight women, or 3:4 (counting from Mount Holyoke's charter as a college and excluding acting president Louise F. Cowles—1889–90). Wellesley, which opened with a 100 percent female faculty, has always had women presidents. Barnard, except for three brief interim or acting appointments (including acting president LeRoy Breunig, dean of the faculty, appointed on the resignation of Martha Peterson in June 1975), has always had female leadership—deans prior to 1953, presidents thereafter. (Jacqueline Anderson Mattfeld was chosen as Miss Peterson's successor in late 1975, becoming the eighth person to head Barnard since its founding in 1889). Vassar has had six men* and one woman (Sarah Gibson Blanding, 1946–64), and Smith's first woman president was inaugurated in October 1975, in time to start it on the second hundred years. Following Mary Lyon's death in 1849 and prior to charter as a college in 1888, Mount Holyoke hired only female presidents or principals, continued the tradition with Elizabeth Storrs Mead (1890–1900) and Mary Woolley (1900–37), then abruptly changed course—the implication being that the women had been incapable of balancing the checkbook—and have not had a woman in the president's office since. (Miss Woolley, an ardent feminist who had practiced all she preached, beginning in 1894 when she was one of the first two women to receive A.B. degrees from Brown University, and who was succeeded in 1937

---

* Including Milo P. Jewett who had helped to persuade Matthew Vassar to establish the women's college, was elected president at the board of trustees' first meeting in February 1861, participated in the planning and organization of the college, then resigned in April 1864, more than a year before the college opened, following a disagreement with the founder.

by Roswell G. Ham, never again set foot on the South Hadley campus she had loved and served so well.) Radcliffe has had four women and two men in Fay House. Bryn Mawr has had three women and two men presidents.*

Of these twenty-eight women, Jill Ker Conway (Mrs. John Conway), was not only Smith's first woman president, but she was also the first woman president of any Seven Sisters institution whose position had at least a temporary necessary priority over her husband's: It was *she* who was recruited by the Smith presidential search committee from the University of Toronto where she had been a faculty member and administrative officer for eleven years, the last three as vice president for internal affairs, and *he*, a distinguished professor of humanities at Toronto's York University, who was willing to job-hunt in the Connecticut Valley. Radcliffe's Matina Horner tells a Harvard horror story, of a faculty meeting at which a well-known woman scholar's name came up during discussion of a faculty appointment but was quickly dropped when it was observed that Harvard couldn't get her because her husband wouldn't come.[20]

Of the twenty-eight Seven Sisters presidents who were women, only two have successfully combined high-powered careers with marriage and family obligations (catch Yale saying that about Kingman Brewster). The first was Millicent Carey McIntosh of Barnard (1947–62)** who had married Dr. Rustin McIntosh, a New York pediatrician and Columbia professor while she was head of the Brearley School for Girls in New York. The second was Matina Horner, an associate professor of psychology at Har-

---

* Mrs. McIntosh was the niece and intellectual heiress of Bryn Mawr's Carey Thomas. When the latter heard of her niece's marriage, she did not entirely approve, but reconsidered when she was assured the young woman did not intend to give up her career. "Millicent," declared Miss Thomas, "can do a great deal for the CAUSE by proving that she can hold down a husband and a job like the headmistress of a big school."[21]

** Harris L. Wofford, whose "worldly credentials" are said to have qualified him for becoming Bryn Mawr's fifth president in 1970, when asked about his claim to the Bryn Mawr inheritance just at the moment of the contemporary women's movement's heaviest impact, laughed charmingly and commented, "It's ironic."[19]

vard who became president of Radcliffe in 1972.* Mary I. Bunting of Radcliffe (1960–72) and Barbara W. Newell of Wellesley (1972–   ) were widows when they assumed the presidencies of their respective institutions.

Those women who married during their presidencies resigned shortly thereafter: Barnard's Emily James Smith (Bryn Mawr '89) had been able to weather professionally her marriage to publisher George H. Putnam, but resigned the deanship in 1900 when her first pregnancy became known—the trustees could not, as the official Barnard history puts it, "risk the charge that Home and Motherhood were slighted for Homer and Miltiades";[23] Wellesley's Alice Freeman (1881–87) resigned in order to marry Harvard philosopher George Herbert Palmer, and Wellesley's Mildred H. McAfee (1936–49) resigned three years after her marriage to Congregational minister Douglas Horton—three years in which they had been kept largely apart by Dr. Horton's professional duties in New York—and Mrs. Horton concluded that her particular marriage and her particular career could not be combined successfully.

The large majority of Seven Sisters presidencies, however, have been filled by the standard academic and social types: men (usually distinguished professors from Harvard, Yale, Columbia, the University of Chicago) whose wives were sort of campus First Ladies (some of them Seven Sisters alumnae) with all the usual societal implications, and by spinsters—bright, scholarly, articulate, personable, but considered just not quite whole. All were men and women who illustrated to students the pages of the text they had memorized long ago: A man could have a marriage or a woman could have a career, but a woman could rarely, without considerable sacrifice to one or the other, have both.

In this day of affirmative action plans and large court awards (some in six figures) to academic women victims of institutional

---

* Mrs. Horner, whose husband, Joseph, is a physicist, tells a revealing story of early sex-role stereotyping: "When my daughter, not yet three, learned that a female friend of the family was a physician, after lengthy silence, she asked, 'Is she still a girl? Well, then, is she still Eric's mommy?' and before going on to other things concluded, 'She must be all mixed up.' "[22]

discrimination, Seven Sisters institutions have been understandably smug about their immunity from some of the requirements of affirmative action: (1) Executive Order 11246, the watershed for all subsequent affirmative action legislation, was signed in 1965, but while it imposed equal employment opportunity requirements on federal contractors, it specified institutions with $50,000 or more in federal contracts, thereby limiting formal adherence to the larger institutions; and (2) traditionally, the Sisters, whether out of a sense of obligation to their own graduates, or because highly qualified male faculty (like highly qualified male students) were more difficult to recruit for a women's college, or because women were cheaper,* have had a more or less common policy of hiring and promoting a relatively large number of women faculty and administrators (relative to men's and male-dominated coeducational institutions). Operating under a kind of voluntary and unwritten system of affirmative action, the Sisters have been known as places where women could find positions approaching their scholarly qualifications, whereas the reverse has been true for women in the men's and coeducational institutions. This is still true. However, while over the past half century the percentage of men has increased substantially in the women's colleges,

---

* Salary discrimination in the early days was no secret. Vassar's President John Howard Raymond openly established a $2,000 annual salary for men professors in the first year of the college and increased it two years later to $2,500 (not including living expenses which have been estimated at $650 per family for rent, coal, and groceries); at the same time astronomer Maria Mitchell, already a distinguished scientist, was offered $800 plus living expenses for herself and her father, and physician Alida Avery was offered $700 plus living expenses; other women instructors were paid $400 to $500 a year, plus living expenses; salary adjustments were finally made some years later when Miss Mitchell and Dr. Avery threatened to resign, partly because of the salary discrimination, partly because they had not been appointed to committees or asked to report their scholarly publication.

Salary discrimination, if it exists, is difficult to document today. Robert Dorfman, Wells Professor of Political Economy at Harvard, was appointed in early 1975 co-chairman of a committee of American Association of University Professors (AAUP) members, supported by the Exxon Education Foundation, to develop a standard method of testing whether female faculty members are paid as much as comparable male faculty on college campuses. Dorfman said he was operating on "the assumption that there is no place where women are getting as much as men."[24]

where males on the faculty was considered a drawing card, the
percentage of women has not increased proportionately in the
men's and coeducational institutions,* where women were considered an impairment.

At the women's colleges, women faculty have had their best if
not always entirely equal opportunities to inherit the senior ranks:
the full and associate professorships, the department chairmanships,
the endowed chairs.** With the increasing presence of men over

---

* In 1919, women made up 100 percent of the Barnard faculty, 55 percent
of the Bryn Mawr faculty, 90.3 percent of the Mount Holyoke faculty, 68.5
percent of the Smith faculty, 80 percent of the Vassar faculty, and 82.2 percent of the Wellesley faculty. Of the 135 Harvard instructors who taught at
Radcliffe, none was a woman; at coeducational Swarthmore, women made
up 30.2 percent of the faculty, at coeducational Oberlin, they made up 29.5
percent; at typical comparable men's institutions—Amherst, Haverford,
Dartmouth, Williams—women made up 0 percent of the faculty.
In 1974–75, women made up 59.1 percent of the Barnard faculty, 40 percent
of the Bryn Mawr faculty, 46.3 percent of the Mount Holyoke faculty,
40.3 percent of the Smith faculty, 39.5 percent of the Vassar faculty, and
55.1 percent of the Wellesley faculty; they made up 21.2 percent of the
Swarthmore faculty and 17.4 percent of the Oberlin faculty (including the
conservatory); they made up 7 percent of the Amherst faculty (which was
on the verge of deciding for coeducation), 12.1 percent of the Haverford
faculty (which had remained single-sex), 13.4 percent of the Dartmouth
faculty, and 15.8 percent of the Williams faculty, both of which had gone
fully coeducational.
** In 1974–75, women made up 52 per cent of the senior faculty at Barnard,
held 51.5 percent of the department chairmanships, and 50 percent of the
endowed chairs; at Bryn Mawr, women made up 38 percent of the senior
faculty, held 29.1 percent of the department chairmanships and 50 percent
of the endowed chairs; at Mount Holyoke, women made up 40.4 percent of
the senior faculty, held 29.6 percent of the department chairmanships, and
55.5 percent of the endowed chairs; at Smith, women made up 29.7 percent
of the senior faculty, held 8.3 percent of the department chairmanships, 35.2
percent of the endowed chairs; at Vassar, women made up 33.3 percent of
the senior faculty, held 26.9 percent of the department chairmanships, and
28.5 percent of the endowed chairs; at Wellesley, women made up 55.1 percent of the senior faculty, held 53.8 percent of the department chairmanships, 60 percent of the endowed chairs.
In the same year, at Swarthmore, women made up 10.1 percent of the
senior faculty, held 10.5 percent of the department chairmanships, and *no*
endowed chairs; at Oberlin, women made up 9 percent of the senior faculty,
held 3.8 percent of the department heads, and *no* endowed chairs.
At Amherst, women made up 4.9 percent of the senior faculty, held 4.1

the past century, these opportunities have declined, of course; they have, however, remained substantially better than at comparable coeducational and men's institutions.

It was not, however, good enough. In 1975, the Massachusetts Commission Against Discrimination (MCAD) decided that Smith had in fact denied tenure to two women members of the English department on the basis of sex and charged that "quite independent of the above, the college . . . has demonstrated a callous disregard for the spirit and letter of the sex discrimination laws,"[26] a decision that Smith, at this writing, was appealing.

The Sisters explain the increasing presence of men on their faculties, particularly in the higher ranks, by citing various periods in academic history that were lean in terms of available women Ph.D's—generally a minimum requirement for teaching there. "Between 1920 and 1960," explained Smith's President Mendenhall in reply to the MCAD's findings, "the proportion of women faculty declined throughout the country as the proportions of higher degrees granted to women declined. In particular after 1945 male veterans with subsidies returned to graduate and professional schools in such numbers that the percentage of women fell to 9 percent and remained under 10 percent through 1960. The availability of women doctorates was at its lowest between 1937 and 1960. Even though the percentage of new women doctorates rose to 13 percent by 1970, by that time they were competed for both by the host of new institutions and by the older colleges and universities who began actively to seek women faculty of all ranks. In short, as qualified women faculty did become slightly more available, more colleges were competing for them."[27]

Less often offered is the explanation that, having institutional psyches almost indistinguishable from those of the non-women's colleges and universities, the Sisters exhibited a similar rigidity in

---

percent of the department chairmanships, no endowed chairs; at Haverford, women made up 5.8 percent of the senior faculty, held 15 percent of the department chairmanships, and no endowed chairs; at Dartmouth, women made up 3.1 percent of the senior faculty, held no department chairmanships, 8.3 percent of the endowed chairs; at Williams, women made up 1.1 percent of the senior faculty, held 6.6 percent of the department chairmanships, and 3.3 percent of the endowed chairs.[25]

the faculty codes, making few adjustments to sex. It was perhaps a little easier for a woman to get a part-time position at Wellesley or Mount Holyoke than it was at the University of Texas or Yale, although part-time teachers did not always enjoy the full prerequisites of their offices, and one finds the Barnard trustees, for example, voting in 1972 to institute part-time professorships only after the part-timers requested the move, and Bryn Mawr was still wrestling in 1974 with the complicated but not insoluble problems of pay scales and tenure for part-timers. Individual faculty members could get pregnancy leaves, and Katharine Mc-Bride, former president of Bryn Mawr, recalled one case where the husband assumed his wife's classroom responsibilities during the last stages of her pregnancy and during confinement. Anti-nepotism rules, if they existed, which kept husbands and wives from joining the same faculty, were largely unwritten (Smith claimed never to have had them; no one at Barnard or Bryn Mawr could recall having had them—which may indicate to some extent the importance attached to them; Vassar and Wellesley dropped theirs in 1973*). The point is that in these women's colleges, there was little official institutional policy of helping women function in their dual roles—and if not here, where? The message was clear: Women scholars were welcomed on the faculty so long as they behaved like men.

"Women scholars," complained Bryn Mawr's Carey Thomas in 1913, "may have spent half a lifetime in fitting themselves for their chosen work and then may be asked to choose between it and

* When it comes to affirmative action, academic administrators claim immunity, the implication being that the high-minded men and women who run the universities ought not to be dealt with like the A&P (a claim HEW has demonstrated to be false); but when it comes to academic politics, there seems to be nothing between these people and undue influence except the anti-nepotism rules. It was not the example of the women's colleges, it was the threats of the federal government to cut off federal contracts that began to move academe in the direction of affirmative action, so that by late 1971 some small gains were being made, with the *Chronicle of Higher Education* reporting in October of that year that SUNY and the universities of New Mexico and Minnesota had modified their anti-nepotism rules, that Harvard and Princeton were changing their tenure policies to allow part-timers to hold it, and at Stanford, women faculty members who gave birth while accumulating seniority toward a tenure appointment could get a one-year extension on the term of their untenured appointments.

marriage. No one can estimate the number of women who remain unmarried in revolt before such a horrible alternative. . . . How many men scholars would there be if we compelled them to make such an inhuman choice?"[28]

By 1971, more than half the married women in the United States were working; women with jobs were acceptable, and the Sisters were taking corrective measures. The outmoded nepotism rules have all but disappeared, and married couples worked together at Bryn Mawr, Wellesley, Mount Holyoke, and Smith, and even at Harvard. Sometimes they even had the same rank, although this was rarer. The woman is often slower to earn her Ph.D.: she may have taken time out to help her husband through graduate school or because she had young children; she is apt to have published less or have less seniority, both of which are considerations in her rank. And in a few cases, in recognition of academe's mating habits, Sisters have been willing to experiment with hiring a married couple for one job. Smith has set up new day-care centers, and young faculty couples are living in the Wellesley dormitories, with children on tricycles spilling into the corridors and dining rooms while their mothers collect their lecture notes for the graduate courses they are taking at Harvard and MIT and attempt to give the happy shambles some organization.

All of which presents a pleasanter picture of post-college opportunities than George Palmer's furtive campus courtship of Alice Freeman in the 1880s. But these are recent developments and the products not of Seven Sisters innovation but of general academic woman's restlessness in the throes of the contemporary women's movement.

Although boards of trustees are not the most visible sector of the college administration, there cannot be a student alive who is unaware not only of the boards' historical domination by men—although this is changing slowly—but by *professional* men, usually with long lists of professional credits, many of them business-men—bankers and brokers—the rationale being that financially precarious institutions need a friend at Chase Manhattan. There is a kind of self-perpetuating myth among women's-college administrators—as if they believed all the clichés pinned on them —that women simply are not capable of keeping accounts; it extends even into the college administration itself, and while there are all sorts of women deans to administrate academic matters, at least until 1975 not a woman treasurer at any of the Seven was to be found. Ever since it was decided to add alumnae representation to the boards of trustees (a pragmatic decision since it has traditionally been the alumnae who foot a goodly percentage of the bills and the trustees who decide financial policy) women have been members; some of them (an increasing number since the contemporary women's movement began) have been elected as regular, non-alumnae trustees. Among the women there is a sprinkling of educators, lawyers, doctors, even an occasional business executive, but the old habits are slow to change, and for the most part, the women are *non*-professionals.

Former student and professional feminist Lucy Stone wondered publicly in 1891, fifty-four years after Mount Holyoke opened, why the college continued to invite men, never women, to speak at Founders' Day, although the founder was a woman. "Well," she decided, "the force of old customs will *sometime* break."[29] Virginia Gildersleeve of Barnard was the first female commencement speaker at Smith—in 1919, 44 years after the college opened. At Bryn Mawr twenty, or 28.5 percent of the commencement speakers at seventy commencements have been women. At Wellesley, of ninety-five commencement speakers, thirteen, or 13.6 percent, have been women. Of seventeen commencement speakers between 1958 and 1974 at Mount Holyoke, four (three of them subsequent to the advent of contemporary feminism), or 23.5 percent, have been women. In 1972, Vassar's Ad Hoc Faculty Committee on Women reported that of the past fifty-seven commencement speakers, nine had been women. The rest were the achievers of this world: men.[30]

All of which, if a young woman is to look to examples for guidance in her choices for living, even in a women's institution, is hardly calculated to alter the traditional images or the traditional and well-worn paths. Or, if Yale or the University of Texas had looked to the women's institutions for guidance in dealing with women faculty, what they saw would hardly be calculated to alter the traditional images or the traditional and well-worn paths.

3

In the social sense at least, the elitism in liberal arts has contributed to a respectable success, preparing Seven Sisters alumnae to mate with Ivy League men, endowing what was once essentially a decorative role with an added intellectual dimension, and forcing some early critics of women's education to admit that not only did this education not unfit her for marriage but may have enabled her to marry better, a situation that has not changed substantially since the turn of the century and was duly noticed by *The New York Times* in 1961, during the earliest days of the Kennedy administration: Not only was the wife of the young president a former Vassar student, but so was her social secretary and so were a number of upper-echelon, including cabinet, wives, putting Vassar, declared the *Times* in one of its more precious comparisons, nearly on a par with Harvard in terms of influence within the new administration.[31]

In the sense of outstanding achievement and/or contribution to society proportionate to the Sisters' academic excellence and their reputations, which is one of the things elitism inherent in liberal arts is all about, the picture is less clear. Bryn Mawr published a comprehensive survey conducted in 1970–71.* Based on an 80.5 percent return of questionnaires from 7,507 alumnae, *A College in Dispersion* quantifies Bryn Mawr alumnae, but makes no attempt at evaluation. Beyond that and notations in alumnae quarterlies and campus newspapers, evidence of Seven Sisters alumnae achievement is scanty, unsystematic, and inconclusive, the field overripe for investigation. The Sisters themselves had produced no meaningful evaluation of their product, and there was no way of assessing with any accuracy whether this expensive and academically demanding type of education had in fact liberated Seven Sisters women beyond the strictly intellectual.

It is true, of course, that each of the Sisters has graduated its share of Superwomen. Helen Keller and Josephine Hull and

---

* 9,330 questionnaires were sent; of 9,695 living alumnae (including the coeducational graduate schools), 200 could not be located and 165 refused to participate; of those surveyed, 6,099 belonged to undergraduate classes from 1896 to 1970, and 1,627 men and women had been enrolled in the Bryn Mawr graduate schools.

Congresswoman Elizabeth Holzman* went to Radcliffe; Margaret Mitchell, Judith Raskin, and Julia Child went to Smith; Elizabeth Janeway and public relations expert Doris Fleischman Bernays went to Barnard; Caroline Bird, Charlotte Curtis, and anthropologist Ruth Benedict went to Vassar, Nobel Peace Prize winner Emily Green Balch and Judianne Densen-Gerber, pioneer in the field of drug rehabilitation, went to Bryn Mawr; Virginia Apgar, developer of an internationally recognized test for determining the health of newborn infants, and movie producer Julia Miller Phillips, who won an Academy Award for her work on *The Sting*, went to Mount Holyoke. But so did Esther Howland, recognized as the first regular publisher, in 1840, of the Valentine, whose popularity was deplored by the administration of Mount Holyoke Female Seminary; student Emily Dickinson reported to her brother in 1848 that "Mistress Lyon arose in the hall & forbade our sending 'any of those foolish notes called Valentines.' But those who were here last year, knowing her opinions, were sufficiently cunning to write & give them into the care of [the postmaster] during the vacation so that about 150 were despatched on Valentine morn."[34] Classical archaeologist Phyllis Williams Lehmann and author Santha Rama Rau went to Wellesley. There are many others to support the claim that Seven Sisters institutions trained leaders.

In fact, M. Elizabeth Tidball (Mount Holyoke '48), professor of physiology at the George Washington University Medical Center, Washington, D.C., conducted a survey of the academic origins of 1,500 women selected at random but in equal numbers from three editions of *Who's Who of American Women*. Pub-

---

* Of the 68 women who, elected in their own right, served full terms in the House of Representatives from 1917 to 1975, 7 were products of Seven Sisters institutions (2 Wellesley, 1 Smith, 1 Barnard, 1 Mount Holyoke, 1 Radcliffe, 1 Bryn Mawr), 10 were products of other women's colleges, 37 were products of coeducational institutions (although not all those 37 received degrees), 11 had no formal higher education, and the education of 3 was unknown; on the Senate side, of the 3 women who were elected in their own right, none has come from a women's college.[32] Ironically, the high point of women in Congress was reached in 1962, prior to the rise of contemporary feminism, when 2 women sat in the Senate and 18 in the House. For the second session of the 94th Congress, which opened in January 1975, there were 19 women in the House, none in the Senate.[33]

lished in the *Educational Record* for Spring 1973, the results of her research indicated that among the alumnae of women's colleges (including the Seven Sisters but not limited to these) there was twice as high a rate of achiever output than among the alumnae of coeducational institutions.

Kenneth R. Hardy, professor of psychology at Brigham Young University, Provo, Utah, in a recent study of the output of 295 baccalaureate institutions (published in *Science* for August 9, 1974 as "Social Origins of American Scientists and Scholars"), found that several women's colleges (Bryn Mawr, Mount Holyoke, Radcliffe, Vassar, Goucher, Wellesley, and Smith) scored high in the production of future doctorate recipients during two separate and limited periods between 1920 and 1961.

Did these women achieve, however, what is measured as worldly success because of or in spite of their experiences in Seven Sisters institutions?

Mrs. Tidball, whose survey indicated that the alumnae of the women's colleges were being entered in *Who's Who of American Women* at a higher rate than the products of coeducational institutions, attributed their success to two major factors inherent in the institutions: the obvious one being the absence of male distractions who provided "a continual and not always subtle reminder that the young woman's collegiate task is to find a suitable mate, to become eventually a wife and mother, and in the interim to experiment in male-female relationships on the supposition that this prelude is necessary to fulfill the expectations of society"; the more important factor, however, being what she found to be a remarkable correlation between the numbers of achievers and the numbers of women on the faculties of their respective alma maters during the critical undergraduate years. "The development," Mrs. Tidball finally determined, "of young women of talent into career-successful adults is directly proportional to the number of role models to whom they have access."*35

* Mabel Newcomer, longtime economics professor at Vassar and student of women's educational history, had reported two decades previously: "There is some evidence . . . that the presence of large numbers of women scholars on the faculties of the women's colleges has been influential in developing scholars among their students. Not only are women faculty more likely to have faith in the intellectual capacity of women students and

The women's colleges, several of which either had recently decided coeducation was not for them or were engaged in serious discussions regarding the desirability and feasibility of admitting men at the time the article was published, were understandably ecstatic at the results of the physiology professor's work, and it has become, not surprisingly, a prominent feature of official public relations at Seven Sisters institutions, a kind of Good Housekeeping Seal of Approval.

Mrs. Tidball's is indeed a seminal piece of research. It is not, however, without problems. First, the measuring stick. Academics will be the first to admit that it is easier for the president of a small college to be included in the various *Who's Who* volumes than it is for the president of a corporation of comparable or even larger size and, equally questionable, neither the eighth (1974–75) or ninth (1975–76) editions of *Who's Who of American Women* included such an outstanding achiever as, for example, tennis player Billie Jean King.

In addition, Mrs. Tidball's research measured women's-college women against other women but failed to consider the position of women's-college women in the larger society. For example, large categories in *Who's Who of American Women* are "civic worker" or "community service," catchalls for a great number of women who would not be included in other rosters; "librarian" is another large—and largely female—category; so is "nurse." The women's colleges did and do indeed train leaders and achievers, but more often than not, they have been leaders of women, achievers among women, not in the larger society. They trained college presidents not for the University of California or Harvard or Cornell but for Wellesley and Radcliffe and Goucher. They even trained military officers, but for the women's services.* But when they trained

---

encourage them to go on with graduate study; they also serve as 'models' for their students. They are living evidence that scholarship is not a masculine monopoly. There is, however, no close correlation between the number of women on the faculty and the number of scholars that have come from different institutions. And unless the women scholars on the faculty are outstanding, their value as models is doubtful. The quality of the faculty is unquestionably of more importance than their sex."[36]

* Julia C. Stimson, Vassar '01, was the first woman officer in the United States Army, a major in the army Nurse Corps; Mildred McAfee, Vassar '20 and later a Wellesley president, was the first commander of the WAVES;

publishers, somehow most of them turned out to be secretaries, when they trained bank presidents, it was largely for women's banks (Madeline H. McWhinney of the First Women's Bank, in New York, was Smith '43), and they trained hardly any union leaders. The elitism was largely among women.

Mrs. Tidball also failed to investigate what Hardy found to be a major factor in the isolation of women's colleges as undergraduate sources of Ph.D. recipients: "A clientele of high socioeconomic status and with strong career orientations, which often lead these women into scientific and scholarly pursuits."[37] Mrs. Tidball rather hastens over the suggestion that "the output of any institution can be no more than a reflection of the input,"[38] that the factors of self-selection and then institutional selection not only through intellectual sifting but also by economic, social, and professional background, has a significant bearing on women's achievement. It is as if Indira Gandhi's election to India's highest parliamentary office had something to do with the numbers of women on the faculty at Somerville College rather than the fact that she was Jawaharlal Nehru's daughter.

Seen in other contexts, this same principle of self-selection may prevail. For example, prior to the 1954–55 United States Supreme Court decisions on public school desegregation, Dunbar High School in Washington, D.C., was the place to be for black youth. Drawing young men and women from all over the city, the Dunbar administration offered rigorous academic programs to the sons and daughters of the city's middle-class blacks, a winning combination that exerted pressures on students to make the most of their opportunities in class and served to enlarge enormously the local black professional pool, at the same time producing a large number of outstanding achievers, including Senator Edward Brooke and William H. Hastie, first black federal judge.[39]

On the flip side of the coin, the open admissions policy of the City University of New York (CUNY) adopted in 1969, while it increased substantially the college-going population of New York City (the large majority from families earning less than $15,000

Ruth Streeter Cheney, first director of the Marine Corps' Women's Reserve, was Bryn Mawr '18; Oveta Culp Hobby of the WACS and later secretary of HEW, went to a small southern women's college.

a year according to the last complete study, in 1972), it has taken
a proportionate toll in academic standards, with many of the local
high school graduates entering CUNY almost completely unpre-
pared for college work, many of them unable to read, write, spell,
or deal with abstractions beyond the sixth-grade level.[40]

Other factors may also influence achievement. Mabel Newcomer, long-time economics professor at Vassar, in a 1950s study
of *American Men of Science* and *Dictionary of American Scholars*, while noting the high achievement of eight (the Seven Sisters
plus Goucher) women's-college alumnae, concluded that "it is the
liberal arts college—not specifically women's colleges—that produces scholars in large numbers. Oberlin ranked below Smith
[which produced five times its expected share], but it still produced three times the number that its enrollment would account
for; Carleton ranked above Smith with six times its quota; and
Swarthmore outdistanced even Bryn Mawr [which produced fifteen times its share] with eighteen times its quota."[41] A study of
women physicians by the Association of American Medical Colleges (AAMC), Department of Academic Affairs, published in
1975, reported still another influence on women's achievement:
"The mothers' education of educationally elite women is particularly higher than that usually attained by most women."[42]

At the Seven Sisters institutions, highest academic standards for
admission begin the process of selecting out. Economics follows
close behind if not parallel; the women's colleges are expensive, not
only in terms of tuition costs but also in terms of the student's
financial ability to luxuriate for four years in undergraduate
study,* not to mention a recognized tendency of the less affluent
to hesitate if not to refuse to commit substantial sums to the higher
education of daughters, even in the mid-1970s. Add to these the
cultural and career orientations which give the children of profes-

---

* In a survey of undergraduate origins of Radcliffe Ph.D's, 1902–1951, the
Radcliffe Committee on Graduate Education for Women attributed the low
proportion of Radcliffe graduate students who had come from state and
municipal universities (35, or 10.9 percent of the total 321 women studied,
as opposed to 176, or 55 percent, from Seven Sisters institutions) to economics: "The expenses of study and the cost of living at Radcliffe are disproportionate to the charges at publicly supported institutions, particularly
for the girl who has been living with her family."[43]

sional parents a significant headstart over first-generation college students, and it is at least possible that the elitism begins for all practical purposes not in Freshman Philosophy at Smith but in the bassinette. What went in came out, intellectually fine-honed but otherwise not noticeably altered.

4

But what of the other 140,000 or so living alumnae of Seven Sisters institutions, that large—by far the larger—mass of women who did not achieve the status of Superwoman?

The arrival of a girl child has rarely aroused the enthusiasm of her family and friends the way the arrival of a boy child has, a hangover, perhaps, from the earliest days of civilization when a boy meant two more hands to hoe and a girl meant a dowry to be put together. Throughout life, the girl's rites of passage, whether baptism or bat mitzvah, traditionally have been less celebrated than those of her brother, including her entry into the labor market—a haphazardly planned-for event in contrast to her brother's which has been, from his first visit to his father's office on the assumption that he will inherit it (figuratively if not literally in recent times), a systematic indoctrination with a sense of purpose.

One result of this casual approach to a woman's work has been, of course, to endow it with an aura of time-killing, an underscoring of the societal statement that while men cannot possibly have enough time in life to fulfill their manifest destinies, women have not nearly enough destiny with which to fill all the time at their disposal, a statement that has gone virtually unchallenged by Seven Sisters institutions over the first hundred years of their existence.

Individual faculty and administrators have, of course, attempted to raise students' aspirations, wheedling and needling them into graduate and professional schools—partly, at least, it is generally recognized in academe, in some subconscious desire to duplicate themselves, and partly, perhaps, because professional and vocational vision from the ivory tower is necessarily somewhat limited. Barnard's Virginia Gildersleeve was instrumental in persuading Columbia to open its professional schools of architecture, journalism, medicine, and law to women, the last two not without a struggle. And Vassar's Professor Abby Leach, who as a young girl had persuaded three Harvard professors to tutor her and thus became an opening wedge in the struggle to establish Radcliffe College, was well known on the Vassar campus for her interest in sending students into scholarly careers. But the Virginia Gildersleeves and the Abby Leaches of the women's-college world were few and far between.

Enrollment in graduate school required some serious commitment to a career and, not surprisingly perhaps, men's and coeducational liberal arts colleges on which Seven Sisters curriculums were modeled, have had more distinguished graduate school records, with a consistently higher percentage of their graduates completing doctoral degrees (Hardy's research, which was limited to two specific periods, notwithstanding). For example, Amherst grants fewer bachelor's degrees each year than any Sister except Bryn Mawr; yet Amherst alumni accounted for 671 doctoral degrees between 1920 and 1966—more than double those of Barnard (314) and Bryn Mawr alumnae (318), nearly double those of Radcliffe (342) to which it is similar in size, and substantially more than those of Mount Holyoke (405), Smith (391), Vassar (422), and Wellesley (465). Haverford grants even fewer bachelor's degrees than Bryn Mawr, yet its alumni managed to account for 432 doctorates during the same period—second only to Wellesley of the Sisters, of which it is about one third the size. Williams alumni, roughly comparable in numbers to Amherst, also came in second only to Wellesley with 460 doctorates. Swarthmore alumni and alumnae, who average slightly fewer bachelor's degrees than Amherst alumni, accounted for 787 doctorates during that period. Oberlin, no more than a third larger than the largest six Sisters and about two thirds larger than Bryn Mawr, was the baccalaureate source of 1,478 doctoral degrees, and Dartmouth alumni, less than double Smith alumnae (the largest of the Seven Sisters), accounted for 1,000 doctorates, or more than double the Wellesley number, which is the highest for the Seven. Harvard, Yale, and Princeton undergraduate alumni are, of course, out of sight.[44]

Similar observations can be made about fellowships awarded seniors for graduate study. In an eleven-year survey (1960–61 through 1970–71) of National Science Foundation grants for first-year graduate study, based on the number of grants as a percentage of the number of bachelor's degrees conferred: Barnard (0.3 percent), Mount Holyoke (0.2 percent), Smith (0.2 percent), Vassar (0.1 percent), and Wellesley (0.3 percent) ranked well behind Amherst (1 percent), Haverford (1.8 percent), Dartmouth (0.6 percent), Princeton (1.7 percent), Yale (1.1 percent), and Williams (0.5 percent) men, and even behind Swarthmore (2.3 percent) women; they ranked roughly even with Oberlin women (0.3 percent). Only Bryn Mawr (0.5 percent) equaled Williams, and only Radcliffe (1 percent) equaled Amherst; none came close to Harvard (2.5 percent), although Radcliffe and Harvard shared faculty and curriculum during that period so that students' opportunities at both institutions ought to have been, at least theoretically, equal.[45]

In a similar survey during the same period of Woodrow Wilson fellowships, which carry a commitment to teaching,* a traditionally feminine occupation, Seven Sisters seniors did slightly better, although again only Bryn Mawr (5.1 percent) and Radcliffe (2.8 percent) outranked, equaled, or approached Amherst (2.7 percent), Harvard (2.8 percent), Haverford (7.5 percent), Princeton (2.9 percent), and Williams (2.1 percent) men, and Swarthmore women (3.6 percent); again, Oberlin (1.1 percent) women were more or less equal to Barnard (1.4 percent), Mount Holyoke (0.7 percent), Smith (1.0 percent), Vassar (1.3 percent), and Wellesley (1.8 percent) women, as were Dartmouth (1.0 percent) and Yale (1.8 percent) men.[46]

Compared with women in a group of universities, where academic excellence may be diffused through a vast system (UCLA, Michigan, Pennsylvania, and Wisconsin) and standards of selection are less stringent where they exist at all, Seven Sisters women did consistently better, outranked by, or nearly comparable to, only the University of Chicago women who averaged 1 percent in National Science Foundation awards and 2.6 percent in Woodrow Wilson fellowships.

Following the rise of contemporary feminism and the social and

---

* The commitment to teaching, although strong, may be loosely interpreted, with the editors of *Woodrow Wilson Fellows 1945–67* captioning a photo of Ralph Nader: "Automakers may wonder whether Ralph Nader, WWF '63, has successfully 'taught' via his book, *Unsafe at Any Speed* (1965)."

political activism of the late 1960s and early 1970s, the nation's law
and medical schools experienced a surge of interest by both men
and women; enrollment of women in medical schools rose from
9 percent in 1969–70 to 15.4 percent in 1973–74, and enrollment of
women in law schools rose from 6.4 percent in 1969 to 13.6 in
1973 (graduate schools of business administration have also experienced an increase in popularity, although not quite so marked);
the interest did not appear to have abated significantly in the
quieter 1970s, and medical school and law school advisors on the
faculties of the Seven have become part of the academic furniture.
But once again, it was not an inner-directed addition but another
response to outside pressures, a restatement of the tendency to
invite others to define them, consumersim at work again.

For the large majority of students, for whom the bachelor's
degree was the end of the academic line, the prefabricated mores
of the professional world went unchallenged, with the stop-gap
career, the time-killer, as the norm, until Prince Charming happened along and again during those golden years when the children
have left and woman was again faced with the frightening prospect
of having to fill her days. But there was little attempt to endow a
woman's life with unity, some sense of long-range purpose outside
marriage, to make some meaningful entity out of all those dis-
combobulated parts.

As Cynthia Propper Seton, Smith '48 and author of *The Mother
of the Graduate*, put it in some reminiscences of college:

I thought rather than shove me along and push me on to being a
grownup fully entitled human being, it allowed me to linger and
dawdle right through Smith as I lingered and dawdled into Smith.

I thought that we were taught really to Think Small. Now I didn't
think everybody did this, by a long shot, a bright girl who had come
from some more liberated family—liberated from middle classness
anyway—or just spunkier or in some psychological way able to take
advantage of what was here, did much better, quite literally understood and learned and took four years worth of really good cultural
learning out, and I didn't do that. . . .

What was I being educated for in the mid-forties? I can only speak
from a very restricted point of view, and I don't think it does justice
to my father and mother or to Smith, but I was not encouraged to be
something beyond a really elegant wife and mother. . . . I was never

encouraged to take a field and make it my own, which would be professionalism of some kind. . . .

. . . Smith . . . said always with great nobility, "We are educating
you to be a finer person, to have a finer mind with more refined values,
that's what we're doing," and they did . . . nobody said, "You're a full
grown grownup, go out and pull your weight." Nobody did. Nobody
expected it of me.[47]

In 1961, more than a decade later, a Smith faculty member
queried his students on what they dreamed for themselves in
1971. Marriage, they answered; two or three children; travel; cultural activity; a vocation *in reserve.* "Nobody," complained the
professor, "wanted to go to the moon; nobody even wanted to be
a millionaire."[48]

And about the same time Mary Ellen Chase, Biblical scholar and
one of Smith's most beloved English professors, articulated the
institutional approach: "I think few, if any, of us indulge ourselves
in the fantastic notions that we shall develop countless master-
minds, or turn out many giantesses in the earth. We are, instead,
inclined to look upon such presumption as a bit ridiculous, and on
the whole, mistrust taking ourselves too seriously."[49] If the Jews,
whose sense of mission may be one of the highest developed in
human history, had said that, think of the consequences for Western ethical traditions. In any event, the Seven Sisters ethos was
hardly calculated to make the college what Clark Kerr called "the
chief port of entry"[50] to the professions, old and new.

Not only was the level of aspirations low. So was the degree of
commitment by professionals to the betterment of society. No one
ever mentioned that the world might be in desperate need of the
talents of a Wellesley girl, that the world's work was for her, too.
Social commitment was for over there, on the side, for the volunteer who was not only perpetuating woman's ancillary role but in
some cases assuring the continued societal dependence on volunteer labor (but more of that later). Social responsibility was an
important item, but it was a separate item, not connected to
careers. The fact that the environment might require a Smith- or
Bryn Mawr-trained biologist was beside the point.

One result was that Seven Sisters students (those who did not
plan to marry immediately following graduation and even some
who did) opted, for lack of any other sense of direction, for the

expedient. Until recent years when feminists became so critical of the academic female as stereotype and at about the same time the bottom dropped out of the academic job market, teaching has been the single, most popular vocation of Seven Sisters graduates. Not education administration, however, except in the women's colleges; these higher-salaried, more prestigious positions have been reserved generally for men. Bryn Mawr's experience is perhaps typical. Its comprehensive survey of all its living alumnae from prior to 1915 to 1970, *A College in Dispersion*, indicates that of the 3,774 alumnae of the undergraduate college reporting full-time jobs (ever), 601, or 15.9 percent, have held positions on college or university faculties; 526, or 13.9 percent, have been independent-school teachers; and 409, or 10.8 percent, have been public-school teachers.* The second highest category is secretarial work (of which the implications of subservience have yet to be properly explored): 434 alumnae, or 11.5 percent. In contrast, only 17, or .5 percent of the Bryn Mawr alumnae became engineers; 18, or .5 percent, became architects; 32, or .8 percent became lawyers; 120, or 3.2 percent, became physicians.

Researchers. Librarians. Social workers. These are other popular items on the Seven Sisters laundry list, a list that lends itself to a career stereotyping that should have been put to rest with Plato—who deplored it—2,300 years ago. Some of them, especially the secretary, are non-ladder positions. Men know they can get into publishing, for example, through a proofreader's door or into business through a salesman's door, both beginning jobs but in a direct line to higher echelons. Women too often are offered secretarial positions which have a lateral rather than a vertical relationship to other beginning jobs, lacking as they do the requirement of long-term commitment, and they become stereotyped as feminine, less perhaps because they assumed the traditional feminine characteristics of dependence, non-competitiveness, and service, than because they were essentially time-killing, ideal for young women whose aspirations and ambitions had not been provoked.

A common institutional complaint about women students is their recognized reluctance to concentrate or major in the "hard"

---

* Because of the possibilities for overlap, these figures cannot be added to discover the total number or total percentage of alumnae who became teachers.

sciences, the explanations usually offered being that women are natural conformists, that they are mentally ill-equipped to deal in quantitative concepts, and that they fear men may be socially ill-equipped to deal with what are assumed to be the Amazonian intellectual abilities of a female physics Ph.D., which is what a physics major must inevitably lead to and which may act just as effectively as a negative dowry as a burdensome financial loan does. A second look at the disciplines in terms of student popularity suggests other causes of this reluctance, at least for Seven Sisters women. One is, of course, the obvious inherent weaknesses of the primarily undergraduate institution: the lack of sophisticated facilities and the lack of excitement that accompanies the commitment to research in a graduate institution. Another cause may have something to do with the common if inaccurate conception of the liberal arts with its connotations of elitist "culture" that do not include hands smelling of formaldehyde. One finds men, in many of the comparable men's and coeducational liberal arts institions, also clustering in the humanities and social sciences. And if the lines are not quite so clear-cut or the contrasts quite so stark as those in the women's colleges, the ratio of English to biology majors, for example, at Amherst, Haverford, Swarthmore, Oberlin, Dartmouth, Princeton, Yale, and Williams is well above the national average. Comparisons of history and chemistry majors follow a similar pattern.* It is a pattern that necessarily perpetuates itself because, based as it must be on a kind of consumerism, the student is often drawn to the large numbers and the eminence of the humanities and social science faculties, as opposed to the little clusters of men and women in the "hard" sciences who sometimes look more like a committee than a faculty.

---

* Actual ratio of English to biology majors from 1960–61 through 1970–71, rounded to the nearest whole number, are Yale 6:1, Harvard and Swarthmore (men) 3:1; Amherst, Haverford, Oberlin (men), Dartmouth, Princeton, and Williams, 2:1; the national average for men is 1:1. Seven Sisters and Swarthmore and Oberlin women's averages range from 6:1 to 2:1 also, with the national women's average 4:1. Comparing history and chemistry majors over the same period, men's institutions ranged from a high of 9:1 at Yale to 2:1 at Oberlin and Swarthmore, with the national men's average 2:1. Seven Sisters and Swarthmore and Oberlin women's ratios ranged from a high of 12:1 at Smith to a low of 2:1 at Mount Holyoke, with 5:1 the national women's average.[51]

All of these are undoubtedly influential in students' choosing of majors; that is, looking toward a future career. But one wonders whether a more significant reason for women's aversion to the hard sciences might not be a feminine hesitation to make the long-term—and lonely—commitment that biology and chemistry and physics demand (at least a Ph.D. if one is to get anywhere at all; a guilty sense of wastefulness if Prince Charming happens along in mid-course or even in mid-career; a heightened sense of frustration if one then abandons one's laboratory) and which English and history and political science do not demand, at least not to such a great extent. So that women's traditional success in the arts—literary products of the Seven Sisters are a dime a dozen—and humanities may have less to do with innate abilities or lack of them than with the institutional direction toward them and away from the commitment required for the sciences.

The institutional assessment of women's life as essentially time-killing except for her reproductive responsibilities was articulated by Wellesley's Margaret Clapp in her president's report for 1956–58: ". . . the important demands of homemaking continue to debar many women from advanced study. However, the greatest difficulty seems to exist not for young married women living near a university and whose husbands approve of their intellectual interests, but for young women who are not married, who naturally wish to marry, who feel that until the central question of marriage is settled they cannot take a long look ahead and so take temporary fill-in jobs." As undergraduates—and even before—Miss Clapp continued, young women must plan further ahead, "flexibly," of course, "in order to be able to fit into their future husbands' careers," and not with any sense of professional or social purpose, but in order to develop "abilities and interests which might well be carried into marriage, set aside in the years of child care, and then renewed without undue difficulty."

Employers caught the institutional mood, only rarely seeking in their annual recruiting visits to Seven Sisters campuses management trainees from whom some sense of commitment was required, but teachers, bank tellers, secretaries, computer operators, editorial researchers, and, in this time of heightening popularity of law schools, paralegals.

"We'll go any place we can to find a chemist," said a personnel officer for a pharmaceutical company that was recruiting on Seven Sisters campuses during the mid-1960s. "It's the graduate schools that are our competition, and, percentagewise, fewer girls go on to graduate work. The so-called snob schools have excellent chemistry and biology programs . . . if we can get one of their girls—the sort who could go on but doesn't—we grab her. And if we can keep her three or four years, we break even." Another company was looking for the bright "bachelor girl who wants maybe a five-year fling in the big city before she gets married."[52] And few within the institutions were disposed to disabuse them of their notions.

It is certainly true that the graduate, male or female, of a liberal arts college, the generalist par excellence, is not the most vocationally viable item in a labor market increasingly demanding of specialists. Added to this, for Seven Sisters graduates, are the traditional economic, social, and political discriminations against women, plus the ambiguities of their own lives. The problem of the generalist, which the Seven shared with the Ivy League, could be coped with if not solved, simply by imitating the men's institutions, although perhaps less successfully. For the first century, however, the sex-related problems were virtually ignored, as the reality of sex beyond a meticulous, not to say defensive, observance of the proprieties had been successfully ignored in other areas of the institutions.

From their earliest days, Seven Sisters institutions have prided themselves on their vocational concern for and services to students and alumnae. Wellesley's first president, Ada Howard, recognized the need for the college to help its graduates "find a suitable situation"[53] in 1878, a year before it even had graduates and, conforming to the fashion of the times, a Teachers' Registry was soon established. As alternatives to teaching became available to women, the Teachers' Registry became the Bureau of Occupations, then the Personnel Bureau, which was superseded in turn by the Placement Office and, finally, Career Services, an office to which 95 percent of the Wellesley senior class ultimately finds its way for counseling and vocational information. Wellesley's operation is not untypical, each of the Seven having set up similar establishments, all with varying degrees of relationship to actual employment offices.

They seemed, however, some sort of appendages to the institutions, remote from the faculty where the intellectual action was and with whom they appeared to have little dialogue. An administrative concession to harsh economic reality not wholly appropriate to the white-gloved self-image.

Consequently, there was until recently little long-range career-planning; the emphasis was on job-getting—called in the argot of gracious living in the early days "accepting appointments"—which was not infrequently tinged with some defeatism at the outset, a defeatism more often laid to the vocational clumsiness of the generalist than to discrimination against women, and putting one's best foot forward meant getting it in the door and under the secretary's desk. Essentially passive, they either relied on alumnae as a kind of "old girl" employment network, or served as gracious hostesses, ladylike liaison, to company men who came to look for the "bachelor girls," but rarely summoned the aggressiveness of spirit that was required to open new areas or to sell their graduates as splendidly equipped to handle such-and-such jobs. They had to be asked to dance.

They grumbled among themselves that their graduates were taking jobs unrelated to their majors, that a Smith theater major was wasting her time as a merchandising trainee at Bloomingdale's or that an American Studies major was teaching physical education at a girl's school; a Mount Holyoke dance major was working as a secretary in a career-counseling office or an English major as a carpenter. And they grumbled into their alumnae magazines that corporate recruitment literature was, as one of their number put it, "explicitly discriminatory," featuring photographs of "young men on the move,"[54] and frequently complained to the companies themselves, not always getting a satisfactory response; but rarely if ever did they publicize the slights. Recruiting discrimination is not much more subtle today; it takes the form of corporate failure to explore—or admit—the fact that Wellesley or Bryn Mawr does not offer engineering majors so that recruiters can add these to their HEW compliance sheets.

The onset of the contemporary women's movement broke down the doors of the vocational offices. The emphasis was no longer on killing time, and serious career counseling was offered. Workshops were presented on a more or less regular schedule to illustrate career options in various fields. Successful alumnae were brought back to campus to share their experiences with students. Internships—or externships, as they were called at Bryn Mawr —were put together, during which a student might spend time during her four years exploring at first hand some field in which she was interested, learning the language, measuring the potential, whetting—or killing—her appetite for that particular field (actually an adaptation to liberal arts of what Oberlin, Antioch, and more recently Simmons had done for years), all in the name of raising women's aspirations.

Once again, however, it was outside forces that brought about the changes rather than some internal momentum which might have coordinated intellectual and vocational problems and realities in some mutually meaningful way. For the vocational offices, despite their bright new look, their increased staff, their new commitments, still seemed appendages to the institutions, constant reminders that it was still a long way from liberal arts to vocational compatibility.

5

In the latter half of the nineteenth century, at the time the Seven Sisters were established, the woman question was already upon us and overripe for investigation and answers. Out of the restless mutterings of the Mary Wollstonecrafts and the John Stuart Mills, the abolitionists and the educators, had emerged a vocal suffrage movement which, over too long a period of time, would prove politically effective. Urbanization and industrialization were recent realities and their consequences were becoming clearer with every blast of the factory whistle. Woman, who on the farm traditionally constituted half the economic structure of the family, was already discovering the potential of the machine to reduce her to a cipher, a condition that, ironically, only war would serve to improve and then only temporarily, until men returned to their peacetime jobs. The old reciprocity was becoming unbalanced, and it was a time of flux, a time for exploring and charting new paths for women before social and economic rigor mortis set in once more.

The women's colleges assigned to themselves the task of intellectual emancipation, unaware, perhaps, that it was not to be accomplished in a vacuum, and, as Radcliffe's Mary Bunting said much later about the education of women in general: "We were willing to open the doors but we did not think it important that they enter the promised land."[55] Leaving the social and economic emancipation to other segments of the society, which in effect left it undone, the women's colleges misinterpreted the reality of sex, and failed even to consider that woman might have some calling in addition to that of wife and mother. On the defensive necessarily at first, they never ventured beyond their original mandate even when the need for proving themselves had passed, but were content to consign their bright young women to secondary roles as the wives of the true leaders.

No one can assess with any degree of accuracy the full consequences of this century of institutional conservatism. It is possible that they increase not arithmetically but geometrically.

The obvious consequence is, of course, the very practical one: the non-utilization of the capacities of the nation's intellectually well endowed and the loss to society—which can ill afford the loss —of potential Newtons and Magellans and Pasteurs and Kants and Frankfurters and Da Vincis and Shakespeares. Or as a member of the Smith class of 1937 complained at her thirty-fifth reunion in 1972: "It was an extremely bright group that didn't make the contribution it was capable of. There should have been more executives, more people in politics and local government."[56] One of the great might-have-beens of history is, of course, what paths the affairs of this not altogether successful planet might have taken, had the second sex had greater input.

An equally obvious and serious consequence may be that the perpetuation of woman's unproductiveness has doomed men to a life of multiplied productiveness, and while the arrangement undoubtedly kept the machismo intact and both sexes bought it with varying degrees of eagerness, such a fate must in fact be as oppressive a one to face every morning while shaving as any a woman has had to face.

Another consequence may be less obvious but not less real. One finds among women at poolsides, in bridge clubs, in small-town hospital auxiliaries, in city citizens' groups, and at the lower echelons of business and government where women have settled,* a certain unsolicited and unspoken but detectable deference to one's Bryn Mawr or Smith or Mount Holyoke background, so that the products of these institutions traditionally have found themselves in the anomalous position of role models to other women.

All of which has meant, over the past century, that the women to be imitated, the holders of the expensive, intellectually demanding, and superior academic credentials, have been largely the sturdy underpinning of the status quo. When teaching is in fashion, they are in graduate school. When the contemporary women's movement drew a bead on business as the next professional domino to fall, they began going into business. Defined by others, they accepted themselves as the second sex, illustrating the truth of everything Erik Erikson and Irving Berlin and Henry James and James Thurber and John Huston and Chic Young and Charles William Eliot said.

So that in one sense, by ignoring the reality of sex, the Sisters only emphasized it, making the social statements of it self-fulfilling, supplying the traditional answers to Henry Higgins' persistent question, and possibly serving actually to retard women's social and economic emancipation. A century after their establishment, sex discrimination remained a reality.

* In the higher echelons of government and business, no one remembers the undergraduate background of personnel except the college public relations officers, and, later, the obituary writers.

6

"Passive acceptance of society's ills by its leaders dooms society."

—RICHARD P. BAILEY, former president
of Hamline University, in
The New York Times, July 1975

HARVARD COLLEGE, the nation's first, was founded in 1636 to assure New England Puritans of a continuing supply of professional clergymen. Although religion and scholarship soon proved to be less than amiable bedfellows (Henry Dunster, first president of the nation's first university, was fired for heresy because he refused to have his son baptized on the grounds that infant baptism was scripturally unsound), the annals of early American education are rife with tales of academic sectarianism, and the atmosphere of American higher education in general was heavily leavened with a sense of Protestant Christianity well into the latter half of the nineteenth century when the Seven Sisters were established. Indeed, a widespread criticism of Cornell, when it opened in 1868 without sectarian ties was its departure from that tradition.

The Sisters, committed only to intellectual adventure and to no other kind, were not about to become spiritual radicals. If there was a prominent feature about them at their founding, it was the commonality of Protestant Christian background and official patronage of the Protestant Christian ethic.

This Christian identification was to prove double-edged, however. Although predicated on social responsibility, orthodox Christianity as an institution has rarely at the same time addressed itself to substantive social change. The focus has been largely on benevolence, charity, noblesse oblige and less on improving either one's own or one's neighbor's earthly status. Indeed, poverty has been held out as a positive virtue, endurance and piety are almost synonymous, and one's earthly condition is ultimately insignificant.

The corollary is, of course, that Christianity has also rarely been a friend to women's struggle for equality, which holds at least the potential for raising questions about the image of God as Father. With exceptions, such as the unknown writer who portrayed Deborah as a liberated woman—part Valkyrie, part Learned Hand—Old Testament authors beginning with "J" who recorded for all time the shaping of Eve from Adam's rib and God's subsequent curse on her, generally reflected the prevailing societal winds by treating women as a legal, economic, and social nonentity at best, more usually as a source of sin and corruption. The cult of the Virgin notwithstanding—which had overtones of chivalry—the direction continued unchallenged and unalterable; subsequent religious leaders, from Paul (especially Paul), Thomas Aquinas, the medieval popes, Martin Luther,* John Wesley, and Cotton Mather, right down into the late twentieth century and the leadership of the Protestant Episcopal Church, which refused priesthood to women in 1974, sanctioned, not to say institutionalized, women's inequality. As H. L. Mencken once put it, Christianity both "libeled women and flattered them, but with the weight always on the side of libel."** Where society led, theology must follow.

So, in the latter half of the nineteenth century, must education. So that while one part of the institutions, steeped in this strong Christian background, argued for a firm sense of social conscience, armed with which the women's-college alumnae marched out to assume responsibility for the world's good works, another part

---

* If anyone in the sixteenth century indulged the hope or thought that the new faith would have beneficial effects on the status of women, he or she had only to read Luther's prior writings. His attitude is summed up in the following: "Men have broad and hairy chests, and small narrow hips, and more understanding than the women, who have but small and narrow breasts, and broad hips, to the end they should remain at home, sit still, keep house, and bear and bring up children."[1]

** Mencken, H. L. *In Defense of Women*. New York, 1918, p. 174.

argued for the status quo* and in fact these institutions may have contributed to the retardation of meaningful social change, a retardation that held serious consequences not only for the social, political, economic, and professional positions of these very alumnae, but for the very society to which they intended to contribute.

To some degree, this religious dimension of the women's colleges was intrinsic to the *in loco parentis* concept which held spiritual nourishment as essential to the growth of young ladies as intellectual, physical, and social nourishment, and which demanded that these *nouveau riche* institutions recognize and establish responsibilities in that important area of feminine personal development. Also, however, it was the genuine religious enthusiasm of the founders, whose deep commitment to Christian morality had dictated the disposal of their wealth to worthy causes.

The diaries of Emily Dickinson, a student at Mount Holyoke Female Seminary in 1848, described Mary Lyon (whose lack of material wealth was abundantly compensated for in energy, determination, and commitment to women's education) as not only teacher and administrator, but also as a saintly if stern shepherdess of souls, concluding, however: "There seems to be much awakening, but not *deep* feeling except in a few cases."[2]

A devout Baptist, Matthew Vassar's great wealth from his breweries** vaguely troubled him, and he had traveled much in search

---

* God-fearing Mary Lyon herself rebuked student Lucy Stone for placing copies of William Lloyd Garrison's anti-slavery magazine *Liberator* in the Mount Holyoke Female Seminary reading room. "You must remember," Miss Lyon admonished Miss Stone, "that the slavery question is a very grave question, and one upon which the best people are divided." (Blackwell, Alice Stone. *Lucy Stone*. Boston, 1930, republished by Grand River Books, Detroit, 1971, p. 40.)

** It was the wealth, not the source of the wealth, that troubled him. He was only too willing to give credit where credit was due, and when asked the secret of his success, he was known to reply, "John Barleycorn, my Joe John."[3] His frankness was not appreciated by the institution he founded, however, and when President Henry Noble MacCracken, in admiration of the founder, had a thousand postcard views of Vassar's Poughkeepsie brewery made for visitors to the college's fiftieth anniversary celebration, a trustee confiscated the lot. Students were not embarrassed, but sang his praises:

> Then here's Matthew Vassar
> Our Love shall never fail,

of some social wrong he might right. An asylum? A school for the poor? A hospital? When he decided upon a college for women, it was not unnatural that he should decide at the same time, as he instructed the first board of trustees four years before the institution opened: While "all sectarian influences should be carefully excluded," the education of his Vassar girls "should never be intrusted to the skeptical, the irreligious, or the immoral."[5]

Dr. Joseph Wright Taylor, whose wealth financed the establishment of Bryn Mawr, is described as a man of quiet charm and infinite humanity whose Quaker conscience drove him to offer education and opportunity to women.

Some found Henry Durant's Christianity oppressive; it drove Katharine Lee Bates (Wellesley, '80, professor of English, 1885–1925, author, "America the Beautiful") "out of church and theology for all time."[6] A prosperous Boston lawyer who abandoned his practice when he could not square the law and the Gospels, Durant transferred his expertise and his considerable zeal into publicly arguing the case for Christ. The ostentation of this move offended Boston's innate sense of good taste and later made Durant's little college at Wellesley an object of local suspicion. Elected a trustee of Mount Holyoke Female Seminary in 1867, Durant had been much impressed by the need for more of the same; he established Wellesley "for the glory of God and the service of the Lord Jesus Christ, in and by the education and culture of women,"[7] presenting every workman on the campus with a Bible on the occasion of the laying of the first foundation stone of College Hall, August 13, 1871.

The religious convictions of the founders were, of course, expressed clearly in the institutions. The Sabbath was strictly observed as a day of religious devotion and total abstinence from pleasures, even from academic concerns. A visiting Amherst student in 1847 complained that at Mount Holyoke Female Seminary, "all but the strictly religious periodicals are carefully put away from Saturday until Monday."[8]

> For well we know that all we owe
> to Matthew Vassar's ale.

—until "fail" and "ale" were censored and changed to "fade" and "aid"[4] by embarrassed authority.

The first Vassar catalogue, 1865–66, described compulsory daily morning and evening prayers, Sunday morning Bible study, Sunday afternoon religious services, and periodical "social meetings for prayer and religious conversation."[9]

"Believing that all education should be for the glory of God, and the good of man," hymn-singing, Bible-reading Sophia Smith dictated in the will that established Smith College, "I direct the Holy Scriptures be daily and systematically read and studied in said College, and without giving preference to any sect or denomination, all the education and all the discipline shall be pervaded by the Spirit of Evangelical Christian religion."[10] Her wishes were carried out without question: Before classes could begin in the earliest years at Smith, students had to attend each morning a short devotional service, "designed," said President Seelye, "especially to nourish and strengthen those spiritual faculties on whose soundness right conduct depends," and ranking "equally in importance with other academic requirements."[11]

At Wellesley, students were required to observe a twenty-minute "silent period" for prayer and meditation twice daily, and a Wellesley tradition has it that the observance was so habit-forming that girls on trains would stop all conversation at the appointed hour. Eleven of the first seventeen members of Wellesley's board of trustees were clergymen, every instructor was required to be able to teach Bible classes as well as the academic disciplines, and Henry Durant was fond of boasting that the first applicant to Wellesley College was the daughter of a missionary.

Bryn Mawr demanded scholarship of its faculty; it also demanded compatibility with its Quaker tone. Woodrow Wilson, a Presbyterian, reported being " 'Thee'd' at a great rate" over lunch with President James Rhoads who was interviewing, in 1884, the future president of the United States for an associate professorship in history. "The Doctor's object was, not so much to discover what I knew as to get a key to my character and an insight into my views on certain points which he considered vital," Wilson reported to his financée. "He was glad to find that I believed that the hand of Providence was in all history; that the progress of Christianity was as great a factor as the development of philosophy and the sciences; and that wars were to be justified only by necessity; and he was careful to ascertain my views as to my personal religion."[12] (Wilson was hired, although he was still two years short of his Ph.D.)

The "silent periods" for prayer are no longer observed at Wellesley, and the Vassar catalogue has toned down its religious thrust considerably, describing religion at Vassar simply as "formal study through courses in the Department of Religion, and through worship and extracurricular activities in association with the Chaplains," of whom there are four: one attached to the college administration and three (Episcopalian, Roman Catholic, and Jewish) independently supported. Key members of the elaborate institutional counseling package, the chaplains today are as much psychologist as preacher, and clerical collars have been superseded by turtleneck sweaters just as Matthew Vassar's old-fashioned evangelism has been superseded by a more personal, individualistic religious style, sometimes with overtones of eastern cults. Few people at Vassar even remember the days of compulsory chapel (voted out by the trustees in 1926), and about the only vestige of religious formality is the more or less non-denominational—though Protestant—Sunday services at which attendance is voluntary and the congregation may or may not outnumber the choir.

When the Smith trustees were looking for a successor to President Marion Leroy Burton, one aspect of the job that troubled Harvard English professor William Allan Neilson, whose religious beliefs were not wholly the prescribed ones, was the fact that the two previous incumbents had been Congregational clergymen. Neilson finally accepted the job* although he refused to conduct formal religious services, but nurtured the spiritual life of the college by larding his chapel talks with religious and moral themes. The college has not had a clergyman in the president's office since.

---

* Neilson, whose friend and employer, Charles W. Eliot, had advised him that his position and prospects at Harvard "promised greater serviceableness for American education and scholarship than the presidency of Smith,"[13] accepted because, having taught for fifteen years at Radcliffe, he was "much interested in the education of women, and believe it to be a matter whose importance is going to increase in the immediate future, and I am confident that I should be keenly interested in the problems involved."[14]

Bryn Mawr's Dr. Rhoads would probably choke on some of the names on the faculty roster today; he would certainly choke on the diversity of religious belief—or lack of it.

The outward and visible signs have disappeared; the inward and spiritual grace remains. The deep tone of institutional morality, established by the founders and embedded in the bricks, has been retained, even nurtured. Like racial memory, it has driven Vassar girls to the barricades for the New York Socialists, to walk picket lines with the Amalgamated Clothing Workers of America, to succor German refugee victims of the Nazis and Hungarian refugee victims of the Communists, as well as William Sloane Coffin. The Vassar Relief Unit followed the infantry to France in 1918 to set up a milk station and clinic at Verdun; a quarter century later, they joined the WAVES, WACS, WAFS, Spars and Women Marines, and created a campus flying club so they could qualify for the WASPS. They set up a local branch of the Consumers League and created a settlement house in downtown Poughkeepsie. In 1935, they marched on Albany to protest passage of a bill requiring oaths of allegiance from college students, and a quarter century later they picketed the local chain stores to protest lunch-counter segregation in their southern branches. To the critics of such unladylike activity, Vassar's Henry Noble Mac-Cracken answered sharply in 1935: "Every college with well-organized departments of economics, political science, and history must expect its students to take a real interest and even to participate in the political movements of their day, just as every college that teaches music must expect to have a glee club that amounts to something in the way of serious music."[15] Combined with a sense of elitism and carried to extremes, this social conscience is capable of creating a Diana Oughton (Bryn Mawr '65), toiler in a Weatherman bomb factory.

However, this institutional sense of responsibility for the less fortunate—a largely noblesse oblige approach—took on other shades of meaning. In keeping with the fundamentally conservative Protestant ethic, it was restated to capitalize on the acceptability of woman as philanthropist, a role made respectable by St. Peter himself when he is said to have raised Dorcas, a woman of Joppa, "full of good works and alms deeds," from the dead. It coincided neatly with woman's natural tendencies* and with the chivalric ideal, which partially compensated for depriving women of political and legal equality by relegating to them the world's "good works" and thereby endowing them with, and cultivating in them, a sense of self-validation that sometimes spilled over into moral superiority. They would make great cosmic mothers of us all.

2

Traditionally, the pride of the women's colleges, their finest product, has been the volunteer whose selfless devotion to lessening the suffering of those less fortunate has been hailed by all, from Alice Freeman—under whose guidance the socially conscious Christian Association was established on the Wellesley campus—to Barbara Newell—Wellesley's tenth president—as the practical statement of the Christian ethic, the outward and visible sign of the inward and spiritual grace; as significant social pioneering typically American in flavor; and as creative leadership of the sex. "We have all," said Mrs. Newell on her inauguration as president of Wellesley in October 1972, "gained from their training and dedication."**[17]

The Sisters' infant years, the late nineteenth and twentieth centuries when the first crops were being graduated, provided fertile soil for indulging social conscience. There was a certain social

* In Vida Scudder's 1903 novel, *A Listener in Babel*, an assistant professor of mathematics at an unnamed women's college (Miss Scudder graduated from Smith, taught for many years at Wellesley) tells the heroine who has just turned down a teaching appointment to take a job in a settlement house: "You are misled by your instincts of a woman; any woman feels restless unless she is taking care of somebody. You have no one near you who needs taking care of, so you want to take care of the poor."[16]

** Although patently widespread, volunteer activity is difficult to quantify and assess. Alumnae replies to the Bryn Mawr questionnaire that resulted in *A College In Dispersion* indicated that of 2,914 Bryn Mawr A.B. degree holders who did not go on to higher degrees, 1,684, or 57.8 percent, had held volunteer jobs, the highest percentages (75.3 percent) from classes 1951–55, the lowest (15.7 percent) from the most recent classes polled, 1966–70.[18] Of the Bryn Mawr A.B. holders with higher degrees from other institutions, 46 percent reported that they had held volunteer jobs.

optimism, born of the new technology, in the already heavily sooted air, a widespread belief in social progress as an evolutionary force, in the perfectibility of life on earth, and at the same time Lincoln Steffens, Jacob Riis, Florence Kelley, Louis Brandeis, and Jane Addams were showing us where the imperfections lay—and there were plenty!

It was a situation well suited to the women's colleges, whose energetic, idealistic, and academically well-trained graduates were beginning to require an alternative to teaching. Seniors were looking beyond the college gates at the bleakness of the serious career opportunities offered them and asking, rhetorically: "What can I do?" "Where can I be useful after leaving college?"

Cornell had established a course in social work in 1885; its usefulness as an outlet for all that youthful feminine restlessness was not lost on the women's institutions. Three years later, Bryn Mawr was offering a course in "Charities and Corrections" which was shortly adopted by Vassar.[19] In 1915, Virginia Gildersleeve of Barnard announced with pride in the *Columbia Quarterly* the creation of a Volunteer Service Department within the Intercollegiate Bureau of Occupations (an early cooperative collegiate enterprise established to aid women job-hunters in New York City). Its purposes, Dean Gildersleeve explained, were to find volunteers for jobs and vice versa, and to begin the process of breaking down "the artificial distinction between women who must 'earn their living' and women who need not . . . The fact that her father or her brother or her husband will provide her living expenses should not and generally does not absolve her from this desire and duty to be of use in the world."[20] By 1929, Wellesley had refined the concept of volunteer social work in a course called "Group Leadership," an early interdepartmental course incorporating social sciences, psychology, and education; its purposes, which were frankly avocational ("to help women to use leisure fruitfully by preparing them to be leaders in group thinking"), were not only to develop "sensitivity to contemporary social problems," but also to show the student how "this social-mindedness may be put into action."[21]

Welfare and social security replaced the old concepts of charity, and the serious study of the sociology of law and poverty and population problems and urbanization replaced "Charities and

Corrections" and "Leadership in Organized Groups." At Bryn
Mawr, Carey Thomas, who was for her time perceptive of
women's requirements and imaginative in filling them, founded
the Bryn Mawr School for Social Work to professionalize the
institutional conscience and offer social-service-minded women
some future independence. Miss Thomas also established the Bryn
Mawr Summer School for Workers in Industry, a modest attempt
to expose to the liberal arts and upgrade the opportunities for
women factory workers that was imitated in some of the other
women's colleges. But the institutional encouragement of voluntarism persisted, and today at Smith, for example, one of the largest
extracurricular groups on campus is the Service Organization of
Smith (SOS), created in 1968 out of the merger of several traditional campus groups. It includes representatives from each dormitory, involves about one quarter of the student body, and boasts
of contributing some 20,000 volunters hours a year in and around
the immediate Connecticut Valley community. SOS posters are
prominently displayed on college bulletin boards; the organization
owned, as of 1974, five automotive vehicles, and its campus-wide
fund-raising events are supported enthusiastically not only by
students but also by administration and faculty who not only
attend but often participate. A fund-raising campaign may collect
as much as $7,000. (In contrast, the Smith swimming team travels
in the coach's car, and in one recent year the entire budget for
intercollegiate sports was $4,300, a parsimoniousness usually re-
ferred to as keeping athletics in perspective.)

The volunteer, traditionally, has had the best of all worlds.
Unlike her sisters on the payroll, she may set her own hours,
adapting them to family responsibilities. However menial her
assignment, it has built-in social approval. A woman with organizational talent may find a challenging outlet. And her own sense of
worth, her usefulness, is heightened by her selflessness, so that
the sex that couldn't make it at Chase Manhattan *could* make it—
big—at the local mental health unit and, like the powerful abbesses
of medieval Europe who suffered political and legal discrimination
along with the rest of their ilk, but who managed enterprises second
in size and complexity only to those of kings and popes, these
women were able to realize the only kinds of independence and
personal fulfillment available outside home and family.

Seven Sisters alumnae, from twenty-five to sixty-five, have volunteered for every conceivable community chore: Consumers League, Junior League, Red Cross, historical societies, art galleries, museums, garden clubs, PTAs, soup kitchens, settlement houses, hospital auxiliaries, mental health units, blood banks, Girl Scout troops. They trudged baskets of food to the poor, nursed the sick and, guardians of the community culture, collected funds for the local symphony. Today they are involved in conservation, voter registration, rape prevention, environmental issues, child adoption, campaigns against alcoholism and drug abuse, and the Equal Rights Amendment.* The Seven Sisters alumnae, trained for leadership, led in keeping the sense of elitism alive along with their social conscience: They not only worked in the garden clubs and the Junior League and the hospital auxiliaries, they organized them and presided over them. "College gave me a social conscience," they are apt to say, sometimes adding with weariness, "It never lets me rest." And a mid-1950s survey of *Who's Who in America* revealed that in the field of voluntarism, the achievements of alumnae of the Sisters plus Goucher (all of whom had not only the social conscience but the leisure and training to achieve) were recognized out of all proportion to expectations on the basis of enrollment numbers.**

These women often bridged the gap between society's and officialdom's recognition of a social problem and since they were articulate, highly skilled women who could define an objective and marshal the arguments for it convincingly, they tended to professionalize wherever they went, so that visiting the sick ultimately became occupational therapy and helping Miss Marian put the books back on the River City library shelves on Saturday afternoon became a legitimate academic discipline. In their inveterate voluntarism, women's college alumnae gave education, as Jane Addams had predicted they would at the Bryn Mawr commencement in 1912, a "civic significance."[23]

* The National Endowment for the Arts, in its 1975 publication *Museums USA*, reported that more than half the museum workers in the United States—57 percent—were unpaid volunteers.

** Bryn Mawr, Barnard, and Vassar, in that order, contributed from twenty-three to seventeen times the expected quota. Radcliffe, Smith, Wellesley, Goucher, and Mount Holyoke, in that order, contributed from ten to five times the expected quota.[22]

And so the cliché is that society is the richer.

But is it?

The possibility that the volunteer keeps a man or woman who must work for a living out of a job and the possibility that voluntarism is reinforcement of the sex stereotypes, while important, miss the main point.

Charity, like power, holds a large potential for corruption. "We need," declared Theodore Parker in 1853, "the justice which removes causes," not the palliative. "If," he continued, "the feminine swallow drives away the flies from a poor fox struggling for life, another set of flies light upon him, and suck every remaining drop of blood out of his veins, as in the old fable. Besides, if the fox finds that a womanly swallow comes to drive off the flies, he depends on her wing, and not on his own brush, and becomes less of a fox."[24]

Suppose, for example, that instead of freeloading on volunteers, society paid for its mental health services, or its symphonies, or its anti-alcoholism campaigns, just as it pays for its post offices. The political system, while subject to frequent and prolonged fits of lethargy, has when pressed demonstrated itself capable of slow but positive response to social need.

Suppose, as a corollary to the above, the Wellesley economics major of, say, the 1950s, instead of spending her considerable youthful energies and expensively acquired skills as a volunteer had been encouraged to go on and get her MBA and in time, did make it big at Chase Manhattan where, armed with what Frances Perkins called her natural "strong social and humanitarian viewpoint,"[25] she was put in charge of, say, overseas investments.

Or suppose she had gone to medical school, and this powerful institutional social conscience had led her into cancer research or a ghetto medical practice.

Or she had gone to law school, and the same strong conscience had led her into government service or politics.

Or she had gone into any one of a thousand fields for which her highly challenging education, with its deep implications of social responsibility, had equipped her to contribute meaningfully.

In which case is society the richer, in which case the opportunities greater for achieving "the justice which removes causes?"

Can we really afford the volunteer? Is the financial saving inherent in voluntarism an illusion; worse, a *delusion*?

The institutional response to the historical imperative of social responsibility and consciousness has been an unsurprising social conservatism which was geared, as were the religious faith from which it came and the clientele that it served, to the maintaining of the status quo.

As Barbara Honeyman Heath, Smith '32, anthropologist, writer, and teacher put it:

I spent fifteen years in Portland at the superficial social level, earnestly wanting to give something to community, and always feeling in the end, no matter what the enterprise was, that I really wasn't solving anything. The problem is we have to do something about the kind of culture that the United States has, and you cannot do that from a topical application of good will, which is really what women's organizations do dispense. I have a feeling that organization women are pretty frustrated, too. They spend an awful lot of time outside of their household duties trying to be good citizens. I see an enormous difference between organization women and women like Dr. Frances Ilg of the Gesell Institute, and Margaret Mead, who are just as much women in every sense, are just as devoted to their families, and probably do a better job of bringing up their children than women who have been persuaded that their place is "in the home."[26]

3

On April 6, 1975, American academe bought a full-page advertisement in *The New York Times* for the purpose of calling the attention of officialdom and of the general public to the need for affirmative action within its ivy-covered walls. The brief message said:

To the Honorable Gerald R. Ford, Jr.

Academic institutions, like other employers, have participated in the unfair treatment of women and minority persons in their employment practices. We urge that the affirmative action provisions of Executive Order 11246 [which prohibits discrimination in employment on the basis of race, color, religion, national origin or sex in all institutions with federal contracts of over $50,000] be implemented in order to remedy such injustices. As the Higher Education guidelines to the order make clear, affirmative action does not require hiring unqualified persons or imposing a quota system. Academic employers are required, however, to make good faith efforts to achieve numerical hiring goals based on the availability of qualified women and minority persons. Without this requirement there is no way to reduce seriously the discriminatory employment practices of universities or other institutions in the United States.

The advertisement had 114 sponsors, including 6 Nobel Laureates; only 2 sponsors were from Seven Sisters institutions: Alberta Arthurs of the Radcliffe administration, and Catharine R. Stimpson of the Barnard English department.

The list of signers consumed the major part of the page—so many of them that their names had been set in the smallest available type. Of the Seven Sisters institutions, only Radcliffe signed as an institution. Eighteen, or 13.1 percent, of the Barnard faculty signed (Martha Peterson, president at that time, since resigned, did not). Three, or 1.6 percent, of the Bryn Mawr faculty signed (Harris L. Wofford, the president, did not). Eighteen, or 8.5 percent, of the Mount Holyoke faculty signed (David B. Truman, the president, did not). Thirty, or 10.3 percent, of the Smith faculty signed (Thomas C. Mendenhall, the president, did not). Eleven, or 4.3 percent, of the Vassar faculty signed (Alan Simpson, the president, did not). Eight, or 4.0 percent, of the Wellesley faculty signed (Barbara W. Newell, the president, signed.*) Yale,

* Mrs. Newell, Vassar '51, traces her initial interest in feminism to undergraduate days when, "bored periodically" with the reading she had been assigned, she spent many hours in a little room off the main reading room of the Vassar library browsing through accounts of earlier women's movements and Seven Sisters beginnings. Latent for a period, her interest revived when she found herself "observing, with the rest of the country, to me, the most crucial human rights movement we've had in close to a hundred years . . . and yet the Seven Sisters were absolutely quiet. And here was a major social movement and institutions which had been vital and alive and have had a resource base that few other institutions have, and they were doing nothing with it. I just couldn't see any excuse for a Vassar of the world not speaking on an issue like this one. And so . . . when the Wellesley search committee said 'won't you come in and talk to us,' I made the decision that I would come to Wellesley and tell them what their obligations were . . . that I really felt that a Wellesley ought to step up to the questions that were being raised in the sixties and seventies. And the thing that surprised me, delighted me, and finally persuaded me to come east [from the University of Pittsburgh where she was associate provost for graduate studies and research] was that the board of trustees were saying the same thing."[27]

with ninety-three signers, or 14.8 percent of the faculty, was ahead of them all.[28]

Such a roll call is not surprising. If the nineteenth and twentieth centuries have any claim to historical distinction, it will be for the two significant human rights movements that emerged then as much as for any other: one, the movement for women's rights, which made its first official public appearance at a women's rights convention in 1848 in Seneca Falls, New York, the long-term effects of which may in fact one day make "man" a generic term; and two, the movement for Negro rights, out of which grew the women's movement of both the nineteenth and twentieth centuries, with its obvious analogies and its training ground for social and political leadership. The Sisters were in the vanguard of neither.

First, the feminist movement.

The Seven Sisters are not and never have been truly feminist institutions, feminism, given the general tenor of society, being a prerequisite to securing woman's proper place in society. Mary Lyon herself set the institutional tone. Confrontation politics was not for her; she had established what amounted to a college, but called it, as ladylike custom demanded, a Female Seminary, explaining that "It is desirable the plans relating to the subject should not seem to originate with *us*, but with benevolent *gentlemen*. If the object should excite attention, there is danger that many good men will fear the effect on society of so much female influence and what they will call female greatness."[29]

By the 1890s, women in fourteen states had won at least some limited voting rights. Elizabeth Cady Stanton, Lucy Stone, and Susan B. Anthony, and others of the National Woman Suffrage Association were taking the case for a constitutional amendment to the House of Representatives. But women's education was still on trial and not about to get mixed up in such dubious causes as suffrage. In 1895, students at Mary Lyon's institution, which finally had been chartered as a college in 1888, took a straw vote and rejected suffrage; some years later Wellesley students followed suit. Some female Smith faculty actually belonged to the Massachusetts Association Opposed to the Extension of Suffrage to Women.

Shortly before Vassar opened, Matthew Vassar's dreams of

glory had led him to couple his name with greatness: "The Founder of Vassar College and President Lincoln—Two Noble Emancipators—one of the Women—the Negro—"[30] he had doodled. In June 1908, James Monroe Taylor, Vassar's fourth president (1886–1914), strictly forbade Vassar students to hold suffrage meetings on campus, and suffragette Inez Milholland, Vassar '09, who was later to ride a white horse down Fifth Avenue to publicize the cause, had to organize her supporters (forty undergraduates, ten alumnae, and two male visitors) in a nearby graveyard.* Vassar legend has it that Miss Milholland retaliated by writing two complete papers for her final ethics examination: "The World As Prexy Thinks It Is," and "The World As It Is," to which the president responded by giving her an "A".[31]

Congressional hearings to consider passage of an Equal Rights amendment to the Constitution in 1929, 1931, 1933, 1945, and 1956 drew testimony from women's professional and political organizations, from unions, religious associations, government personnel, and educational associations. From the Seven Sisters, only Bryn Mawr's Carey Thomas showed interest, sending a letter of support when she was unable to appear.

In 1970, as the contemporary women's movement was getting down to serious business, and women's education was no longer standing trial, the United States Congress again was considering passage of a Constitutional amendment "to provide equal rights for men and women." The women's colleges were conspicuous by their absence. While congressmen, union representatives, bar associations, feminist leaders, the Business and Professional Women, ZONTA, and even John Mack Carter for the *Ladies Home Journal* trekked to Washington to testify before the appropriate judiciary committees considering ERA, no one from Barnard, Bryn Mawr, Mount Holyoke, Radcliffe, Smith, Vassar, or Wellesley appeared, and in 1975, a congressional aide grumbled that the

---

* Four years later, in 1912, President Taylor allowed a mass suffrage meeting on the Vassar campus, and in 1914 the faculty and a board of trustees committee that was operating the college between presidents, gave students permission to form a Woman's Suffrage Club. However, as late as 1917, her head of hall reprimanded a young Vassar instructor for taking a group of students to a suffrage rally on the eve of New York's ratification of the Nineteenth Amendment.

only interest the women's colleges had in ERA was not its effect, for good or ill, on women or men or the larger society, but upon the legality of their single-sex status, a status Smith, Mount Holyoke, and Wellesley together hired a legal firm to explore.

Whether through lack of interest or encouragement (to testify before a congressional committee, one need only offer assurances of one's expertise on relevant matters and of one's sanity) the Sisters have not in fact been prominent in pursuing women's interests politically or, equally important, in offering their considerable expertise in the education of women to those who might use it legislatively.

Some for-instances: In the spring of 1962, Congressman Herbert Zelenko's Select Subcommittee on Labor held hearings on bills to prohibit discrimination in the payment of wages on the basis of sex, bringing to town witnesses from the AAUW, the United Nations Commission on the Status of Women, the National Women's Party, unions, the National Council of Churches, the International Association of Policewomen, and the Country Music Association, but not from any of the Seven Sisters.* In 1969, Congressman John H. Dent's General Subcommittee on Labor held hearings on bills to further equal employment opportunities for workers, bringing to town witnesses from WEAL and NOW, but not from the Seven Sisters. (Senate hearings on related bills drew similar representation.)

In June 1970, Congresswoman Edith Green's special Subcommittee on Education held hearings on "Discrimination Against Women" particularly in "administrative, professional, and executive employment." Victoria Schuck, professor of political science at Mount Holyoke and the only witness from (although not a representative of) one of the Sisters, discussed discrimination against women in political science. In 1973, appropriate committees in both Senate and House held hearings on a proposed Woman's Educational Equity Act designed to improve vocational, physical education, and community education programs for women, draw-

---

* An informal study of witnesses before congressional committees over the past decade indicates that whenever such items as equality of opportunity or nondiscrimination in payment of wages are discussed, academe in general is sparsely represented; when federal assistance to higher education is discussed, academe in general is well represented.

ing women from WEAL, NOW, NEA, the National Women's Political Caucus, Georgetown University, the University of Minnesota, as well as Billie Jean King. But no one from any of the Sisters appeared. The same year Congresswoman Martha W. Griffiths presided over a joint Economic Committee looking into the "Economic Problems of Women"; Carolyn Shaw Bell, Katharine Coman professor of economics at Wellesley, testified on the inequities of social security as an independent economist but not as a representative of Wellesley College. In 1974, a House special subcommittee on education investigated the "Civil Rights Obligations" of higher education institutions. How these obligations were ultimately defined was to have a bearing on eligibility for various federal programs. Faculty and/or administration testified from a number of colleges and universities, from the major minority and women's groups, from Congress and HEW, but not from any of the Seven Sisters. There are others, but these are the major relevant hearings conducted in Washington over the past decade.

In December 1961, President Kennedy established his Commission on the Status of Women with 26 members including Mary I. Bunting, then president of Radcliffe and the only member at that level from a Seven Sisters institution. Mrs. Bunting was chairman of the committee on education; none of its other members came from Seven Sisters institutions. Of the 74 members of the other six committees, none came from a Seven Sisters institution. In addition to these committees, the commission included 4 consultants, a total of 142 women; one, Mrs. Robert Bishop of the Wellesley College Career Services Offices (since retired), came from a Seven Sisters institution.

In February 1975, President Ford appointed seventeen persons to a newly created Advisory Council on Women's Educational Programs whose purpose was to "advise the Commissioner of Education with respect to general policy matters relating to the administration of women's educational equity; advise and make recommendations to the Assistant Secretary for Education concerning the improvement of educational equity for women; make recommendations to the commissioner with respect to the allocation of any funds . . . and develop criteria for the establishment of program priorities." Its members, of whom four were men, came from state education departments, women's groups, coeducational universities, educational associations, small private liberal arts institutions (Amherst, for example), and other women's colleges (Texas Woman's University, Mississippi University for Women, College of Saint Teresa, and Chatham College).[32] When asked about the omission of all Seven Sisters institutions, a spokesman for the Office of Education, where the list had been assembled, said the omission had not been noticed, that their inclusion "never occurred to us."

It is true that the Sisters have political representation through such education lobby groups as the Association of American Colleges, which included a Project on the Status of Women. It is also true that academic matters took priority in small, independent institutions. But what of their role as examples to others?

It is equally true that the concept of affirmative action has not worked over the decade or so during which it has been ordered and legislated, and in 1974 the United States Commission on Civil Rights, followed in 1975 by the General Accounting Office and the Carnegie Council on Policy Studies in Higher Education* pronounced it a failure on the part of both academe and the federal government.

And it is not as if the Sisters were incapable of acting in concert, as evidenced by their quick and unanimous reaction—a petition to Congress—[33] to passage in late 1974 of a federal law that gave students access to their confidential student files.

"Oh, this academic fatalism!" cried Vida Scudder's heroine to the faculty of an unnamed women's college in her 1903 novel, *A Listener in Babel*, "Why is it that thinking seems to congeal the circulation? Where's audacity? Where's adventure?—You think yourselves free, because you enjoy daring theories; but you are bound hand and foot with moral hesitancy. It is your type of fatalism which kept our best men for years out of politics, which has turned over the shaping of American life to the instincts of the illiterate majority."[34]

In May 1975, Princeton University, Higher Education Re-

---

* Whose twelve members included three women: Rosemary Park, professor of education, University of California, Los Angeles (former president of Barnard); Lois Rice, vice president, College Entrance Examination Board; and Pauline Tompkins, president of Cedar Crest College.

sources (HERS), and the Central New Jersey chapter of NOW, with support from the Russell Sage Foundation, sponsored an eastern region conference of "Women in Higher Education Administration" which featured workshops and panel discussion on such questions as "Responsibility for Female Administrators for Affirmative Action," "Involving Men in Women's Issues," "The 'Old Boys Network' and the 'New Women's Network'" and others led by women from Rutgers, Princeton, Chatham College, Wesleyan, SUNY, Connecticut College, the University of Maryland, and the University of Pennsylvania. In April 1976 the National Archives sponsored a conference on women's history, with speakers from various academic institutions: Oklahoma State University, University of Missouri, SUNY, Duke, University of Minnesota, University of Iowa, Coppin State College, University of Illinois, and the University of Rochester.

In August 1975, the American Association of University Women updated its roster of eighty-eight professional women's groups. Seven Sisters faculty held chairmanships of just two of the women's committees of these organizations.

With this level of visibility on women's issues among faculty and administration, it is hardly surprising that contemporary feminism has drawn apathetic responses from students. At Barnard and Radcliffe, where the presences of Columbia and Harvard may be catalytic, the apathy was less apparent. In the early 1970s, Barnard opened a Women's Center which maintained a women-oriented library, published an annual bibliography of research on women, and assembled both academic and non-academic meetings and conferences to address women's issues; Radcliffe established an Office of Women's Education in 1973 "to maintain contact with the students and to improve the quality of life of every undergraduate woman in the Harvard community."[35] But Kate Millett was appalled at the low level of enthusiasm for women's issues that she found on 1970 visits to Vassar and Smith, and the Wellesley Women's Congress, a campus organization planned to acquaint students with the concerns and activities of local and national women's organizations, folded because of lack of student interest. Bryn Mawr students today, concluded Catharine Stimpson, Bryn Mawr '58 and associate professor of English at Barnard, in _Change_ in 1974, "find the new feminism irrelevant to Bryn Mawr, irritatingly preachy, unfair to mother-hood, or excessively frank about sexuality."[36]

Interestingly, several of feminism's leaders, then and now, came out of the Seven Sisters: Lucy Stone, Mount Holyoke Female Seminary; Harriot Stanton Blatch, Vassar '78;* Gloria Steinem and Betty Friedan from Smith, Sheila Tobias from Wellesley, and Caroline Bird from Vassar. Betty Friedan attributed her dedication to the cause of women to "the influences at Smith . . . a kind of osmosis to commit your abilities to some purpose larger than yourself."[38] But a more prevalent attitude toward contemporary feminism among alumnae is that illustrated by a 1971 Mount Holyoke survey: Only 3.3 percent of those returning the questionnaire had ever participated in a women's liberation group.[39]

The women's colleges were established for a single purpose: to provide young women with academic opportunities equal to those provided for young men, and thereby to prove women the intellectual equals of men. Having completed this mission, they abandoned ship in much the same manner women in the larger society abandoned feminism for a third of a century as soon as they got the vote. The Sisters attempted to produce intellectual superwomen; everything else was irrelevant, and they deluded themselves, perhaps, into believing, more as an article of faith than a plan of action, that professional, legal, political, and social equality would be achieved—in much the same way women in the larger society fooled themselves into believing that suffrage was the panacea. There seemed to be a widespread optimism that the tangible gains—first education, then suffrage—would automatically translate themselves into the intangibles. That is one explanation for the Sisters' less than feverish enthusiasm for feminism.

Another is the one articulated by Bryn Mawr's Carey Thomas, one of the exceptions within the Seven Sisters, who frankly and

---

* In his memoirs, *A Hickory Limb,* Vassar's President MacCracken recalled lunching with Mrs. Blatch on the 50th anniversary of her graduation. "It seems strange," she told Mr. MacCracken, "to be in the President's House at Vassar. For many years I was banned by my own college. I could not speak on the campus. We were regarded as unworthy of our education, and now the cause we fought for has become the law of the land."[37]

ardently embraced the feminist cause at the same time she attempted to broaden post-graduate opportunities for Bryn Mawr
students. The real objection to women's suffrage—and she might
easily have substituted "women's movement" for "suffrage"—
is that it is "the symbol of a stupendous social revolution and we
are frightened before it."[40]

4

On June 16, 1897, in a page one story from Poughkeepsie, *The
New York Times* informed its readers that "The graduates and
students of Vassar College are much disturbed over a report that
one of the members of the senior class of '97 was of colored
parentage."

You've come a long way, Baby!

Or have you?

Officially, black is beautiful on the Vassar campus and on the
campuses of her six Sisters. A surface serenity makes it difficult
to recall that only a few years ago these institutions, like so many
others across the nation, were the scenes of an uncommon racial
conflict.

It is true that the races are sharing dormitories and classrooms
and the offices in College Hall. Although the subtler forms of
racism remain—the condescension and the patronization—overt
incidents have largely disappeared. You don't hear a Harvard
professor tell a black Radcliffe girl any more that Harvard
lowered its standards to admit her; professors are more subtle than
that now; they are more apt, as one at another of the Sisters actually did, to tell a student how well done her term paper is, then
give her a C—.

However, social revolution it's not. Far from living together
productively, the races do little more than coexist, like oil and
water in the same glass. They talk, but they have little conversation. The sharing is purely physical, the sharing of space on the
campus; there is little sharing of cultures, concerns, interests, or
goals. And there is little detectable enthusiasm on the part of
either race for meaningful relationships, only for the perpetuation
of what, in the past decade, have developed into parallel campus
institutions—one black, one white, each with its own administra-

tion, faculty, and students—a kind of "separate but equal" arrangement, a resegregation that mirrors the larger society in which black banks, black magazines, black real estate firms, have proliferated, symbols of rejection to both black and white. There was a kind of ghettoization of the campuses—which varied only in degree from institution to institution, dependent usually on the size of the black group, the critical mass—and if these new ghettos lacked the physical accoutrements of big city slums, the psychological accessories lingered.

For all their keen sense of social conscience—that same conscience that insisted Matthew Vassar find some social wrong to right, the one that sent Vassar women to the barricades for labor and academic freedom and the Socialist party and peace—the leaders in higher education for American women missed the second great social movement of their time. They blew it. Remote not only physically, but academically, historically, and institutionally from the slums of Boston and Springfield and North Philadelphia, and imprisoned by their middle-class assumptions, they lacked the vision to act imaginatively, and only *re*acted to the social upheaval in which they found themselves suddenly embroiled. It was crisis management of disruption, a strategy that had become all too familiar throughout the 1960s and throughout the nation, rather than visionary handling of a social movement for human rights, first aid where major surgery was required.

There is an attitude that even if Harvard were 70 percent female, it would still be a man's school, and the corollary is that if Mount Holyoke or Smith or Bryn Mawr or Barnard or Wellesley or Vassar were 70 percent black, it would still be a white middle-class school, with the emphasis on middle-class, that hefty segment of society for which Mary Lyon determined early in her career to labor, containing as she declared it did, "the main springs, and main wheels, which are to move the world."[41] Joseph Wright Taylor, the Quaker physician who lavished his fortune on Bryn Mawr, wrote frankly in his will that he intended the institution to serve "the advanced education of young women and girls of the higher and more refined classes of society," and there are tales of early Bryn Mawr students bringing their maids to college. A survey[42] at regular intervals, 1872 through 1939, of the occupations of the fathers of Vassar students revealed the six leading occupations to be those most commonly associated with middle class: lawyers, doctors, clergymen, businessmen, educators, and farmers. There were not many daughters of tailors or pharmacists or carpenters or clerks or construction workers or union leaders taking afternoon tea in the Victorian drawing rooms of Main, and upper classes still largely relied on finishing schools, often abroad, to educate their daughters. What was left was the middle class: economically relatively affluent, ethnically WASPish, morally and educationally conservative, and numerous girls who looked, as one of them put it much later, as if they had been "born under the clock at the Biltmore."[43]

From the beginning the alumnae of the Seven labored diligently to raise scholarship money, but not many bricklayers' daughters applied, and when they did, there was often the question of whether they could be truly happy among their economic and social betters, so that the awards tended to go to applicants only a little less fortunate financially than the paying guests, the daughters of poor missionaries, or businessmen down on their luck, underpaid college professsors or lawyers in government service with several children to educate—young ladies who already entertained middle-class ambitions. The alumni of the men's colleges have been somewhat more successful in discovering and rewarding potential academic brilliance in lower social classes; however, it must also be remembered that the bricklayer himself believed much more in the importance of education for his son than for his daughter.

The Seven have always prided themselves on the diversity of their enrollments, and each year's admission statistics carefully include the geographical distribution of the entering freshman class as if this factor had some deep social meaning. From the beginning the Seven have aspired to and have succeeded in attracting a national clientele, and more than half the 353 students who entered Vassar in 1865 came from outside New York State, 1 from as far away as Hawaii.[44] Foreign students have long been an honored tradition; however, until recently, "foreign" meant middle-class Western European, Latin American, and Hong Kong Chinese—not African. And although the girls came from Cincinnati, Los Angeles, Atlanta, even Oslo, Caracas, and New Delhi, they were still the daughters of lawyers, doctors, businessmen, and clergymen; the diversity was all horizontal, rarely vertical, the differences superficial, and the girls enjoyed a rapport they probably could not have established with many girls who came from their own hometowns, a few geographical but hundreds of cultural miles away.

Intellectually, the students have been similar: high scorers on entrance examinations—about 200 points or 25 percent ahead of the national norm on the College Entrance Examination Board SATS—and leaders in their secondary schools. Even in lean years, when numbers of applications dropped, it was still a problem for admissions officials to separate the best from the better rather than the better from the merely good.

The faculties and adminstrations, mostly Ivy League and Seven Sisters until outside events of the late 1960s forced the institutions to cast a wider net, only perpetuated the middle-class identity.

All of which has resulted in a kind of self-propelling institutional homogeneity. One didn't achieve middle-class status through quality education, one already belonged when one applied to Wellesley. And while the entire American nation, given a leg up by the waves of immigration and the new industrialism of the late nineteenth and early twentieth centuries, appeared to be engaged in some vast upward-moving social operation, the Seven Sisters—and to a lesser extent but still generally the Ivy League and others like them—continued to attract and serve the same clientele, so that today's middle class educated, subsidized, and thereby insured the continued influence of tomorrow's middle class.

And so the Seven Sisters came to the mid-twentieth century ill-equipped to deal in any mutually meaningful way with the social revolution, which came clothed in the persons of a critical mass of students who had prepped not at Dana Hall or Miss Porter's but in the public schools and in the streets of Harlem, Watts, and North Philadelphia.

It was class, not race, for which the institutions were so badly prepared. Historically reflecting its clientele, if there was any racism at all, it had been a sin of *o*mission, not of *co*mission, what Derek Bok of Harvard, borrowing a phrase from one of his former faculty members, described to the NAACP in 1974 as a policy of institutional "benign neglect."[45]

It was the Negro colleges that had the reputation for producing racial role models: Martin Luther King, Jr., and Maynard Jackson went to Morehouse, Thurgood Marshall to Lincoln University and Howard; Edward W. Brooke went to Howard, and John Hope Franklin and Constance Baker Motley went to Fisk; and Medgar Evers went to Alcorn A&M.

Nevertheless, white colleges accepted, if they did not actively recruit, academically prepared and financially able blacks before the Civil War: Amherst graduated a black student in 1826, five years after the college opened; Oberlin had a similar record; Vassar's reaction to the news of a black girl in the class of '97 notwithstanding, Smith graduated, with less fanfare, its first black student in 1900; and "qualified" blacks—carefully selected, bright, affluent—have been sprinkled ever since through the student bodies of the Seven.* In her 1947–48 presidential report Sarah Gibson Blanding of Vassar urged more blacks to apply, and in 1963, Wellesley tried to recruit black students by enrolling nine girls from southern Negro colleges for a term—a program Wellesley called "Junior Year in the North."[47] But the number of blacks was small—two or three regular students on a campus at one time.

Faculty and administrative positions were rarely denied on the basis of color alone, and if black teachers were not actively sought, at least those few blacks with doctorates, like women, were sometimes able to find jobs at Seven Sisters institutions when many other institutions of higher learning frankly discriminated on the basis of race.

Blacks, in those days, played by white rules, color was politely disregarded, and as late as 1964, the withdrawal of middle-class blacks from the black community was decried. At Columbia, for example, of the seventy active members of the Congress of Racial Equality (CORE) in early 1964, none was black; and Hilton Clark, son of psychologist Kenneth B. Clark, the chairman of a new student group calling itself the Student Afro-American Soci-

---

* At a reunion of Bryn Mawr's black alumnae in 1975, Lillian Russell, Bryn Mawr '34, recalled that when she was an undergraduate, racial restrictions in the dormitories (since abandoned) precluded her living on campus. For the first few days, she lived in the home of the president, Marion E. Park, then found a room in the home of a local black woman who worked at Bryn Mawr.[46]

ety, complained of the "apathy among educated, or so-called Ivy League Negroes to our race's outstanding struggle."[48]

Black students wore pressed hair, Pringle sweaters, pearls, and plaid skirts, and were, except for skin color which was "overlooked," indistinguishable from the other girls in the dormitories. They sang in the college choral groups, played field hockey, and wrote for the college newspapers. At Smith a black girl was elected head of Student Council for the academic year 1951–52. As a black woman, Smith '40, put it when interviewed in the 1970s: "I was never a black student at Smith. I was a student at Smith."[49]

As middle-class success-oriented as their white classmates, they competed on a par academically and, according to a study in the 1950s of Negro and white drop-out rates, blacks at integrated, high prestige institutions (Ivy League, Big Ten, Seven Sisters, Amherst, Oberlin, and Dartmouth), obtained their bachelor's degrees at a greater rate than their white counterparts.[50] They were, as we used to say down home, "a credit to their race."

Inside, they wore their middle-class values perhaps compulsively, certainly more aggressively than even their white roommates did. Margaret Mead described a group of young blacks she met at a conference in the fifties as the "Arrow-collar men. They looked much more like Arrow-collar men than the Arrow-collar ad looks like an ordinary group of white men."[51]

Black college students of the fifties, "do not wish to recall their past" in slavery, explained E. Franklin Frazier in *Black Bourgeoisie*. "As they ride to school in their automobiles, they prefer to think of the money which they will earn as professional and businessmen. For they have been taught that money will bring them justice and equality in American life and they propose to get money."[52] Which finalized their claim on middle-class status, of course.

On May 12, 1954, the nine justices of the United States Supreme Court (Justice Robert H. Jackson had left his hospital bed to sit with his brethren on this historic occasion) declared that separate but equal facilities had "no place" in American life, thereby setting in motion a broad social revolution which had been brewing for half a century and which was to challenge the validity of all America's existing racial assumptions and was to peak in 1968 in nationwide racial confrontations, one direct result of which was the presence on Seven Sisters campuses of a new Negro, one who proudly called herself "Black" and who strove in a very different fashion to be "a credit to her race."

Nearly a decade after that Supreme Court decision, the racial consciousness in higher education began to be aroused, and while observers agree that blacks continued to be underrepresented in higher education in terms of their numbers in the total United States population, their numbers increased substantially. From 1964 to 1969, the number of blacks enrolled in college increased 110 percent; between 1964 and 1968, the proportion of blacks aged eighteen to twenty-four in college increased from 8 to 15 percent.

In the fall of 1963, Ivy League and Seven Sisters institutions undertook an unprecedented joint "talent search,"[53] sending an assistant admissions director from Yale on a four-week trip through the Deep South to solicit applications from bright black students, by opening lines of communications with high school guidance counselors and offering financial aid. Undergraduates from northern colleges visited Negro high schools to publicize the availability of opportunities at their prestigious institutions. By 1965, the Cooperative Program for Educational Opportunity, as this talent search was known, was able to place forty-five girls in Seven Sisters institutions.

That same year Barnard and Mount Holyoke reported the number of Negroes applying had tripled over the past year, and the Seven, aided by the National Scholarship Service Fund for Negro Students (NSSFNS) as well as the Cooperative Program, included 152 blacks in the total of 4,687[54] girls they accepted for admission—hardly enough to make even a cosmetic change in the resident establishment, but a substantial increase over the class that had entered, say, in 1946, about which a Wellesley alumna said: "I was the only black student in my freshman class."[55]

Enough also to begin to group together, to find identity in blackness, security in organization, and to turn inward in an attempt to solve common problems, so that by 1967 a spokesman for the Harvard–Radcliffe Association of African and Afro-American Students (AAAAS) predicted "a confrontation with the university itself because we are trying to keep the black students out of the mainstream of campus since traditionally being in the mainstream has meant putting black people second."[56]

Then the tragedies of the Medgar Evers assassination, of church bombings in the South, of the murder of Reverend Martin Luther King, Jr. in 1968, combined with the heady political wine of successful freedom rides and sit-ins plus the bravado that so often overlays a desperate search for identity in youth—and plus, perhaps, a pinch of guilt because of their relatively privileged positions as students—gave that prediction a terrible reality. The normally serene colleges were turned into hostile camps, albeit characterized by a surface gentility, at least by Columbia standards, with the dean of Radcliffe hospitably offering chairs to the neatly dressed young women who sat in at Fay House in December of 1968, demanding larger black enrollments and changes in admissions policies.

Led by Barnard, with 78 blacks on campus, or 4.4 percent of its total enrollment, the Seven Sisters shared 329 blacks on their campuses, or 2.9 percent of their total 11,272 enrollment in the fall of 1968—all disenchanted with and alienated from the traditional American way of life, which was symbolized graphically by the middle-class status-conscious institutions they had entered.

Even the middle-class black girls were politicized. One who came to Barnard in 1968, expecting her Barnard B.A. four years later to open all doors, wrote: "From the first I felt uncomfortable . . . the social life—Freshman Orientation program, floor parties, mixers, luncheons, teas—was geared to the incoming white freshman, completely ignoring the different needs of the black students." It was the most invidious form of racism, she charged, the fact that "everyone was so willing to 'overlook' the fact that we were black."[57] Twenty years ago she would have smiled ingratiatingly and held out a white-gloved hand; now she was angry, a development for which deans, professors, and white students were not prepared.

There is education and then there is education. The corridors of power are no less evident in the city streets than they are in the city halls. These young blacks had learned that political power, not money, would bring them justice and equality in American life, and they proposed to get political power. Gaining a measure of security in their increasing numbers and a new self-confidence—some would say arrogance—born in the achievements of the Civil Rights movement, and an awareness of the potential in confrontation politics, these black girls, like black students in many of the nation's colleges and universities, recognized the opportunities for manipulation of the institutions.

"What this generation is reacting to, and what it is saying," James Baldwin, a kind of intellectual "Superfly," told anthropologist Margaret Mead in *A Rap on Race*, "is they realize that you, the white people, white Americans, have always attempted to murder them. Not merely by burning them or castrating them or hanging them from trees, but murdering them in the mind, in the heart." Young blacks today, Baldwin declared, reject "the entire theology."[58]

The national gesture of rejection was the sit-in. At Vassar, 35 of the school's 51 black students occupied Main for three days, and, in the spirit of Five-College cooperation, 200 black students from Smith, Mount Holyoke, Amherst, Hamsphire, and the University of Massachusetts occupied four buildings at Amherst.

Specifically, they demanded increased black enrollments achieved not necessarily through talent searches but through more flexible admissions policies; black studies for their ideological as much as for their educational value; black faculty as much for their color as their academic utility; and separate living quarters for their psychological security. What they were really demanding was power for the previously powerless, some standing in court for those whose lives only a few years before would have been defined by outside events before they were six years old. And through power, identity. Black Wellesley, as one of their number put it, would no longer be a carbon copy of white Wellesley.

Black Wellesley—or black Barnard or black Vassar or black Bryn Mawr—had not enrolled for the traditional academic advantages, or if it had, it would have been politically and socially tactless, not to say disastrous, to admit it. Black Wellesley had enrolled, black Wellesley declared, only to explore the complacent white middle-class world and to learn not to live in it but to deal with it. Black Barnard demanded not quality education but recognition as blacks and a measure of political leverage in academic decision-making; they would have soul food in the cafeteria and ghettos in the dormitories, identity first, education second.

Disturbances were always commonplace at men's institutions: Harvard annals recount with glee such occasions as the Great Butter Protest of 1766 and the Rotten Cabbage Rebellion of 1807. Until the 1960s, however, such upheavals had been aimed at redressing specific grievances and not at altering the character of the institutions. Never had such bizarre behavior been seen on the genteel women's-college campuses.

Such unaccustomed displays of defiance traumatized both educators and the larger society. Nursing a sense of guilt not untinged by fear and expediency, academe went on a binge of atonement. Implicit in it was black acceptance of the posture, gratitude for its substantial benefits and ultimate mutual embrace —the traditional middle-class noblesse oblige approach to the less fortunate, or in the case of racial condescension, the underground railroad approach.

And the Sisters, lacking a real sense of mission beyond the narrowly academic, or any heightened sense of social purpose that might have channeled the energies of these young black women —many of whom could ill-afford the luxury of an education that got them all dressed up with no place to go—responded similarly.

There were some who said the institutional behavior represented finesse and good judgment. Others said it represented precedent-setting and unacceptable capitulation to illegal behavior, beneficial in the end to no one. And there were still others who declared that while blacks were ostensibly being pampered, their deeper problems were being studiously ignored. It was not so dissimilar, in the case of the women's colleges, to the way in which the woman question had been traditionally handled.

As far as budgets allowed, black demands were met. Scholarship funds were diverted, and admissions offices were enlarged to accommodate black assistant directors. Admission standards were altered to accommodate academically and culturally disadvantaged students. Admissions officials unanimously refused to specify their standards and commonly described them as "different" rather than lower. It is fair to say, however, that suddenly sensitive to the middle-class orientation of standard entrance examinations, admissions officials began, in the case of black applicants, to rely more on high school performance and other factors which they considered relevant to the predictability of a candidate's college performance, a practice they claimed not to have had occasion to regret, although the institutions were also close-mouthed about the attrition rates of preferentially admitted students and unanimously refused to supply data. These practices, which white college applicants call "reverse discrimination" and admissions officials call "affirmative action," were unsuccessfully challenged in the United States Supreme Court during the 1973–74 term.

The rate of return on this substantial institutional investment was not extremely high. Nationwide competition for the best minority students, in response to nationwide sit-ins, was heavy, and these culturally disadvantaged applicants, whose College Entrance Examination Board scores did not always reach the 600s, were streetwise in the ways of playing institution against institution for the available financial aid—a practice that most private colleges in the northeast have since learned to deal with by collaborating on certain aspects of their admissions and financial aid programs.

Nevertheless, by the 1972–73 academic term, Radcliffe, leading the pack in percentages, had an 8 percent black enrollment (an 11.1 percent total minority enrollment which included Orientals, American Indians, and students with Spanish surnames), and announced it had more black women on campus that year than it had blacks among its 18,500 living alumnae.[59] Generally on Seven Sisters campuses, the percentage of black students rose from negligible to 5 or 7 percent. Sensitive to accusations that they once set quotas (in at least a partial confession that they once did, Wellesley now claims to be the first to have removed the question of religion from its application form in 1948) admissions officials refused to reveal how many minority students they would accept, although they made clear they had not reached a saturation point and were continuing hard-sell recruitment of minority students. After 1973, minority enrollments dipped; admissions officials blamed continuing competition for minority students, rising tuition costs, and decreasing purchasing power of the available financial aid in uncertain times; black students blamed weakened white commitment.

Recognizing the necessity for unity, they banded together in what they called Afro-American organizations—the Harvard–

Radcliffe Association of African and Afro-American Students; at Vassar the Student Afro-American Society (SAS); Ethos at Wellesley; Sisterhood at Bryn Mawr; and at Barnard, perhaps the most honest of all, the Barnard Organization of Soul Sisters (BOSS). Mutual ethnic-interest groups, from Hillel and Newman Clubs to Smith's Texas Independence Society established during the presidency of Texan Benjamin F. Wright, have always flourished on Seven Sisters campuses; none of these, however, represented a way of life as did the black organizations, and none of these ever had the institutional support—the gift of a college house for meetings and social events and even living quarters was common—that these black organizations won. They developed parallel to the long-established campus-wide student government units which were largely boycotted by black students and tight-knit as Tammany became the black wards' source of power not only in relation to the white establishment but also in relation to their own black constituencies. (It was a rare and courageous freshman who could resist its promise of security or its threat of ostracism.) From this enviable position these black groups were able to demand and usually get whatever they wanted, from soul food to separate living arrangements. Regular student government organizations, less unified, less militant, more ladylike, had labored for years for minor institutional concessions, and the relatively recent phenomenon of controlled student input to college policy was the result of a century of proving their political maturity.

One item high on the list of demands was black studies. The achievements of the most obscure Greeks and Romans, even of some Asians, were treated elaborately and with dignity, declared these militant young women, but the mention of a W. E. B. DuBois elicited only blank stares. Up to that point, there are some obvious analogies with the traditional academic approach to women's issues, problems, and achievements, but the similarity ends there. The women's-studies advocates were able to add a few courses specifically about women here and there, to incorporate what was known about women into existing courses and even, on occasion, to begin to add to the knowledge about women through academic research. Black students, highly politicized and able to exploit an institutional sense of guilt that rarely existed on women's issues, were able to construct, in some cases,* an entire curriculum, parallel to the standard curriculum, around the body of black knowledge and experience—especially experience—of, by, and for blacks. As one faculty member put it, "When you study the Civil War in black studies, you don't study what Abraham Lincoln did, you study what your grandmother did. The black person is the center of the study . . . you look at Lincoln as he impacted on black people."[60] Amid intense controversy over their scholarly versus their ideological and psychological value, black studies was grafted—sometimes overhastily—on to the traditional liberal arts curriculum. In time, the courses, even if they were not really integrated into the curriculum and were not always the most intellectually exciting courses offered in the catalogues, were made at least intellectually respectable.

An assumption that underlay the introduction of black studies to the curriculum was white insensitivity to racial nuances, a factor that dictated, of course, the hiring of black faculty to teach the black experience.

Faculty recruitment has never been easy for the small, private liberal arts colleges where salaries and research opportunities cannot compete with those of the large universities. *Black* faculty recruitment from a much smaller pool (in 1972, approximately 2,500 institutions were bidding for the services of the 1,200 blacks with doctorates or the equivalent who, in addition to being scarce, were concentrated in fields of education, far less in the physical sciences) is much more difficult, and a Smith or a Bryn Mawr is consistently and handily outbid** by a Harvard, a Michigan, or a

---

* At all except Barnard and Bryn Mawr, black studies majors were assembled; usually they were interdepartmental; at Smith and Mount Holyoke, they were intercollegiate as well, an example of Five College cooperation, with the two Sisters, Amherst College, Hampshire College, and the University of Massachusetts at Amherst sharing responsibility for a single concentration.

** Bidding, in this case is an appropriate image. Richard A. Lester, in a report prepared for the Carnegie Commission on Higher Education, said in 1974: "From 1968 on . . . a kind of special market tended to develop for black faculty. Many universities offered appointments to black faculty at salaries well above those for whites with equivalent or better qualifications. In some cases the salary offers were $3,000 or $4,000 a year higher for blacks at the assistant professor level and $5,000 to $8,000 higher at the associate

Stanford, also under pressure from students and the Department of Health, Education and Welfare to hire minority group members. Departments had long tended to hire on the "old boy" system, becoming dependent on a few sources of supply; liberal ideology had traditionally declared faculty-raiding at Negro colleges to be taking unfair advantage, and it sometimes became an excuse for procrastination.

Nevertheless, occasionally willing to overlook the absence of a Ph.D., all Seven of the Sisters managed to hire intellectually respectable black faculty, largely to teach black studies, and to hire black administrators, largely to serve in such newly created positions as special presidential assistants for "black affairs," as buffers and interpreters of this new campus community (black, usually urban and poor, often angry) which had suddenly appeared in the entrenched, older campus community (white, usually suburban or rural, and well-to-do, often baffled and angry).

By fall 1974, looser admissions policies in graduate as well as undergraduate schools had squeezed an increasing number of black scholars through the Ph.D. pipeline, and young blacks eager to teach French literature and biological sciences were showing up in faculty applicant pools. However, while these young instructors were being hired with increasing frequency to teach within their disciplines, they continued to complain that faculty deans still tended to see color first, scholarship second, and to assume a young black Ph.D. who was qualified to teach physics or constitutional law was equally qualified—and anxious—to teach black studies. (Of the Seven, the only institution required by the amount of its government contracts—in excess of $50,000 a year—to file an affirmative action plan of faculty hiring with HEW was Radcliffe—that is, Harvard; in the spring of 1975, Walter J. Leonard, special assistant to the president of Harvard and director of the university's affirmative action program, charged that Harvard, though it had filed a plan, had failed to meet its obligations to

and full professor levels. . . . Among the most extreme instances of reverse discrimination were the offer of associate professorships to blacks just completing their Ph.D.'s and the case of a black assistant professor of philosophy on full-time appointment at a yearly salary of $13,000 at Yale in 1971–72, who was discovered to have also a full-time tenure appointment at the New York State University at Stony Brook at double the salary—$26,000."[61]

minorities in many areas, including administrative appointments, departmental hiring policies, and graduate admissions.)

As mentioned earlier, black students demanded—and got—on Seven Sisters campuses some form of separate housing, as they did at most other American colleges, on the grounds that, as the Barnard Organization of Soul Sisters put it, "It is a strain—academically, socially, and therefore psychologically, for us, black women, to live apart from one another in the dormitories."[62] They were tired of meeting at the swimming pool. It was euphemistically called a cultural shock absorber, a halfway house (to integration), everything but what it was: an unimaginative and hasty solution to a significant social problem, and the New York State Board of Regents, after a battle with Vassar students, administration, and trustees, finally forced the institution to close its black house on the grounds that "setting apart black, brown, or other minority students is to the detriment of both minority and majority students because it violates the open pursuit of knowledge, truth, and experience which is the foundation of the educational process."[63]

Black sisterhoods and black cultural centers have proliferated; so have black literary magazines, black arts festivals, black concerts; student newspapers have black columnists. Black students have all but boycotted white activities and held their own parties. (In a survey of black students at predominantly white colleges in the 1950s, it was found that about two thirds of the black students participated in three or more extracurricular activities; in 1972, nearly twenty years after the Supreme Court declared separate facilities inherently unequal, a survey of black students on white college campuses found that black social life tended to be limited to interaction with other blacks and almost half of those questioned reported not having been in a racially mixed group within the prior six months.)[64] White students, who were accused of ignoring minority student interests in the planning of extracurricular activities, have gotten the signal that they were not welcome at black activities. A black social life, long a serious problem to black students in predominantly white colleges, has developed, the problems of dating alleviated by the larger numerical presence of black men at surrounding institutions, and it is unlikely that a Mount Holyoke dean will ever again (as one did in the late 1940s) have to summon a black student from her dormitory because a black man had arrived unexpectedly at a campus party and might decide to dance with a white girl.[65]

Suspicious of a career counseling system geared to sending middle-class white girls into academe and genteel occupations (as opposed to careers) in publishing, the arts, and government, and suspicious of campus corporate recruiters who might be more interested in interviewing their quotas of minority students than in actually hiring anyone, black students all but boycotted vocational offices on Seven Sisters campuses even though the vocational office staffs were expanded to include a black assistant director, and some institutions resorted to holding separate workshops and conferences for blacks and whites.

Reunions of black alumnae have become popular—black seniors at Wellesley threatened in 1973 to create a separate black alumnae association "to better direct Wellesley in its supportive obligation to its black students"[66]—and it has become *de rigeur* to elect a black to the board of trustees.

This parallel campus structure, based on the questionable premise of race, had a fragility about it, as if it had been placed there temporarily, all of it able to be dismantled easily, without putting too much strain on the superstructure as, in a sense, it had been added without much real strain: an assistant dean of black affairs here, an assistant professor for black studies there, an assistant director of admissions, an assistant director in the vocational office; rarely, although a few exist, a black dean for an entire class, a black professor of chemistry, or a black official actually integrated into the power structure. Instead of leading, academe appeared to lag behind the larger society where we had become accustomed to black policemen and black mayors and black congressmen. All of which raised some questions: Did the holders of these newly created positions have much influence on campus-wide policy and decision-making or were they thought of only in terms of representing a constituency; how much opportunity were they offered for advancement? The implications in the answers were important factors in racial self-images, both black and white.

The character of the Sisters has not been altered. Black concerns have been diverted rather than dealt with, and the institutions continue to serve the needs and priorities of their traditional clientele, the white middle-class majority student and, by easy transference, the white middle-class community, the only community they have equipped themselves to serve.

That they were class institutions was their "misfortune," declared Vida Scudder, Smith '84, teacher of English at Wellesley for forty years, who had had her own experiences with institutional bias.* "We are all segregated in the prison of class. More than we recognize, our inner life is shaped by the traditions of the group to which we happen to belong; and until we escape from such a prison, at least through imagination, or better far through personal contacts, our culture is bound to remain tragically cramped and incomplete."[68]

5

"Academic life is but half life," Supreme Court Justice Oliver Wendell Holmes told a young Felix Frankfurter, when in 1913 the latter was considering an invitation to join the faculty of Harvard Law School. "It is withdrawal from the fight in order to utter smart things that cost you nothing except the thinking them from a cloister."[69] Frankfurter ignored the advice, accepted the appointment (which he held until he was appointed to the Supreme Court in 1939), and went on to turn his particular ivory tower into an intellectual Grand Central Terminal from which his ebullient person emerged variously as legal fighter for social causes, author of progressive legislation, and liberal advisor to

---

* In 1912, Miss Scudder, along with Ellen Hayes, professor of astronomy, traveled to Lawrence, Massachusetts, and the woolen mill strikes where, to the chagrin of her employer, she visited, in her ostrich-plumed hat, the homes of the striking workers and even addressed a labor meeting. Wellesley did not fire her for her radicalism, of which this was not the first example (previously a Wellesley president had told her she was a "detriment to the institution"); however, Miss Scudder was required to drop temporarily her popular "Social Ideas in English Letters" course, for which she substituted Arthurian romance, considered ideologically less damaging to adolescents. And when her close friend Katharine Lee Bates, author of *America the Beautiful*, later resigned the chairmanship of the English department, she did not recommend Miss Scudder to assume that responsibility largely because, Miss Scudder explained, "she never again quite trusted my classroom judgment."[67]

congressmen, governors, and presidents. His extracurricular activity was only the natural extension of his curricular, a mobilization of all the resources of the law—of which he had an almost mystical vision—to the service of society. Which is what academic elitism is all about.

It was part of the vocabulary of Bryn Mawr's Carey Thomas—eccentric, autocratic, even tyrannical; impulsive, even arbitrary; a despot in every sense of the word, but absolutely committed to the improvement of the status of women. "We are a woman's college," she declared in 1921, "and as such it is very important for Bryn Mawr to continue to lead in women's educational movements, national and international."[70]

Mount Holyoke's Mary Woolley knew what elitism meant, and although she came late to the feminism of her time, she was able to translate that concept into something bigger, telling the Peace Congress of Women held at Carnegie Hall in 1907 that "The achievement, the distinction of the representative womanhood of today, is that it unites the intellectual and the emotional for some larger social end than the world has ever known before. Her opportunity extends from neighborhood nursing to world organization in the cause of peace."[71]

Barnard's Virginia Gildersleeve, dean from 1909 to 1947, was reminded every time she passed Columbia's Low Library, with its inscription "for the advancement of the public good" that education was not to be dispensed in a vacuum; and while Miss Gildersleeve is not remembered as an ardent feminist, she is remembered as an ardent internationalist, serving the cause of international intellectual cooperation through the League of Nations, later the United Nations, and the International Federation of University Women which she was instrumental in establishing. Looking back over the long span of her involvement, which had been precipitated by World War I, Miss Gildersleeve observed, "Perhaps it would have been better if I had adopted as my chief hobby the cultivation of chrysanthemums or the breeding of West Highland white terriors or even . . . the collection of Japanese swordguards. But no,—I am glad to have lived fully in the main current of my times, making some effort to grapple with our most vital problems."[72]

The confessions of Richard P. Bailey, president of Hamline

University, 1968–75, appeared in *The New York Times* (reprinted from the *Minneapolis Star*) in July 1975 under the title "Why I Quit:"

Resignations are followed by a listing of personal accomplishments. One item only on my list; for seven years I survived.

The stack of things I did not accomplish mounts skyward in a miserable monument.

I was much too timid; I spoke too little and too softly; I wrote too seldom and with much too much caution; and when there was a need for an educational leader to step forward I often waited for someone else to do it.

There is no excuse. Passive acceptance of society's ills by its leaders dooms society. And education must be the cutting edge of society's scalpel, ever ready to perform the exploratory or corrective surgery necessary.[73]

7

I'm Radcliffe! Fly Me!

WRITING IN 1922, Sinclair Lewis made Verona Babbitt a Bryn
Mawr alumna; he might as well have been discussing a brand of
washing machine as a brand of education for all the significance
it had (except to enhance her social status in Zenith). Mary
McCarthy described "the group" (Vassar '33) as intellectually,
professionally, socially, and morally unimportant at best. Philip
Roth made the heroine (a heroine only in the strictest technical
sense) of *Good-bye Columbus* a student at Radcliffe, but she
could as easily have been a student at Slippery Rock State Teachers College. Alison Lurie (Radcliffe '47) made Erica Tate, also a
Radcliffe alumna, a dilettante at life and love.

This is us. Mrs. Tidball's army of achievers notwithstanding.
This is how others see us, how we have impacted on our society,
and, equally important, how we have impacted on our own inner
selves.

The question asked at the beginning of this book was whether
the women's colleges can survive or whether they are an anachro-
nism; whether Mrs. Tidball's achievers or the Erica Tates are the
representative alumnae. The answer lies in the ability of the institutions, as institutions, to shed their century-old habits of dependence and docility and to become truly self-reliant so that they can
lead their students into similar self-reliance.

Radcliffe's Matina Horner, a psychologist by training and profession, recognized, as a graduate student and lecturer in psychology at the University of Michigan, that there was a significant body of data on men's achievement motives but only sparse footnotes on women's. Researchers, predominantly male, apparently had decided, Mrs. Horner concluded, "as Freud had before them, that the only way to understand women was to turn to the poets."[1]

In an effort to expand the data to include the second sex, Mrs. Horner began an exploration of sex differences in achievement motivation, an exploration that ultimately resulted in what has become known as a largely feminine characteristic—the "motive to avoid success." Simplified, this motive to avoid success implies that woman—more frequently than man, who traditionally has received precisely the opposite societal signals—learns early in life that "it really isn't ladylike to be too intellectual," according to Mrs. Horner, who attributed her own scholarly and academic successes to the influence of her father and husband, both true believers in woman's responsibility for self-fulfillment. "She is warned," Mrs. Horner continued her description of modern woman, "that men will treat her with distrustful tolerance at best, and outright prejudice at worst, if she pursues a career. She learns the truth of Samuel Johnson's comment, 'A man is in general better pleased when he has a good dinner upon his table, than when his wife talks Greek.' So she doesn't learn Greek, and the motive to avoid success is born."[2] Achievement and masculinity may be synonymous, but Mrs. Horner discovered achievement and femininity are viewed by many women to be mutually exclusive. It was hardly a new discovery, Carey Thomas herself having been warned as a girl that a college education would scare away bachelors and, as one writer put it, "she fancied it might make her a 'sort of woman devil.' "[3]

Mrs. Horner conducted her research at a time of heightened interest in women, and she had hit a tender spot. As soon as her research became known, other investigators began their own researches into women's achievement motivation, the result of which is that her basic findings have been both elaborated on and refuted. However, her findings carry meaning for the Seven Sisters as institutions.

It is only a very short step from hypothesizing that women, traditionally defined by others, have a motive to avoid success to the corollary that the academic, social, and moral docility which has characterized the Sisters as institutions reflected this same emotionally repressive psychological feature.

And the motive persists in the sex and in the institutions for much the same reason perhaps—the belief in the need for acceptance by men. Had they been more aggressively intellectual, more morally daring, the rationale goes, the institutions would have lost not only their clientele, which was notable for its conservatism, but also the men who ran them (trustees, presidents, faculty) and, not least important, the financial indulgence of Harvard, Yale, and Amherst husbands, a generosity impossible for most alumnae to duplicate in a discriminatory labor market (a situation not without its paradoxical implications). So that as institutions, they were content to put a good dinner on the table, and they would forgo the Greek—in effect, emasculating at the same time they thought they were preserving the male prerogatives, and mortgaging their own aspirations for a traditional kind of security, when the only real security lay in self-reliance. Even the present attempts, to create new knowledge about women and to broaden opportunities, while considerable, are only being carried on within the acceptable definitions of contemporary feminism so that few stereotypes are really being disputed. It is only another face put on the old consumerism, and only to a Calvin Coolidge could the women's colleges appear to be "hotbeds of radicalism."[4]

All of this institutional timidity has not been without its effect on the social and political progress of this often wayward planet. For if these Seven, the recognized leaders among women's educational institutions, accept themselves as academic Adam's ribs, who at Harvard or the University of Michigan or Chase Manhattan or the American Medical Association would—or could—argue? And their collective institutional contribution to the failure of the larger society to balance the sexual equation, while not quantifiable, may be significant, another fact, given the Sisters' origins in academic radicalism, that is not without its paradoxical implications.

The problem of the Seven Sisters is deeply rooted in the institutional psyche and has little to do with such specifics as coeducation versus single-sex, whether or not the colleges offer certain courses or how they are taught. These questions are only pointers to a more serious imbalance within the organism. The real problem of the Seven Sisters is that singly and collectively they found themselves consistently faced with the same dilemmas women in the larger society faced, and they chose to solve them in the same way, demonstrating institutional timidity and humility and becoming severely limited within the obvious societal and academic parameters. Their survival depends less on whether they adopt some specific methodology or whether they can secure certain foundation grants and more on whether they can liberate themselves from a hundred years as second-class citizens. And if they do, whether they can become truly innovative, can begin to think in terms of lowering the water instead of routinely raising the bridge, in terms of curriculum, faculty, financing, administration; whether they have dreams in their heads, and whether they can discover the means of making them come true.

What they need is what Donald H. J. Hermann of the Harvard Law School said Harvard and the American society needs: "An ethic of aspiration" which can come only "from individuals [and institutions], gifted, perceptive, and ambitious. . . ."[5]

Notes

CHAPTER I

1. Letter, March 20, 1791, from Abigail Adams to her sister, in Abigail Adams, *Letters of Mrs. Adams, Wife of John Adams* (Boston, 1848), p. 358.
2. Bennett, p. 13.
3. *Godey's Lady's Book*, July 1870, p. 42.
4. Converse, p. 21.
5. James Monroe Taylor, p. 92.
6. Greene, p. 3.
7. Meigs, p. 41.
8. Rogers, p. 50.
9. Seelye, p. 51.
10. Thwing, p. 16.
11. *Report to the President from the University Committee on the Education of Women, 1973–74*, p. 40.
12. Starrett, *After College*, pp. 7–8.
13. Anonymous; in Sheila Cunningham, "Working with Western Electric," *Bryn Mawr Alumnae Bulletin*, Winter 1975, p. 11.
14. Gildersleeve, *Crusade*, p. 132.
15. Cole, p. 71.

CHAPTER 2

1. *Annual Report of the President of Columbia College to the Board of Trustees*, 1881, pp. 76–77.
2. Thomas, "The College," p. 21.
3. Finch, p. 64.
4. Finch, p. 280.
5. Thomas, "The College," p. 21.
6. Friedan, p. 142.
7. Meigs, p. 42.
8. Editorial, *Change*, June 1974, p. 10.
9. Doermann, *Crosscurrents*, p. 156.
10. *Wellesley Alumnae Magazine*, Summer 1975, p. 9.
11. *The New York Times*, April 23, 1971, pp. 1 and 45.
12. Doermann, *Crosscurrents*, p. 2.
13. College Entrance Examination Board, *College-Bound Seniors 1974–75*, p. 12.
14. Plum and Dowell, p. 59.
15. American Association of University Professors, *Bulletin*, Summer 1966, p. 153 and Summer 1975, p. 138.

16. *School and Society*, January 22, 1966.
17. Chesler, p. 4.
18. Alan Simpson, *Report of the President, 1964–70*, p. 11.
19. Roger Ascham, *The Schoolmaster* (Ithaca, 1967), pp. 56–57.
20. McCarthy, *The Group*, p. 30.
21. *The New York Times Magazine*, December 31, 1964, p. 31.
22. Conway, pp. 241–242.
23. Eliot, pp. 17–18.
24. *Amherst College Semi-Centennial Exercises*, pp. 79–80.
25. Seelye, p. 49, footnote 1.
26. McAfee, *Sociology*, p. 17.
27. *The New York Times Magazine*, March 26, 1933, pp. 4–5.
28. *The New York Times*, June 12, 1949, p. 53.
29. *Saturday Review*, April 20, 1963, p. 66.
30. *The New York Times*, March 19, 1961, p. 69.
31. The story of the Vassar-Yale negotiations was assembled from a number
    of sources: an author's interview with Alan Simpson in October 1973;
    Mr. Simpson's presidential report of 1964–70; Vassar Alumnae magazines,
    particularly the issues of February 1967 and April 1967; Vassar *Miscel-
    lany News* for 1966 and 1967; the report of Elga R. Wasserman, special
    assistant to the president on the education of women at Yale and chair-
    man of the University Committee on Coeducation, in the *Educational
    Record*, Spring 1970; *Coeducation 1969–70*, a progress report also by
    Elga Wasserman; *The New York Times* for 1966–67, particularly the
    issues of December 17, 18, and 25, 1966, and October 22, November 21,
    and November 26, 1967; *Newsweek* of December 12, 1966 and December
    4, 1967; but above all, Chesler *et al* in *The New Journal* of April 28,
    1968.

    Miss Blanding revealed her former "ambivalent feelings" in an inter-
    view with the Vassar *Miscellany News* published November 30, 1973,
    p. 7.
32. *Choragos*, September 11, 1975, p. 1.
33. Mount Holyoke Alumnae Quarterly, Winter 1972, p. 248.
34. Simpson, *Report 1964–70*, p. 13.
35. Ann Sutherland Harris, "The Second Sex in Academe." In Stacey *et al*,
    p. 294.
36. Elga R. Wasserman, *Coeducation 1969–70*, pp. 3, 5, 6, 18. National aver-
    age SAT scores in College Entrance Examination Board, *College Bound
    Seniors 1974–75*, p. 12.
37. Bryn Mawr attrition rate figure supplied by the college.
38. Faculty data were assembled from the Vassar College Catalogues, 1967–68
    and 1973–74.
39. The *Miscellany News* reported in detail the campus controversy over
    the recruiting film; particularly relevant were articles on October 26,
    1973 and November 9, 1973, in addition to the author's interview with
    Richard D. Stephenson, director of admissions at that time.

40. Data on the Pulitzer Prizes were assembled from the 1975 *Information Please Almanac*, pp. 797–805, from the announcements of winners each year—published the first Tuesday in May in *The New York Times*, and from *The New York Times* obituaries.

41. McCarthy, *The Group*, pp. 218–219.

42. Data on course offerings through 1930–31 were collected from Foster, p. 83; from the Vassar College Catalogue for 1974–75.

43. Data on bachelor's degrees were assembled from United States Office of Education, *Earned*, 1950 through 1967.

44. Data on fellowships were collected from *Woodrow Wilson Fellows 1945–1967*, from annual reports of the National Science Foundation, and from the annual reports of the John Simon Guggenheim Foundation.

45. Simpson, *Report, 1964–1970*, pp. 45–51.

46. *The New York Times*, November 19, 1974, p. 78.

47. Vassar figures supplied by the Vassar Public Information Office; Yale figures were found in the *Report to the President from the University Committee on the Education of Women, 1973–74*, p. 28.

48. *Report of the Trustee Committee on Coeducation*, February 4, 1975.

49. "Smith College and the Question of Coeducation," *A Report with Recommendations Submitted to the Faculty and Board of Trustees by the Augmented College Planning Committee, April 1971*, p. 1.

50. Chinoy, p. 2; "Smith College and the Question of Coeducation, pp. 17–18.

51. Special questionnaire on Seniors' Attitudes Toward College (the Princeton–Smith High School Survey) and "College Planning Committee Survey of Attitudes toward Coeducation at Smith."

52. Chinoy, pp. 4–5.

53. Chinoy, pp. 35–36.

54. Chinoy, p. 87.

55. *The New York Times*, February 22, 1970, p. 69.

56. "Smith College and the Question of Coeducation," pp. 17–18.

57. "Smith College and the Question of Coeducation," pp. 15–16.

58. Chinoy, p. 79.

59. Smith College *Alumnae Quarterly*, April 1972, p. 2.

60. *The New York Times*, May 18, 1967, p. 43.

61. Simpson, p. 32.

62. During the academic year 1974–75, the *Bryn Mawr–Haverford News* published a series of articles analyzing the progress of cooperation, department by department; the conclusions drawn here are based on these articles and from the author's observations and interviews during a five-day visit to the Bryn Mawr campus in January 1974.

63. *Amherst Student*, reprinted in *Choragos*, April 18, 1974, p. 4.

64. *The New York Times*, April 25, 1937, section ii, p. 6.

65. North Burn, "Five Years with Five Colleges," p. 3 (undated and unpaged insert in the Spring 1793 local alumnae magazines).

66. Conclusions drawn on the successes and failures of the five colleges were based on the author's interviews during visits to Smith and Mount

Holyoke in 1973–74, from "Five Years with Five Colleges," and from articles in student newspapers, alumnae quarterlies, and presidential reports.

67. Lewis, *The New York Times*, pp. 38–40.
68. Radcliffe College, *Acre*, pp. 9–13.
69. Lewis, *The New York Times*, p. 17.
70. Letter, Eliot to Benjamin Wheeler, in Buck, pp. 45–46.
71. Faculty figures from Byerly, pp. 234–235.
72. Thomas, *Education*, p. 30.
73. Ann Sutherland Harris, "The Second Sex in Academe," in Stacey *et al*, p. 294.
74. Author's interview with Robert H. Gardiner, Radcliffe treasurer, October 1974.
75. Mary I. Bunting, "What Is It Like Under the New Agreement with Harvard?" *Radcliffe Quarterly*, June 1972, p. 3.
76. HEW Office of Civil Rights to Nathan M. Pusey, December 31, 1970.
77. Gornick, "Why Radcliffe . . .," p. 60.
78. *The New York Times*, March 4, 1888, p. 1.
79. Report by Connie J. G. Gersick of the Radcliffe Office of Women's Education and Katharine A. Hutchins, assistant director, Office of Career Services and Off-Campus Learning, March 5, 1974; Strauch Committee Report, February 26, 1975, pp. 17 and 33; *Harvard Crimson*, May 9, 1975, 1.
80. *Smith College Monthly*, October 1894, pp. 36–37.
81. Strauch Committee Report, p. 33.
82. *Womensports*, September 1974, p. 39; *Athletic Opportunities for Women at Harvard and Radcliffe*, Fall 1974.
83. Author's interview with Robert H. Gardiner, Radcliffe College treasurer, October 1974.
84. *Harvard Crimson*, March 27, 1975, p. 5.
85. Julia Ward Howe, p. 64.
86. Author's interview with Patricia A. Graham, at that time professor of education and director of the education program, Barnard College, February 1974.
87. *The New York Times*, November 19, 1894, p. 7.
88. Meyer, p. 7.
89. Alice Duer Miller, pp. 18–20.
90. Anthony Lewis, p. 17.
91. Gildersleeve, *Crusade*, pp. 66–67.
92. Patricia A. Graham, "Women in Academic Life," in *Successful*, *p*. 234.
93. *Barnard Reports*, February 1973, p. 1.
94. Applications data was supplied by the respective admissions offices; also *Sense of the Six*, November 1973, pp. 1, 3; *The New York Times Encyclopedic Almanac*, 1970, p. 521.
95. National Merit Scholarship Corporation, *Annual Reports*: 1965, pp. 63–66; 1973, pp. 28–33.
96. *The New York Times*, February 18, 1921, p. 11.

97. American Association of University Professors, *Bulletin*, Summer 1975, pp. 138–183; *Supplementary Tables*, 1973–74, pp. 30–35.

CHAPTER 3

1. Clarke, p. 129.
2. Wollstonecraft, *Vindication*, p. 7.
3. O'Neill, *The Woman Movement*, p. 170.
4. "The Subjection of Women, in John Stuart and Harriett Taylor Mill, *Essays on Sex Equality* (New York, 1970), p. 182.
5. Rauh, p. 53.
6. Clarke, p. 33.
7. Clarke, p. 40.
8. Clarke, p. 39.
9. Clarke, pp. 41–48.
10. Clarke, pp. 49–54.
11. Clarke, p. 123.
12. Clarke, pp. 126–128.
13. Clarke, p. 127.
14. Clarke, p. 157.
15. Clarke, pp. 62–63.
16. Elliott, p. 151.
17. Julia Ward Howe, p. 89.
18. Clarke, pp. 77–83.
19. *Letters from Old-Time Vassar*, pp. 14–15; Julie Ward Howe, pp. 191–195; Vassar College *Catalogue*, 1865–66, p. 35.
20. Julia Ward Howe, p. 197.
21. Orton, pp. 246–247.
22. Julia Ward Howe, p. 199.
23. Julia Ward Howe, p. 41.
24. Julia Ward Howe, p. 28.
25. Julia Ward Howe, p. 95.
26. Julia Ward Howe, p. 70.
27. Duffey, pp. 71–72.
28. Julia Ward Howe, pp. 157–158.
29. Wollstonecraft, *Vindication*, p. 179.
30. McCurdy, pp. 137–150.
31. *Addresses at the Inauguration of Rev. L. Clarke Seelye, President of Smith College, July 14, 1895*, (Springfield, Mass., 1875), pp. 28–29.
32. *Harper's Magazine*, August 1876, p. 327.
33. Seelye, p. 51.
34. *Smith College Alumnae Register, 1875–1975*, Necrology, p. 1.
35. *Health Statistics*, pp. 74–78.
36. Matthew Vassar to James Renwick, Jr., January 11, 1862. In Haight, p. 72.
37. Raymond, *Life*, p. 563.
38. *Harvard Crimson*, February 18, 1975, p. 4.
39. *The New York Times*, June 2, 1937, p. 26.

40. *Choragos*, May 8, 1975, p. 3.
41. Brown, pp. 231–232.
42. Alan Simpson, "Vandals and Vandal-Worship." Address, special convocation, Vassar College, April 16, 1975, p. 4.
43. Hackett, p. 283.
44. Matthew Vassar to Rev. Rufus Babcock, October 23, 1961. In Haight, p. 65.
45. Plum and Dowell, pp. 8 and 12; Raymond, *Life*, pp. 532–534; *Vassar Quarterly*, May 1921, pp. 172–173; *Letters from Old-Time Vassar*, pp. 10–21; Lossing, p. 165.
46. Thomas, "Present Tendencies," p. 68.
47. *Intellectual Honesty*, p. 14.
48. Chase, p. 300.
49. Arlen, p. 63.
50. Anne N. Chamberlin, "Diary of a Mad Alumna," *Vassar Quarterly*, Winter 1974, p. 6.
51. Simpson, *Report, 1964–70*, p. 33.
52. *The New York Times*, May 1, 1976, p. 14.
53. *Washington Post*, August 3, 1975, p. E 1–2.
54. Hamilton, p. 346.
55. Terman, p. 321.
56. Warren B. Miller, pp. 5 and 6.
57. Elizabeth Aub Reid, "How has coresidential living affected Radcliffe Women?" *Radcliffe Quarterly*, June 1973, pp. 15 and 17.
58. Mead, *Blackberry*, p. 103.
59. Author's interviews with physicians at Barnard, Bryn Mawr, Mount Holyoke, Smith, and Vassar; Lee, p. 92; *Harvard Crimson*, April 26, 1974, p. 2.
60. Caroline W. Bynum, "The Motive to Avoid Love," *Radcliffe Quarterly*, December 1974, p. 19.
61. Author's interviews with deans of residences or their equivalents at Barnard, Mount Holyoke, Smith, Vassar, and Wellesley; chaplains at Vassar and Smith; also with the physicians enumerated above.
62. Horton, p. 23.
63. *The New York Times*, January 24, 1966, p. 32; *Harvard Crimson*, December 10, 1974, pp. 1 and 5; *Harvard Crimson*, February 25, 1974, p. 1.
64. American Association of University Women, *Campus 1970, Where Do Woman Stand?* (Washington, 1970), p. 9.
65. *Bryn Mawr–Haverford News*, November 2, 1973, p. 12.
66. Vassar College *Catalogue, 1865–66*, p. 32.
67. Harris L. Wofford, *Report of the President, 1970–73*, p. 37.
68. *Life*, May 9, 1949, p. 79.
69. *The New York Times*, March 20, 1927, Section ix, p. 16.
70. Riesman and Jencks, p. 57.
71. *Choragos*, March 14, 1974, p. 3; *Bryn Mawr–Haverford News*, January 17, 1975, p. 1.

72. *Wellesley News*, September 23, 1971, p. 3; October 14, 1971, p. 1.
73. Smith College *Bulletin*, 1974–75, p. 36; Mount Holyoke College *Catalogue, 1974–75*, p. 239; *Choragos*, April 25, 1974, p. 3.
74. Editorial, *Smith College Monthly*, November 1893, p. 29.
75. *Choragos*, February 13, 1975, p. 8.
76. Newcover, *A Century*, p. 121.
77. Neilsen, "Should Women," p. 105.
78. *Washington Post*, August 4, 1975, p. A4.
79. *Wellesley News*, April 12. 1974, p. 4.
80. *Report of the Trustee Committee on Coeducation*, February 4, 1975, p. 2.
81. *Wellesley News*, February 28, 1975, p. 3.
82. *Wellesley News*, May 2, 1975, p. 7.
83. Riesman and Jencks, p. 308.
84. Riesman and Jencks, pp. 307–308.

CHAPTER 4

1. Whitehead, pp. 138–139.
2. Mount Holyoke *Alumnae Quarterly*, Fall 1973, p. 176.
3. Wellesley commencement address, 1971, p. 4.
4. Phoebe Kendall, p. 174.
5. Vassar College *Catalogue, 1865–66*, p. 23.
6. Vassar College *Catalogue, 1865–66*, p. 16.
7. Raymond, *Life*, p. 567.
8. Thomas, *Education*, p. 24.
9. Robinson, p. 108.
10. Van Voris, p. 198.
11. These statistics were compiled from the appropriate annual reports of the foundations cited.
12. These figures were supplied by the Ford Foundation.
13. Author's interview with Mrs. Conway, August 1975.
14. Cross, p. 135.
15. Richard Gettell, "A Plea for the Uncommon Woman." Inaugural Address of November 1957; reprinted in *School and Society*, June 7, 1958, pp. 259–260.
16. Carnegie Commission, *Less Time*, p. 19.
17. Bunting, "A Huge Waste," p. 23.
18. *Successful*, p. 196.
19. Information regarding the Radcliffe Institute was compiled from *Radcliffe Institute 1960–71*; various press releases from the institute; *Harvard Crimson*, January 12, 1974, p. 3; and author's interview with Patricia A. Graham, director, October 1974.
20. Details and quotes regarding the Sarah Lawrence Continuing Education Program were collected from Richter and Whipple.
21. Details and quotes regarding Minnesota Plan were collected from Schletzer *et al.*
22. Alberta Arthurs, Radcliffe dean of admissions, in *Harvard Crimson*, May 2, 1975, p. 1.

23. Smith College *Alumnae Quarterly*, Spring 1975, p. 22.
24. Schletzer *et al*, p. 74.
25. Woodrow Wilson, Journal, October 1887, in *The Papers of Woodrow Wilson*, Arthur S. Link, ed. (Princeton, N. J., 1968), Vol. 5, p. 619.
26. *Barnard Bulletin*, February 28, 1974, p. 6.
27. Liz Schneider, "Our Failures Only Marry." In Gornick and Moran, *Woman in*, p. 586.
28. Finch, p. 57.
29. Mendenhall, p. 436.
30. Rosovsky, p. 4.
31. All material on writings on women's education is from author's survey of educational publications.

CHAPTER 5

1. Seelye, p. 127.
2. John Henry Newman, *The Uses of Knowledge* (New York, 1948), p. 10.
3. Pusey, p. 198.
4. McAfee, "Segregation," pp. 20–21.
5. *The New York Times Magazine*, May 1, 1932, p. 6.
6. *Radcliffe Quarterly*, September 1975, p. 1.
7. *Mount Holyoke College, The Seventy-fifth Anniversary*, p. 113.
8. Smith College *Alumnae Quarterly*, August 1975, p. 1.
9. *Wellesley News*, April 11, 1975, p. 4.
10. Van Voris, p. 120.
11. *Harvard Today*, Spring 1975, p. 4.
12. *The New York Times*, July 28, 1946, p. 40.
13. Thomas Wentworth Higginson, "Woman and Her Wishes. An Essay." In *Women's Rights Tracts*, No. 4, p. 10.
14. Riesman, "Two Generations," pp. 712–713.
15. Rosemary Park, Report to the Barnard trustees, 1962–64. Reprinted in *School and Society*, January 22, 1966, p. 38.
16. Bernard, p. 6.
17. *The New York Times*, October 31, 1929, p. 18.
18. Putnam, pp. 69–70.
19. Author's interview with Harris L. Wofford, January 1974.
20. Gornick, "Why Radcliffe," p. 61.
21. Anne Goodman, p. 95.
22. Horner, "Fail," p. 63.
23. Marian C. White, p. 47.
24. Newcomer, *A Century*, pp. 161–164; *Harvard Crimson*, February 14, 1975, p. 1.
25. Faculty data were compiled from the appropriate catalogues in these years.
26. Schroeder *et al* versus Smith College. Massachusetts Commission Against Discrimination Findings of Fact and Conclusions of Law and Order, December 30, 1974, p. 31.
27. Letter from Smith College, February 1975, p. 3.

28. Cross, p. 172.
29. Cole, p. 182.
30. Facts about commencement speakers were supplied by the respective colleges.
31. *The New York Times*, January 30, 1961, p. 10.
32. Author's survey of educational backgrounds of women in Congress.
33. *The New York Times*, August 25, 1974, Section iv, p. 2.
34. Leyda, pp. 137–138.
35. Tidball, pp. 132 and 133.
36. Newcomer, *A Century*, p. 198.
37. Hardy, p. 501.
38. Tidball, p. 132.
39. *Washington Post*, June 23, 1975, p. C1.
40. *The New York Times*, June 23, 1975, p. 27.
41. Newcomer, *A Century*, pp. 190–200.
42. Ayers D'Costa, and Rosemary Yancik, *Planning for Follow-up of AAMC Longitudinal Study of Medical Students of the Class of 1960*, Phase 3, February 1975, p. 63.
43. *Graduate Education*, p. 14.
44. Ph.D. figures compiled from National Academy of Sciences, *Doctorate Production in the United States, 1920–62 and 1958–66*.
45. National Science Foundation grants data compiled from annual press releases supplied by the foundation.
46. Woodrow Wilson Fellowship figures compiled from *Woodrow Wilson Fellows, 1945–67*, and subsequent annual reports of the Woodrow Wilson Foundation.
47. Van Voris, p. 151.
48. Boroff, p. 183.
49. Boroff, p. 183.
50. Kerr, p. 111.
51. Comparisons of English, biology, history, and chemistry majors were compiled from the appropriate volumes of *Earned Degrees Conferred*, published by the Office of Education.
52. *Business Week*, May 18, 1963, pp. 117–118.
53. *Wellesley Alumnae Magazine*, Spring 1975, p. 17.
54. Jane Schwarz Gould, "Discrimination in Employment," *Barnard Alumnae*, Spring 1970, p. 29.
55. Bunting, "A Huge Waste," p. 109.
56. *The New York Times*, June 24, 1972, p. 20.

CHAPTER 6

1. Martin Luther, *The Table Talk of Martin Luther* (London, 1875), p. 299.
2. Leyda, p. 133.
3. "Then here's . . . aid"; MacCracken, p. 47.
4. MacCracken, p. 47.

5. Matthew Vassar, statement to first board of trustees, February 26, 1861. Lossing, p. 93.
6. Selden, "Half a century," p. 10.
7. Hackett, p. 31.
8. *The Library of Mount*, unpaged.
9. Vassar College *Catalogue, 1865–66*, p. 37.
10. Seelye, p. 225.
11. Seelye, p. 35.
12. Woodrow Wilson to Ellen L. Axon, November 27, 1884. In *The Papers of Woodrow Wilson*, Arthur S. Link, ed. (Princeton, N.J., 1967), Vol. 3, p. 490.
13. Eliot to Neilson, August 8, 1917. In Thorp, p. 159.
14. Neilson to Eliot, August 9, 1917. In Thorp, p. 155.
15. *The New York Times*, March 3, 1935. Section ii, p. 5.
16. Scudder, *A Listener*, p. 51.
17. *Wellesley Alumnae Magazine*, Fall 1972, p. 13.
18. Ann F. Miller, p. 29 and Appendix, Table 37, p. 139.
19. Newcomer, *A Century*, p. 99.
20. Gildersleeve, *Columbia University Quarterly*, September 1915, p. 397.
21. Foster, pp. 104–105.
22. Newcomer, *A Century*, p. 230.
23. Jane Addams, "The Civic Value of Higher Education for Women." Address, Bryn Mawr commencement, June 1912. In *Bryn Mawr Alumnae Bulletin*, June 1912, p. 61.
24. Parker, p. 9.
25. Frances Perkins, Mount Holyoke College, Centenary Anniversary Exercises, 1937, p. 29.
26. Van Voris, p. 89.
27. Author's interview with Mrs. Newell, October 1974.
28. *The New York Times*, April 6, 1975, Section 4, p. 5.
29. Lansing, p. 110.
30. Matthew Vassar, May 1864. In Haight, p. 42.
31. MacCracken, *Hickory*, p. 26.
32. White House news release, February 27, 1975.
33. *Harvard Crimson*, November 4, 1974, pp. 1 and 3.
34. Scudder, *Listener*, p. 57.
35. *Radcliffe Quarterly*, June 1974, p. 19.
36. Stimpson, p. 30.
37. MacCracken, *Hickory*, p. 164.
38. Van Voris, p. 119.
39. *Choragos*, February 15, 1973, p. 3.
40. Finch, p. 250.
41. Cole, p. 19.
42. Rogers, pp. 31–33.
43. Greenfield, p. 43.
44. Vassar College *Catalogue, 1865–66*, p. 15.
45. *Harvard Crimson*, November 18, 1974, p. 2.

46. Bryn Mawr *Alumnae Bulletin*, Summer 1975, p. 20.
47. *The New York Times*, September 22, 1963, Section iv. p. 9.
48. *The New York Times*, February 20, 1964, p. 53.
49. Van Voris, p. 112.
50. Clark and Plotkin, pp.15–17.
51. Mead and Baldwin, p. 19.
52. Frazier, pp. 84–85.
53. *The New York Times*, October 20, 1963, Section iv, p. 9.
54. *The New York Times*, April 22, 1965, p. 26.
55. *Wellesley News*, April 19, 1973, p. 3.
56. Vassar *Miscellany News*, November 8, 1967, p. 9.
57. *Barnard Alumnae*, Spring 1969, p. 15.
58. Mead and Baldwin, p. 17.
59. *Radcliffe Quarterly*, June 1973, p. 6.
60. *The New York Times*, April 21, 1974, pp. 1 and 47.
61. Lester, p. 49.
62. *Barnard Alumnae*, Spring 1969, p. 10.
63. *Minority Access to and Participation in Post-Secondary Education*, State Education Department, Albany, May 1972, p. 9.
64. Willie and McCord, p. 15.
65. William S. McFeely, "History 265: Black and White Americans," Mount Holyoke *Alumnae Quarterly*, Spring 1974, p. 17.
66. *Wellesley Alumnae Magazine*, Summer, 1973, p. 19.
67. Scudder, *Journey*, pp. 183–184; Hackett, pp. 184–188.
68. Scudder, *Journey*, pp. 67–68.
69. Holmes to Frankfurter, July 1913. In Alexander M. Bickel, "Applied Politics and the Science of Law: Writings of the Harvard Period"; in Wallace Mendelson, *Felix Frankfurter: A Tribute* (New York, 1964), p. 165.
70. Thomas, "The Next President of Bryn Mawr." In Bryn Mawr *Alumnae Bulletin*, May 1921, p. 7.
71. Marks, p. 77.
72. Gildersleeve, *Crusade*, p. 123.
73. *The New York Times*, July 30, 1975, p. 29.

CHAPTER 7

1. Horner, "Fail," p. 36.
2. Horner, "Fail," p. 62.
3. Cross, p. 34.
4. Bernard, p. 83.
5. *Harvard Crimson*, March 19, 1974, p. 3.

Bibliography

Interviews: Between October 1973 and August 1975, the author spent several days on each of the Seven Sister campuses talking—sometimes formally with a tape recorder, at other times informally over lunch or dinner—with administration, faculty, and students. Interviews were also conducted with selected alumnae and trustees.

Campus Publications: Various issues—as cited—of officers' reports, catalogues, bulletins, newspapers, newsletters, alumnae registers, alumnae quarterlies, reunion reports, anniversary proceedings, inauguration proceedings, memorial exercises, and commencement exercises.

Other Published Sources:

Addams, Jane. "The Civic Value of Higher Education for Women." *Bryn Mawr Alumnae Bulletin*, June 1912, pp. 59–67.

Arlen, M.J. "The Girl With the Harvard Degree." *The New York Times Magazine*, June 10, 1962, pp. 16 ff.

Astin, Alexander. *Who Goes Where to College?* Chicago, 1965.

Astin, Helen S., and Bayer, Alan E. "Sex Discrimination in Academe." *Educational Record*, Spring 1972, pp. 101–118.

Bardwick, Judith M., ed. *Readings on the Psychology of Women*. New York, 1972.

Barzun, Jacques. *The American University*. New York, 1968.

Beecher, Catherine. "Women's Profession Dishonored." *Harper's New Monthly Magazine*, November 1864, pp. 766–68.

Bennett, Helen M. "Seven Colleges—Seven Types." *Woman's Home Companion*, November 1920, pp. 13 ff.

Berman, Ronald. "An Unquiet Quiet on Campus." *The New York Times Magazine*, February 10, 1974, pp. 14 ff.

Bernard, Jessie. *Academic Women*. University Park, Pa., 1964.

Bird, Caroline. "Women's Colleges and Women's Lib." *Change*, April 1972, pp. 60–65.

Blackwell, Elizabeth. *The Laws of Life*. New York, 1852.

Blakeley, Bertha E. *The Library of Mount Holyoke College* (1837–1937). Unpublished.

Blanchard, Phyllis, and Manasses, Carlyn. *New Girls for Old*. New York, 1930.

Boas, Louise Schutz. *Woman's Education Begins.* Norton, Mass., 1935.

Boroff, David. "Smith: a College for ARG's (All-Round Girls) with High IQ's." *Mademoiselle*, March 1961, pp. 122 ff.

Bowles, Frank H., and de Costa, Frank A. *Between Two Worlds.* New York, 1971.

Brackett, Anna C., ed. *Woman and the Higher Education.* New York, 1893.

Brown, Rollo Walter. *Dean Briggs.* New York, 1926.

"Bryn Mawr Raises Its Torch." *Fortune*, April 1943. pp. 107 ff.

Buck, Paul. "Harvard Attitudes Toward Radcliffe in the Early Years." Paper read at the May 1962 meeting of the Massachusetts Historical Society.

Bunting, Mary I. "A Huge Waste: Educated Woman-Power." *The New York Times Magazine*, May 7, 1961, pp. 23, 109, 112.

———; Graham, Patricia A.; and Wasserman, Elga R. "Academic Freedom and Incentive for Women." *Educational Record*, Fall 1970, pp. 386–391.

Byerly, W.E. "Radcliffe College Thirty Years After." *The Harvard Graduates' Magazine*, December 1909, pp. 233–35.

Call, Annie Payson. "The Greatest Need of College Girls." *Atlantic Monthly*, January 1892, pp. 102–109.

Carey, Henry R. "Career or Maternity." *North American Review*, December 1929, pp. 737–44.

——— "Sterilizing the Fittest." *North American Review*, November 1929, pp. 519–24.

Carnegie Commission on Higher Education. *Less Time More Options.* New York, 1971.

——— *Opportunities for Women in Higher Education.* New York, 1973.

——— *Reform on Campus.* New York, 1972.

Centra, John A. "Black Students at Predominantly White Colleges: A Research Description." *Sociology of Education*, Summer 1970, pp. 325–38.

——— *Women, Men and the Doctorate.* Princeton, N.J., 1974.

Chase, Mary Ellen. *A Goodly Fellowship.* New York, 1939.

Chesler, Ellen; Weisman, Steven; and Winger, Michael. "Vassar-Yale: What Happened?" *The New Journal*, April 28, 1968, pp. 3 ff.

Chinoy, Ely. *Coeducation at Smith College.* A Report to the President and the College Planning Committee. October 1969.

Claghorn, Kate H. "Bryn Mawr." *Outlook*, June 23, 1894, pp. 1148–49.

Clark, Kenneth B., and Plotkin, Lawrence. *The Negro at Integrated Colleges.* New York, 1963.

Clarke, Edward H. *Sex in Education or a Fair Chance for the Girls.* Boston, 1873.

Cole, Arthur C. *A Hundred Years of Mount Holyoke College.* New Haven, 1940.

Comfort, George F., and Comfort, Anna Manning. *Woman's Education and Woman's Health.* Syracuse, 1874.

Comstock, Sarah. "A Master-Mistress of Education." *World's Work,* September 1913, pp. 579–87.

Conant, James B. *The Citadel of Learning.* New Haven, 1956.

Converse, Florence. *Wellesley College.* Wellesley, Mass., 1939.

Conway, Jill Ker. "Coeducation and Women's Studies: Two Approaches to the Question of Woman's Place in the Contemporary University." *Daedalus,* Fall 1974, pp. 239–49.

Cooney, Barbara. *Twenty-five Years A-Graying.* Pepperell, Mass., 1963.

Cousten, T.C. "Female Education from a Medical Point of View." *Popular Science Monthly,* December 1883, pp. 214–28, and January 1884, pp. 319–34.

Cross, Barbara M., ed. *Educated Woman in America.* (Classic in Education, Number 25) New York, 1965.

Cunningham, Ann Marie. "Do Women's Colleges Need Men? Second Thoughts." *Mademoiselle,* February 1974, pp. 122 ff.

Daniels, Arlene Kaplan. *A Survey of Research Concerns on Women's Issues.* Washington, 1975.

Dealey, Hermione L. "College Women and Emotional Attitudes." *Education,* April 1920, pp. 511–19.

Doermann, Humphrey. *Crosscurrents in College Admissions.* New York, 1969.

——— "The Market for College Education." *Educational Record,* Winter 1968, pp. 49–57.

Dube, W.F.; Stritter, Frank T.; and Nelson, Bonnie C. "Study of U.S. Medical School Applicants, 1970–71." *Journal of Medical Education,* October 1971, pp. 837–57.

Duffey, Mrs. E.B. *No Sex in Education.* Philadelphia, 1875

Eddy, S.S. "Education of Women." *Cornell Review,* March 1874, pp. 286–94.

Education and a Woman's Life. Proceedings of the Itasca Conference on the Continuing Education of Women, Itasca State Park, Minnesota, 1962. American Council on Education, Washington, D.C. 1963.

Eliot, Charles W. *A Turning Point in Higher Education.* Cambridge, Mass., 1869.

Elliott, Charles W. "Woman's Work and Woman's Wages." *North American Review*, August 1882, pp. 146–61.

Ephron, Nora. "Women." *Esquire*, October 1972, pp. 57–62.

Farber, Seymour M., and Wilson, Roger H.L. *The Potential of Woman*. New York, 1963.

Finch, Edith. *Carey Thomas of Bryn Mawr*. New York, 1947.

Flexner, Abraham. *The American College*. New York, 1969.

Flexner, Eleanor. *Mary Wollstonecraft*. New York, 1972.

Flexner, Helen Thomas. "Bryn Mawr: A Characterization." *Bryn Mawr Alumnae Quarterly*, January 1908, pp. 5–17.

Flynn, James J. *Negroes of Achievement in Modern America*. New York, 1970.

Ford Foundation. *Four Minorities and the Ph.D.* New York, 1973.

Foster, Grace R. *Social Change in Relation to Curricular Development in Collegiate Education for Women*. Waterville, Maine, 1934.

Frazier, E. Franklin. *Black Bourgeoisie*. Glencoe, Ill., 1957.

Freeman, J. "Women's Liberation and Its Impact on the Campus." *Liberal Education*, December 1971, pp. 468–78.

Friedan, Betty. *The Feminine Mystique*. New York, 1974.

The Fund Committee of the American Alumni Council. *An Alumna Fund Survey*. Ithaca, New York, 1932.

Gallup, George, and Hill, Evan. "The American Woman." *Saturday Evening Post*, December 22–29, 1962, pp. 15–32.

General Education in a Free Society. Cambridge, Mass., 1950.

Gildersleeve, Virginia C. *A Hoard for Winter*. New York, 1962.

—— *Many a Good Crusade*. New York, 1954.

—— et al. "The Question of the Women's Colleges." *Atlantic Monthly*, November 1927, pp. 577–85.

Goodman, Anne L. "Mrs. Mac of Barnard." *Harper's Magazine*, May 1951, pp. 92–100.

Goodman, Paul. "For a Reactionary Experiment in Education." *Harper's Magazine*, November 1962, pp. 61–72.

Gornick, Vivian. "Why Radcliffe Women are Afraid of Success." *The New York Times Magazine*, January 14, 1973, pp. 10 ff.

—— and Moran, Barbara K., eds. *Woman in Sexist Society*. New York, 1971.

Graduate Education for Women. The Radcliffe Ph.D. Cambridge, Mass., 1956.

The Graduates. Princeton, N.J., 1973.

Graham, Patricia A. "Women in Academic Life." *Annals of the New York Academy of Sciences*, March 15, 1793, pp. 227–36.

Greenbaum, Lucy. "Vassar Picks a Woman and Breaks Tradition." *The New York Times Magazine*, March 31, 1946, pp. 18ff.

Greene, Louisa Dickinson. *Foreshadowings of Smith College*. Privately printed, 1928.

Greenfield, Meg. "The Revolt that Failed." *The Reporter*, July 19, 1962, pp. 43–46.

Guidelines for Creating Positive Sexual and Racial Images in Educational Materials. New York, 1975.

Guitar, Mary Anne. "Knitted Brows on the Subway. A Profile of New York's Barnard College." *Mademoiselle*, April 1964, pp. 169 ff.

——— "The Seven Sisters: Is the Ivy Overgrown?" *Mademoiselle*, August 1967, pp. 268 ff.

Hackett, Alice P. *Wellesley: Part of the American Story*. New York, 1949.

Haight, Elizabeth Hazelton, ed. *The Autobiography and Letters of Matthew Vassar*. New York , 1916.

Hamilton, G.V. *A Research in Marriage*. New York, 1929.

Hardy, K.R. "Social Origins of American Scientists and Scholars." *Science*, August 9, 1974, pp. 497–506.

Hartnett, Rodney T. *The New College Trustee: Some Predictions for the 1970s*. Princeton, N.J., 1969.

Health Statistics of Women College Graduates. Report of a Special Committee of the Association of Collegiate Alumnae, with statisical tables collated by the Massachusetts Bureau of Statistics of Labor, Boston, 1885.

Hechinger, Fred M. "Academic Freedom in America," *Change*, November/December 1970, pp. 32–36.

——— "Student Targets: Professors Are Next." *Change*, January/February 1969, pp. 36–40.

Heilbron, Louis H. *The College and University Trustee*. San Francisco, 1973.

Hermann, Helen Markel. "The Saga of Sophia Smith." *The New York Times Magazine*, October 16, 1949, pp. 14, 15, 54, 55.

Herring, Hubert. "Neilson of Smith." *Harper's Magazine*, June 1938, pp. 50–61.

Hesburgh, Theodore M. "Resurrection for Higher Education." *Educational Record*, Winter 1972, pp. 5–11.

Holsendolph, Ernest. "Black Colleges Are Worth Saving." *Fortune*, October 1971, pp. 104 ff.

Holtby, Winifred. *Women and a Changing Civilization*. New York, 1935.

Horner, Matina S. "Fail: Bright Women." *Psychology Today*, November 1969, pp. 35 ff.

——— "Toward an Understanding of Achievement-Related Conflicts in Women." *Journal of Social Issues*, volume 2, number 2, 1972, pp. 157–74.

Horton, Mildred McAfee. "Myths About Women's Colleges." *The New York Times Magazine*, February 5, 1950, pp. 10 ff.

Howard, Bruce. "Turning Toward the Professions." *Change*, October 1974, pp. 19–23.

Howe, Florence. "No Ivory Towers Need Apply." *Ms*, September 1973, pp. 46 ff.

Howe, Julia Ward. *Sex and Education*. Boston, 1874.

Howes, Bertha Bell. "The Oldest Occupation." *Vassar Alumnae Quarterly*, November 1920, pp. 15–21.

Hutchins, Robert M. *The Higher Learning in America*. New Haven, 1936.

Isaacs, Stephen. "What Happened to Harvard?" *Washington Post*, November 25, 1973, pp. C1 and C4.

Jacobi, Mary Putnam. "Shall Women Practice Medicine?" *North American Review*, January 1882, pp. 52–75.

Jaffe, A.J.; Adams, Walter; and Meyers, Sandra G. *Negro Higher Education in the 1960s*. New York, 1968.

Janeway, Elizabeth. *Man's World, Woman's Place*. New York, 1971.

Jewett, Milo P. *The President's Visit to Europe*. New York, 1863.

Jones, Ann. *Uncle Tom's Campus*. New York, 1973.

Jones, Mack H. "The Responsibility of the Black College to the Black Community: Then and Now." *Daedalus*, Summer 1971, pp. 732–44.

Jordan, David Starr. "The Higher Education of Women." *Popular Science Monthly*, December 1902, pp. 97–107.

Kendall, Elaine. "Founders Five." *American Heritage*, February 1975, pp. 33–48.

Kendall, Phoebe Mitchell. *Maria Mitchell, Life, Letters, and Journals*. Freeport, New York, 1971.

Kennedy, Gail, ed. *Education at Amherst*. New York, 1955.

Kerr, Clark. *The Uses of the University*. Cambridge, Mass., 1963.

Kilson, Martin. "The Black Experience at Harvard." *The New York Times Magazine*, September 2, 1973. pp. 13 ff.

Lansing, Marion. *Mary Lyon Through Her Letters*. Boston, 1937.

Lee, Richard V. "What About the Right to Say 'No'?" *The New York Times Magazine*, September 16, 1973, pp. 90–92.

Lelyveld, Joseph. "Mr. Simpson of Vassar." *The New York Times Magazine*, December 13, 1964, pp. 31 ff.

Lester, Richard A. *Antibias Regulations of Universities*. New York, 1974.

"Letter from a Father to his Daughter." *American Journal of Education*, November 1836, pp. 503–505.

Letters from Old-Time Vassar. Poughkeepsie, N.Y., 1915.

Lever, Janet, and Schwartz, Pepper. *Women at Yale*. Indianapolis, 1971.

Lewis, Dio; Stanton, Elizabeth Cady; and Chadwick, Dr. James Read. "The Health of American Women." *North American Review*, December 1882, pp. 503–24.

Lewis, J. Anthony. "Harvard Goes Co-ed, But Incognito." *The New York Times Magazine*, May 1, 1949, pp. 17. ff.

Leyda, Jay. *The Years and Hours of Emily Dickinson*. Vols. 1 and 2. Hamden, Conn., 1970.

The Library of Mount Holyoke College. 1837–1968. Pamphlet prepared for dedication of renovated building, November 8, 9, and 10, 1968.

Little, Clarence C. "Women and Higher Education." *Scribner's Magazine*, August 1929, pp. 146–50.

Longstreth, Bevis, and Rosenbloom, H. David. *Corporate Social Responsibility and the Institutional Investor*. New York, 1973.

Lossing, Benson J. *Vassar College and Its Founder*. New York, 1867.

Luce, Clare Boothe. "The 21st-Century Woman—Free at Last?" *Saturday Review/World*, August 24, 1974, pp. 58–62.

Lydon, Susan. "The Case Against Coeducation, or, I Guess Vassar Wasn't so Bad After All." *Ms*, September 1973, pp. 53 ff.

McAfee, Mildred H. "Educating Daughters." *The Atlantic Monthly*, February 1942, pp. 211–18.

——— "Segregation and the Women's Colleges." *American Journal of Sociology*, July 1937, pp. 16 ff.

McBride, Katharine E. *Higher Education and the Pace of Change*. Pittsburgh, 1972.

McCabe, Lida Rose. *The American Girl At College*. New York, 1893.

McCarthy, Mary. *The Group*. New York, 1964.

——— "The Vassar Girl." *Holiday*, May 1951, pp. 46 ff.

McCord, David. *An Acre for Education*. (A later edition of *An Acre for Education* originally published by Radcliffe College in 1938). Cambridge, 1958.

——— "Radcliffe—and Education for Women." *The New York Times Magazine*, December 5, 1954.

MacCracken, Henry Noble. *The Hickory Limb*. New York, 1950.

McCurdy, Persis Harlow. "The History of Physical Training at Mount Holyoke College." *American Physical Education Review*, March 1909, pp. 138–50.

McGrath, Earl J. *The Predominantly Negro Colleges and Universities in Transition*. New York, 1965.

Magill, Edward H. *An Address upon the Co-education of the Sexes*. Philadelphia, 1873.

Malkiel, Burton G., and Quandt, Richard E. "Moral Issues in Investment Policy." *Harvard Business Review*, March/April 1971, pp. 37–47.

Marks, Jeannette A. *Life and Letters of Mary Emma Woolley*. Washington, D.C., 1955.

Mead, Margaret. *Blackberry Winter*. New York. 1972.

—— and Baldwin, James. *A Rap on Race*. New York, 1971.

—— and Kaplan, Frances B., eds. *American Women*. Report of the President's Commission on the Status of Women and Other Publications of the Commission. New York, 1965.

Measurement and Evaluation of Change in College Women. Poughkeepsie, New York, 1961.

Meigs, Cornelia L. *What Makes a College? A History of Bryn Mawr*. New York, 1956.

Mendenhall, Thomas C. "Women's Education and the Educated Woman." *School and Society*, November 19, 1960. pp. 436–39.

Mertins, Paul F., and Baker, Leonard S. *Financial Statistics of Institutions of Higher Education*. Washington, D.C., 1970.

Meyer, Annie Nathan. *Barnard Beginnings*. Boston, 1935.

Miller, Alice Duer. *Barnard College. The First 50 Years*. New York, 1939.

Miller, Ann F., ed. *A College in Dispersion*. Report of the 1970–71 Survey of Bryn Mawr College Alumnae/Alumni. 1974.

Miller, Warren B. "Sexuality, Contraception and Pregnancy in a High-School Population." *California Medicine*, August 1973, pp. 14–21.

Millett, Kate. "Libbies, Smithies, Vassarites." *Change*, September/October 1970, pp. 42–50.

—— *Sexual Politics*. New York, 1970.

Mills, Herbert E. *College Women and the Social Sciences*. Freeport, N.Y., 1971.

Mills, Mary Higley. *The First Hundred Years. 1872–1972*. South Hadley, Mass., 1973.

Mommsen, Kent G. "Black Ph.D's in the Academic Marketplace." *Journal of Higher Education*, April 1974, pp. 253–67.

Morison, Samuel Eliot. *Three Centuries of Harvard.* Cambridge, Mass., 1936.

Myrdal, Gunnar. *An American Dilemma.* Vols. 1 and 2. New York,

National Academy of Sciences. *Doctorate Production in United States Universities, 1920–1962.* Washington, D.C., 1963.

—— *Doctorate Recipients from United States Universities, 1958–66.* Washington, D.C., 1967.

National Science Foundation. *Women in Scientific Careers.* Washington, D.C., 1961.

Nearing, Scott. "Who's Who Among College Trustees." *School and Society,* September 8, 1917, pp. 297–99.

Neilson, William Allan. *Intellectual Honesty.* Litchfield, Conn., 1940.

—— "Should Women be Educated Like Men?" *The Forum,* February 1929, pp. 102–105.

Newcomer, Mabel. *A Century of Higher Education for American Women.* New York, 1959.

—— and Gibson, Evelyn S. "Vital Statistics from Vassar College." *American Journal of Sociology,* January 1924, pp. 430–42.

Newell, Barbara W. "Enter Now and Pay Later." *Educational Record,* Winter 1970, pp. 57–59.

Noble, Jeanne L. *The Negro Women's College Education.* New York, 1956.

Oltman, Ruth M. *Campus 1970. Where Do Women Stand?* Washington, D.C., 1970.

O'Neill, William L. *Everyone Was Brave.* Chicago, 1969.

Orton, James, ed. *The Liberal Education of Women.* New York, 1973.

—— *The Woman Movement,* New York, 1969.

"Ought Women to Learn the Alphabet?" *Atlantic Monthly,* February 1959, pp. 137–50.

Parker, Theodore. "A Sermon on the Public Function of Women." Preached at the Music-Hall, Boston, March 17, 1835. In *Series of Woman's Rights Tracts,* No. 1, undated.

Parkinson, Margaret B. "Bryn Mawr's Barefoot Intellectuals." *Mademoiselle,* October 1962, pp. 127–29.

"The Past and Future of Mount Holyoke College." *Harper's Weekly,* February 20, 1897, p. 186.

Perlman, Daniel H. "Faculty Trusteeship." *Educational Record,* Spring 1973, pp. 115–28.

Pifer, Alan. *The Foundation in the Year 2000.* New York, 1968.

Plum, Dorothy A., and Dowell, George B. *The Magnificent Enterprise.* Poughkeepsie, N.Y., 1961.

Pollard, Josephine. *Co-Education.* New York, 1883.

President's Commission on the Status of Women. *Report of the Committee on Education.* Washington, D.C., 1963.

Pringle, Henry F., and Pringle, Katharine. "They're Using Lipstick at Harvard Now." *Saturday Evening Post*, January 30, 1954, pp. 34 ff.

Pusey, Nathan M. "The Exploding World of Education." *Fortune*, September 1955, pp. 96 ff.

Putnam, Emily Jane. *The Lady.* New York, 1910.

Radcliffe College. *An Acre for Education*, Cambridge, Mass., 1938 (The forerunner of McCord, *An Acre for Education*, 1958).

Rama Rau, Santha. "Harvard's Girl Friend—Wellesley." *Holiday*, April 1954, pp. 48 ff.

Rapoport, Roger. "New Myth on Campus." *Esquire*, September 1974, pp. 93 ff.

Rauh, Morton A. *The Trusteeship of Colleges and Universities.* New York, 1969.

Raymond, John Howard. *Life and Letters of John Howard Raymond.* New York, 1881.

———— *Vassar College.* New York, 1873.

Reuther, Rosemary Radford, ed. *Religion and Sexism.* New York, 1974.

Richter, Melissa L., and Whipple, Jane B. *A Revolution in the Education of Women.* Bronxville, N.Y., 1972.

Riesman, David. "Permissiveness and Sex Roles." *Journal of Marriage and Family Living.* August 1959, pp. 211–17.

———— "Two Generations." *Daedalus*, Spring 1964, pp. 711–35.

———— and Jencks, Christopher. *The Academic Revolution.* Garden City, N.Y. ,1968.

———— and Stadtman, Verne, eds. *Academic Transformation.* New York, 1973.

Roberts, Mary Panton. "When the College Girl Comes Home to Stay." *The New York Times Magazine*, January 26, 1913, p. 8. ff.

Roberts, Willa. "Euthenics at Vassar." *Woman's Home Companion*, November 1926, pp. 14 ff.

Robinson, Mabel Louise. "The Curriculum of the Woman's College." United States Bureau of Education *Bulletin*, 1918 (No. 6). Washington, D.C., 1918.

Rogers, Agnes. *Vassar Women.* Poughkeepsie, New York, 1940.

Rosen, Norma. "Mount Holyoke forever will be Mount Holyoke forever will be For Women Only." *The New York Times Magazine*, April 9, 1972, pp. 36 ff.

Rosovsky, Henry. *A Letter to the Faculty on Undergraduate Education.* Cambridge, Mass., October 1974.

Rossi, Alice, ed. *Academic Women on the Move.* New York, 1973.
——— "Equality Between the Sexes." *Daedalus*, Spring 1964, pp. 607–49.
Sale, J. Kirk, "Men of Low Profile." *Change*, July/August 1970, pp. 35–39.
Sanford, Nevitt, ed. *The American College.* New York, 1962.
Sayre, Nora. "The Radcliffe Girl." *Holiday.* December 1962, pp. 109–113.
Schletzer, Vera M.; Cless, Elizabeth L.; McCune, Cornelia W.; Mantini, Barbara K.; and Loeffler, Dorothy L. *A Five-Year Report 1960–65 of the Minnesota Plan for the Continuing Education of Women.* Minneapolis, 1967.
Schroeder, Mary C., and Adams, Maurianne versus Smith College. Hearings before the Massachusetts Commission Against Discrimination, January through May 1973. In 12 volumes. Springfield, Mass., 1973.
Schuck, Victoria. "Sexism and Scholarship: A Brief Overview of Women, Academia, and the Disciplines." *Social Science Quarterly*, December 1974, pp. 563–85.
Scudder, Vida D. *A Listener in Babel.* Boston, 1903.
——— *On Journey.* New York, 1937.
Seelye, L. Clark. *The Early History of Smith College 1871–1910.* Boston, 1923.
Selden, Charles A. "Bryn Mawr the Cosmopolitan." *Ladies Home Journal*, September 1925, pp. 32 ff.
——— "Half a Century of Wellesley." *Ladies Home Journal*, June 1925, pp. 10 ff.
——— "Vassar." *Ladies Home Journal*, May 1925. pp. 14 ff.
——— "What Radcliffe Has Done and Is Doing." *Ladies Home Journal*, October 1925, pp. 33 ff.
——— "Why Smith College is Different." *Ladies Home Journal*, August 1925, pp. 21 ff.
Seton, Cynthia Propper. *The Mother of the Graduate.* New York, 1970.
Sherwood, Margaret. "Undergraduate Life at Vassar." *Scribner's Magazine*, June 1898, pp. 643–60.
Simon, John G.; Powers, Charles W.; and Gunnemann, Jon P. *The Ethical Investor.* New Haven, 1972.
"Smith College." *Scribner's Monthly*, May 1877, pp. 9–17.
Smith, Florence. *Mary Astell.* New York, 1916.
Stacey, Judith; Bereaud, Susan; and Daniels, Joan, eds. *And Jill Came Tumbling After.* New York, 1974.

Starrett, Helen Ekin. *After College, What? For Girls.* New York, 1896.

—— *Letters to Elder Daughters.* Chicago, 1888.

Sternick, Joanna H. " 'But I Love It Here.'—Coeducation Comes to Dartmouth." *Journal of the National Association for Women Deans, Administrators, and Counselors,* Spring 1974. pp. 140–44.

Stevens, Edward I. "Grading Systems and Student Mobility." *Educational Record,* Fall 1973, pp. 308–12.

Stimpson, Catharine R. "Women at Bryn Mawr." *Change,* April 1974, pp. 25 ff.

Stoddard, George D. *On the Education of Women.* New York, 1950.

"Successful Women in the Sciences." *Annals* of the New York Academy of Sciences, March 15, 1973.

Swarthmore College. *Critique of a College.* Reports of the Commission on Educational Policy, the Special Committee on Library Policy, and the Special Committee on Student Life. Swarthmore, Pa., 1967.

Taylor, Harold. "Are Women's Colleges Obsolete?" *The New York Times Magazine,* September 7, 1958. pp. 24 ff.

Taylor, James Monroe. *Before Vassar Opened.* Boston, 1914.

Terman, Lewis M. *Psychological Factors in Marital Happiness.* New York, 1938.

Thierry, Adelaide H. *When Radcliffe Was Teen-Age.* Boston, 1959.

Thomas, M. Carey. "The College." Paper read before the International Congress of Arts and Sciences, Louisiana Purchase Exposition, St. Louis, Mo., September 1904.

—— "Education of Women." Department of Education for the United States Commission to the Paris Exposition of 1900. 1899.

—— "The Next President of Bryn Mawr." *Bryn Mawr Alumnae Bulletin,* May 1921, pp. 1–22.

—— "Present Tendencies in Women's Education." *Educational Review,* January 1908, pp. 64–85.

—— "Should the Higher Education of Women Differ from that of Men?" *Educational Review,* January 1901, pp. 1–10.

Thorp, Margaret Farrand. *Neilson of Smith.* New York, 1956.

Thwing, Charles Franklin. *The College Woman.* New York, 1894.

Tiball, M. Elizabeth. "Perspective on Academic Women and Affirmative Action." *Educational Record,* Spring 1973. pp. 130–35.

Tresemer, David. "Fear of Success; Popular but Unproven." *Psychology Today,* March 1974, pp. 82–85.

United States Commission on Civil Rights. *The Federal Civil Rights Enforcement Effort—1974.* Washington, D.C., 1975.

United States Office of Education. *Biennial Survey of Education in the United States*. Washington, D.C. (Various issues as cited.)

—— *Earned Degrees Conferred*. Washington, D.C. (Various issues as cited.)

Van De Warker, Ely. *Women's Unfitness for Higher Coeducation*. New York, 1903.

Van Voris, Jacqueline, ed. *College. A Smith Mosaic*. West Springfield, Mass., 1975.

Warner, Joseph B. "Radcliffe College." *The Harvard Graduates' Magazine*, March 1894, pp. 329–45.

Wasserman, Elga R. "Coeducation Comes to Yale College." *Educational Record*, Spring 1970, pp. 143–47.

Watley, Donivan J. *Black and Nonblack Youth*. Evanston, Ill., 1971.

White, Lynn T., Jr. "Do Women's Colleges Turn Out Spinsters?" *Harper's Magazine*, October 1952, pp. 44–48.

—— *Educating Our Daughters*. New York, 1950.

White, Marian Churchill. *A History of Barnard College*. New York, 1954.

Whitehead, Alfred North. *The Aims of Education and other essays*. New York, 1929.

Whiting, Albert N. "Apartheid in American Higher Education." *Educational Record*, Spring 1972, pp. 128–31.

Willie, Charles V., and McCord, Arline Sakuma. *Black Students at White Colleges*. New York, 1972.

Willig, John. "Class of '34 (Female) 15 Years Later." *The New York Times*, June 12, 1949, pp. 10 ff.

Wolfe, W. Beran. "Why Educate Women?" *The Forum*, March 1929, pp. 165–68.

Wollstonecraft, Mary. *A Vindication of the Rights of Woman*. New York, 1856.

——*Thoughts on the Education of Daughters*. Clifton, N.J., 1972.

Women in Higher Education. Background papers for participants in the 55th annual meeting of the American Council on Education. Washington, D.C., 1972.

Wood, Francis A. *Earliest Years at Vassar*. Poughkeepsie, N.Y., 1909.

Woody, Thomas. *A History of Women's Education in the United States*. Vols. 1 and 2. New York, 1966.

Woolley, Mary E. "Educational Problems in the Colleges for Women." *Education*, May 1918, pp. 650–54.

Yoder, Robert M. "Station-Wagon College." *Saturday Evening Post*, October 8, 1949, pp. 41 ff.

Yost, Edna. "The Case for the Co-Educated Woman." *Harper's Monthly Magazine*, July 1927, pp. 194–202.

Index